THOMAS HARDY AND RURAL ENGLAND

Thomas Hardy
and Rural England

Merryn Williams

First edition 1972
Reprinted 1974, 1977

Published by
THE MACMILLAN PRESS LTD
London and Basingstoke
Associated companies in Delhi Dublin Hong Kong
Johannesburg Lagos Melbourne
New York Singapore Tokyo

ISBN 0 333 13346 3

Printed in Great Britain by
REDWOOD BURN LIMITED
Trowbridge & Esher

To

Diana Forrest

Contents

Preface

This book was originally written as a thesis at Cambridge University and I have been given invaluable help by some of the scholars there. I have to record my special thanks to Mr L. G. Salingar, Mrs Gillian Beer and Dr Raymond Williams from the English Faculty, and Mrs J. Howarth from the History Faculty. The late Professor C. B. Joslin also gave me some very kind advice. Miss Phyllis Deane helped me with the population statistics in the first chapter. I also had a long and very helpful talk about nineteenth-century rural life and literature with Mr Adrian Bell.

Nobody else, though, is responsible for any errors that I may have made. The book is my own original work, except that in some parts of Chapter 1 I have consulted and to some extent depended on the historical authorities referred to in the text.

M.W.

Introduction

By 1922, near the end of his life, Thomas Hardy had given up hoping that literary critics would understand him. He had ceased to write novels years before – he said he had been cured of it by the assaults on *Jude the Obscure* – and he was convinced by this time that 'critics approached his work with an ignorant prejudice against his "pessimism" which they allowed to stand in the way of fair reading and fair judgement'.[1]

It is very understandable that he should have felt like this, for the great majority of contemporary critics had abused or failed to see the point of his most important works. The Victorians wanted him to go on and on writing novels like *Far from the Madding Crowd*,[2] which one critic called a 'picturesque romance of rural life'.[3] Edmund Gosse in his review of *Jude* complained, 'We wish he would go back to Egdon Heath and listen to the singing in the heather'.[4] They continually abused his best and most serious work because they would have liked to reduce him to a mass entertainer, giving support to their own conventional and misleading views of what the English countryside was like.

I think that twentieth-century criticism has not got far enough beyond this; Hardy's greatness, and his central significance in the history of the English novel, is not understood even today. I'm not thinking only of T. S. Eliot's really vicious attack on him, or Dr Leavis's exclusion of his work from 'the great tradition', for even the growing number of critics who admire Hardy often fail to understand what he is writing about. It is generally taken for granted that he was a pessimist,* just as it was in his own day. But instead of treating his 'pessimism' as a personal idiosyncrasy, several modern critics – and this is where I quarrel with them – have given it a precise definition by relating it to the great

---

* Roy Morrell in *Thomas Hardy: The Will and the Way* argues very convincingly that Hardy was nothing of the sort. His analysis of *Far from the Madding Crowd* has had some influence on my own.

events which were transforming English rural society during his life. Douglas Brown calls this 'the contemporary agricultural tragedy',[5] and other critics betray a romantic view of the old rural England which is equally distorting. Irving Howe in a recent book illustrates this most clearly:

> The world of Thomas Hardy's youth . . . was another world, an earlier England. It was rural, traditional, fixed in old country ways, rituals and speech. England was then deep into the convulsive transformations of the Industrial Revolution; the reform movement known as Chartism was stirring many people and frightening many more; but in the Dorset country-side . . . one might almost have supposed that human nature was changeless, unaffected by history or technology, flowing through the centuries like a stately procession of verities and recurrences.[6]

Nobody would suppose from reading this that Hardy grew up in a locality which was still buzzing with the trial of the Tol-puddle Martyrs, or that the last labourers' revolt had been sup-pressed, brutally, in Dorset only ten years before he was born. The deep conflicts which existed within rural society, long before industrialism changed the face of England, are ignored com-pletely by this kind of criticism. A. J. Guerard sums up what he thinks is Hardy's attitude:

> One of Hardy's great 'subjects' was of course, the sad passing of the stable rural life, the decay of old customs and of local traditions, the death of ghost stories and the death of village choirs. The agricultural labourers in *Under the Greenwood Tree* . . . belong to that stable and cheerful old England.

In *Tess of the d'Urbervilles*, 'the farm labourer has lost not only his ancient memories and folk customs but also the reason-able comforts of life'.[7] Guerard himself realises that this was not the true situation in rural England, but many other critics assume that it was. So the critical confusion about both Hardy's inten-tions and the actual state of things in nineteenth-century rural England persists.

This confusion makes it possible for Brown to see the central theme of Hardy's novels as 'the tension between the old rural world and the new urban one',[8] and for Arnold Kettle to say that 'the subject of *Tess* is the destruction of the peasantry', and that Hardy is writing with 'the pessimism of the Wessex peasant who sees his world and his values being destroyed'.[9] My own discussion of the novels tries to challenge these views. But I think that Brown and Kettle are two of the best Hardy critics, because they relate Hardy to the society he lived in instead of studying him in isolation as most critics do.

The version of Hardy which has become established sees him as the novelist of a vanishing way of life, with a nostalgic yearning for old-fashioned rural simplicity and a deep hostility to the disruptive forces of urbanism, industrialism, even education (Brown thinks that 'he found the "more perfect insight into the conditions of existence", which education brought to bear, to be stunting to life'). Rural society up to about 1870 is seen as essentially good. A few critics question this view, for example John Holloway:

> They (the novels) suggest not just a growing preoccupation with the rural problem, nor even a growing sense that an earlier way of life was inevitably vanishing. They suggest something more disquieting: a gathering realisation that the earlier way did not possess the inner resources upon which to make a good fight for its existence. The old order was not just a less powerful mode of life than the new, but ultimately helpless before it through inner defect.[10]

The popular version, however, is still firmly established and needs to be examined and refuted in further detail. My purpose is to study Hardy's 'novels of character and environment' in the light of his conception of rural society. It is my argument that when they are read in this way, a very much greater and more complex artist emerges than has been recognised before.

Because of the amount of controversy about conditions in rural England between 1840 (the year Hardy was born) and 1900 (after he had stopped writing fiction) it seemed necessary to go back to the beginning and give a brief account in the first chapter of what was happening in the countryside during those years. Not being a historian I had to rely fairly heavily on modern histories of agriculture, as well as my reading from the period itself, and the chapter makes no claim to be original. The same is true of the first chapter of Part Two, which studies the history, agriculture and geography of the region which Hardy called Wessex in order to relate it to the novels in a new way.

The first half of the book attempts to give a context to Hardy's novels, by studying the work of other writers on the same themes. The primary aim is to find out what their attitudes to change in the countryside were. It was impossible within the limits of this book to go much further back than the year 1840, which meant that writers like Clare, Crabbe and Cobbett had, regretfully, to be left out. Non-fiction is studied in the second chapter; the history of the country novel in Chapter 4 – which tries to show in what ways these novels differed from Hardy's, even when they were dealing with the same material, and how it is possible to see Hardy's work as the culmination of a tradition. Chapter 3 concentrates on Richard Jefferies, a remarkable and unjustly neglected writer who has often been compared with Hardy as a novelist and an observer of country life. Chapter 6 is a special case. The 'theme of seduction', which comes up over and over again in discussions of country life during this period, demanded a chapter to itself, so I have studied the developments of attitudes towards it in a comparison of three novels, *Adam Bede*, *A Village Tragedy*, by Margaret Woods (a very interesting book which modern readers are unlikely to know about) and *Tess of the d'Urbervilles*. I felt that this comparison showed that Hardy had gone a long way beyond other nineteenth-century writers on the same theme.

In the second half, where Hardy's novels are studied in more detail, readers are invited to bear the first half in mind and to keep drawing comparisons between Hardy and the other writers, fictional and non-fictional, who have been discussed here. Perhaps then we shall be better able to see how much he had in common with these writers and how far he rejected them. My own view is that, although much material of great value had been written on the subject before him, his novels are the first to transform the life of rural England into great and imperishable art.

Part One

1 Rural England 1840–1900

In the last sixty years of the nineteenth century the population of England and Wales more than doubled. But the numbers of those employed in agriculture kept dropping, in tens and hundreds of thousands, after the peak census year of 1851. In 1840 agriculture was the most important of all industries, absorbing over twenty per cent of the labour force. By 1900 it employed less than ten per cent and it was widely believed that if the present trends went on the countryside would soon be depopulated and British farming would come to an end.

What had happened was that the agricultural labourers had shown quite clearly that they refused to stay on the land if there was any alternative. The growth of industrial towns had offered them better-paid jobs; railways had given them a means of leaving their native villages, and education – it was claimed – had made them dissatisfied with their conditions. Joseph Arch's Union (which we shall discuss later) had encouraged many thousands of labourers to move to the towns or to emigrate abroad. During this period their living standards had gone up somewhat and their condition had improved in other ways. Education had become compulsory after 1870; labouring men had been given the vote in 1883 and by the end of the century female and child labour had almost disappeared.

The changes in English society over these sixty years were so enormous and far-reaching that they can only be summarised briefly in this chapter. The aim is not so much to analyse the rural crisis in depth as to get some idea of the kind of society Thomas Hardy was writing about.

We shall get a good rough idea of conditions in rural England in the middle of the century by looking at James Caird's map, published in 1852.* This map is an illustration of Caird's argument – a controversial one at the time – that the growth of towns, so far from being a threat to agriculture, was actually a stimulus to its development. It showed that 'the marked inequality in wages and poverty . . . bisects the kingdom by unmistakeable lines into two great geographical divisions'[1] – the north and the south.

The reason why labourers in the north were so much better paid was that there were mines and large industrial cities there where they could find work if their wages were not high enough:

> The influence of manufacturing enterprise is thus seen to add 37 per cent to the wages of the agricultural labourers of the Northern counties, as compared with those of the South. The line is distinctly drawn at the point where coal ceases to be found.[2]

So labourers had everything to gain from the Industrial Revolution:

> We constantly hear expressions of regret, on the part of those who do not look beneath the surface, that the agricultural labourer, hitherto accustomed to the peace and plenty of his Arcadian lot, is year after year being withdrawn from it by the increasing demands and more tempting wages of the manufacturer. But, when we look to the facts, we find that in the manufacturing districts agricultural rents and wages have kept pace with each other; while in the purely agricultural counties the landlord's rent has increased 100 per cent, and the labourers' wages not quite 14. In the Northern counties the labourers are enabled to feed and clothe themselves with respectability and comfort, while in some of the Southern counties their wages are insufficient for their healthy sustenance.[3]

* Sir James Caird (1816–92) was one of the most distinguished agriculturists of his day. In 1850 *The Times* asked him to do a survey of English agriculture after the repeal of the Corn Laws. Caird investigated thirty-two counties in what was the only comprehensive survey between Arthur Young's in 1770 and Henry Rider Haggard's in 1902. Though himself a tenant farmer, he supported free trade and industrial growth. He was a strong advocate of scientific farming, conversion of arable land to pasture and the free movement of labour. 'The agricultural improver cannot stand still', he wrote, 'if he tries to do so, he will soon fall into the list of obsolete men'.

Outline Map of England

Shewing the distinction between the Corn and Grazing counties; and the line of division between high and low Wages.

All to the East of the black line, running from North to South, may be regarded as the chief Corn Districts of England; the average rental per acre of the cultivated land of which is 30 per cent less than that of the counties to the West of the same line, which are the principle Grazing, Green Crop, and Dairy districts.

The dotted line, running from East to West, shows the line of Wages; the average of the counties to the North of that line being 37 per cent higher than those to the South of it.

(Source: Caird's Map of England, 1852).

The reason for this was that labourers in the south of England – although many were unemployed and nearly all badly paid – had no alternative source of employment. There was very little industry in the south, railways were new and strange and it was psychologically impossible for many people to leave the villages where their ancestors had lived for generations. They knew nothing about the life outside it. As Hardy said in *The Mayor of Casterbridge*, 'To the liege subjects of Labour, the England of those days was a continent, and a mile a geographical degree'. At the time Caird was writing there was scarcely any emigration from the south to the north, although this would have solved many labourers' problems. He himself urged the government 'to enable and encourage the free circulation of labour throughout England', adding – prophetically, as it turned out:

> As labourers begin to withdraw, employers will soon discover, under the pressure of higher wages, that the surplus was not as great as they led themselves to believe.[4]

The other thing which Caird's map shows clearly is that the south and east were mainly corn-growing districts while the north and extreme west specialised in cattle farming. Conditions varied widely in fact from region to region, from county to county and from small farm to small farm:

> Much of English farming was 'mixed', which is to say that the cultivation of arable crops was associated with the fattening of cattle and sheep . . . While there were many pasture farmers who had little or no arable acreage, there were relatively few arable farmers who did not keep some sheep or cattle . . . There was also a considerable degree of regional specialisation . . . The farmers of the eastern and southern counties depended mainly on arable products, particularly on wheat . . . The western half of the English lowland area, south-western England and the border areas, were largely given over to grass . . . Finally the farmers of the upland areas, the Pennines, Yorkshire moors, Welsh hills and the remote north, depended largely on sheep.[5]

By the end of the century the agricultural map of England would have looked very different from Caird's as a great deal of arable land had been converted to pasture. A struggle for supremacy had been going on between the corn-growing farmers and the 'graziers', who specialised in meat and dairy produce. Their interests were not identical; often they were strongly opposed. The Anti-Corn Law League drew much of its support from dairy farmers who wanted cheap grain for their cattle (as well as from urban workers who wanted cheap bread). The repeal of the Corn Laws in 1846 was in the long run a bitter blow to the arable farmers of England.

In the next thirty years, however, English agriculture was very prosperous. Production went up and was increased by the modern methods of farming which were coming into use. During these years the price of wheat remained fairly stable because foreign countries were not yet in a position to compete with it. The price of meat and dairy produce rose steadily because the working classes were becoming more prosperous and could afford better food. But after 1875 a series of disastrous harvests coincided with an influx of cheap grain from America and caused heavy losses among the corn farmers. (The pasture farmers also had some competition in the shape of Danish butter and American canned meat, but this was much less serious. Farmers who traded only in perishable products like milk and eggs were in the strongest position of all.)

There were two 'great depressions', in 1875–84 and 1891–9, and these made it clear that the independent corn industry could not keep going unless there was a return to Protection, which was politically impossible. Also, labourers had begun to migrate in large numbers since the early seventies (their reasons for doing so will be discussed in the next section). On top of their other difficulties the farmers had to cope with an acute labour shortage and to raise the wages of those workers who stayed on the land. But few of them were actually ruined (Table 2 shows that the numbers of farmers between 1840 and 1900 remained much the same). The natural solution to their problems was to convert arable land to pasture, especially as a dairy farm required only about half as many workers. They also began to use much more labour-saving machinery during the nineties – by which time the exodus of the labourers had slowed down.

By the end of the century things appeared desperate to observers like Rider Haggard who saw only the farmers' point of view. But in fact English agriculture was on the verge, not of ruin, but of a small-scale revival. Between 1900 and the outbreak of war in 1914 prices began to rise again and the numbers of agricultural workers, and the population of many rural areas, went up for the first time in many years. The farming interest had survived – despite the most gloomy predictions – and adapted itself successfully to the needs of a modern industrial economy in which it had necessarily to play a subordinate role.

The Structure of Rural Society

The aristocracy – 'a group of rather over 300 landed families which contained wide differences of wealth'[6] – constituted in the 1840s the backbone of the English ruling class. Land ownership carried a prestige which the rising urban capitalists (like the Stoke-d'Urbervilles in *Tess*) were very anxious to buy:

> In the nineteenth century a new class was beginning to invade the countryside, the rich manufacturers from the Midlands and North, wanting to . . . make their sons into gentlemen on their new country estates.[7]

Ranking just below the great landlords was the much larger class of small country squires. The combined property of these classes was immense, the New Domesday Survey of 1873 showed that 'four-fifths of the land of the United Kingdom was owned by less than 7000 persons'.[8] The Anglican clergy was linked to these landed gentry by many family and property ties. It was virtually alienated from the labourers; radicals tended to be Methodists or attached to some other nonconformist sect.

About half of all English farmers were tenants holding land from the squires. The others were smallholders, or 'family farmers' who employed hardly any outside labour and formed a relatively independent class.

Most villages also contained a small group of rural craftsmen, described by Hardy in *Tess*:

> The village had formerly contained, side by side with the agricultural labourers, an interesting and better-informed class, ranking distinctly above the former . . . and including the carpenter, the smith, the shoemaker, the huckster, together with nondescript workers other than farm labourers; a set of people

who owed a certain stability of aim and conduct to the fact of their being life-holders . . . copyholders, or occasionally small freeholders.*

This was the class which suffered most from the dwindling of the village market and the industrialisation of neighbouring towns. The farmers resented its semi-independent position (it was this class, significantly, which provided most of the leadership of the early trade unions), and persecuted it in petty ways. By the twentieth century it had practically disappeared.

We can see from this survey that the class structure of rural society was rather complex. The gap between rich farmers and landless labourers was immense, but social mobility was possible on a limited scale. A small farmer might lose his capital and sink to being a bailiff, whereas a shepherd might *rise* to being a bailiff or even to renting a small farm of his own. Members of the small group of rural craftsmen might easily lose their homes and jobs and become ordinary labourers. The fluctuation of individuals between classes is one of the central themes in Hardy.

The Labourers

The condition of the labourer in the 1840s has been summed up:

He was given starvation wages, overlong hours of work, disgraceful housing, little or no education, and was generally treated as of lowly estate and as being of no account, an object of charity, perhaps, but with no prospect of improving his lot.[9]

As a general picture this is true enough, although we must make some qualifications. There were skilled workers, for instance, like shepherds and carters, who earned an extra shilling a week. The regional differences, as we have seen, were also very striking. In 1837 a survey showed the Cheshire labourers as the most prosperous in the country with 13s a week and the Dorsetshire labourers worst off with 7s 6d.[10] During the next sixty years wages rose everywhere, but not steadily or uniformly, for the

* Life-holders rented their cottages for the duration of three lives, unlike the ordinary labourers who could be turned out whenever the farmers wished. But when the last life ended they were often forced to leave. Hardy shows this happening in *The Woodlanders* and *Tess*.

eastern arable region and the backward western counties of Dorset, Wiltshire and Devon always lagged behind the rest. Besides, in areas of underemployment (the south-west was particularly bad) these wages were not constant, and after 1834 those who could not manage were sent to the hated workhouse. Unmarried mothers and old people past working were often forced to go there, but able-bodied men preferred to steal sheep, or to poach.

Poaching was very popular – in spite of the savage penalties – because a labourer's family only rarely got the chance to eat meat. The great staple of their diet was bread, helped out by cheese and potatoes, beer and tea. Meat and dairy produce only became widely available in the 'great depression' years.

Cottages were usually small, dirty and overcrowded (two or three generations might be living under the same roof). They were let by the farmers exclusively to their own labourers, which meant that anyone who lost his job would be turned out at once. As late as 1884 Jesse Collings wrote that this

> subjects the men to great hardships. It frequently compels them to accept lower wages and submit to unjust treatment rather than be turned out of their houses. It puts them at the mercy of the farmers.[11]

At the beginning of our period it was normal for women and children to work in the fields. The farmers sometimes used their labour as a cheap substitute for men's, but when both children and their parents were employed the family was comparatively well off. Women did much of the roughest work. Children started very young, sometimes at younger than six. They were usually given the lighter jobs, such as bird-scaring, but even these could have disastrous effects on their health. Joseph Arch wrote:

> The sickly son of an agricultural labourer had as little chance of growing up to a healthy manhood as had the sickly son of a miner or a mill hand . . . The life of poor little Hodge was not a whit better than that of a plantation nigger boy.[12]

The most notorious exploitation went on in the eastern counties where gangs of children and teenagers roamed the countryside doing casual labour. (The moral atmosphere of these gangs was described by Marx in a passage we shall study in the next chapter.) In the sixties there was a public outcry which led to their suppression. The Agricultural Children's Act of 1873, and the coming of compulsory education, did away with child labour in its old form. This was not always popular. Many labourers resented the loss of their children's earnings and this was one reason why they became much more militant around this time.[18]

Trade Unionism

The 'last labourers' revolt' in the southern counties in 1830 had ended in widespread hangings and transportations. Four years later, in Tolpuddle (a few miles from Hardy's birthplace), six men who tried to form a trade union branch were transported. For the next thirty years the labourers remained largely apathetic:

> Their isolation from the main stream of working class life concentrated in the towns was the result of their geographical separation and their dispersal in small scattered groups under the eyes of their employers.[14]

In the late 1860s, however, union branches began to appear again in the underpaid south. By far the most important was Joseph Arch's National Union, founded in Warwickshire in 1872.* This happened, Arch tells us, only because the men were half-starved and at the end of their tether. 'Oppression, and hunger, and misery, made them desperate, and desperation was the mother of Union'.[15]

The Union spread like wildfire over the poverty-stricken southern counties. Within a few months it had fifty thousand members and had forced up wages in several areas. The

* Joseph Arch (1826–1919) was the son of a Warwickshire shepherd and grew up in a condition of grinding poverty which made him hate both the exploiting class and the Anglican Church. He left school at nine and got a job scaring birds, but went on reading all he could and 'managed to pick up piecemeal what was then considered a fair education'. He became a skilled piece-worker earning good money, but agreed out of sympathy to organise the Warwickshire labourers when they became desperate in February 1872. Though a moderate man he became a bogy-figure to the farmers. After the Union's collapse he was a Liberal M.P. for some years. His *Life* (1898) is one of the great documents of labour history. Hardy wrote in 'The Dorsetshire Labourer' that 'nobody who saw and heard Mr. Arch ... ever forgot him and the influence his presence exercised over the crowds he drew'.

labourers' new-found militancy came as a profound shock to
observers:

> It was as if the dead had come to life... The agricultural
> labourer had seemed hopeless. The serfs of the plough had
> lost even the aspiration to be free men. Such at least was the
> prevailing opinion when Joseph Arch arose.[16]

The movement was very different from the previous outbursts
of rick-burning and machine-smashing among the labourers. It
was scrupulously legal and non-violent, and was led in most cases
by skilled, responsible men. Organisers on all levels tended to be
small rural craftsmen or tradesmen who were independent of the
farmers both economically and intellectually (several of them
were Dissenters) – that is, members of the class in which Hardy
was so interested.

> The management of a union branch demanded a degree of
> education that was rare among labourers, and more likely to
> be met with among the shopkeepers (who had emerged some
> time before as a distinct and superior class).[17]

The nature of the leadership explains the Union's emphasis on
self-respect and self-government. Its propaganda concentrated
powerfully 'on education and temperance, on demands for the
franchise and the nationalisation of the land'.[18] Arch repeatedly
urged the labourers to educate themselves and their children.
Another of their leaders, Heywood, said

> they must not neglect the claims of the mind in favour of the
> claims of the body. They must learn to read, read the Bible,
> read good books, and good newspapers, and they must not
> only read, but read thoughtfully'.[19]

The effect of this 'revolt of the field', as it was called, was to
push up wages by twenty to thirty per cent. Where this could not
be done the Union helped men to move to the towns to find work.
Many of them had never left the village before, and their new
mobility represented a psychological liberation:

> The labourer, through the Union, was now able to break the
> chain of poverty, fear and debt, which had tied him by the leg

to one place. He would hobble off elsewhere, and soon he would learn how to walk erect – a free man.[20]

Others went to the Dominions or America, where they helped the foreign market to outsell English produce. 'The very men that the farmers said seven years ago they would starve into submission, are those who are now helping foreign growers to compete with the farmers at home',[21] Arch said at a meeting in 1878.

Helping the labourers to migrate or emigrate was really the central achievement of the Union, for it turned out to be too difficult to fight the farmers on their own ground. Only about a quarter of the labour force ever joined the Union, there were internal quarrels and in 1884 it collapsed. But it was impossible for the labourers ever again to be treated as they had been. They continued to leave the land in increasing numbers* and this forced an improvement in the conditions of those who remained behind.

Most observers, including Arch himself, watched the depopulation of the countryside with dismay, but there was nothing they could do about it. Probably the only thing that could have kept the labourers on the land would have been the opportunity to possess land of their own. The Union voiced the popular demand that each man should have 'two acres and a cow', but this never happened. Towards the end of the century, allotments were granted in several places but they made very little difference to the rate of migration. Many people (we shall be studying some of them later) would have liked to see a return to a society based on the land, but this was not suited to the needs of England in the twentieth century:

> More than Acts of Parliament were needed to turn a centuries-old rural proletariat into a race of peasant cultivators. The labourer remained a labourer, although he now had a cheap and somewhat better cottage, an allotment, education, better access to the amenities of towns, and after 1883 the vote.[22]

Yet the impact of the modern world which broke up the old static village community had, in a very important sense, set the labourer free. In the 1840s he had been, in the words of a popular pamphlet

* It has been established by John Saville that those who left tended to be young people, especially girls.

a tiller of the soil, a scarer of birds, a keeper of cows and sheep, follower of the plough, a producer of wealth, that my masters might live in idleness and luxuriousness all the days of their lives.[23]

By the end of the century he was able and willing to leave the village at an early age and become absorbed in the working class of the towns. Those who remained on the land freely chose to do so, and their standard of living was higher than ever before. They were aware of, and in touch with, the world outside the village. They had learned to read and write, they were able to vote. The English countryside in the year 1900 was still poor and backward, but it had at least got rid of the worst evils of a system which 'keeps the labourers bound and therefore ignorant; ignorant and therefore bound'.[24]

Table 1: Population of England and Wales, 1840–1900

1840	15,731,000
1850	17,773,000
1860	19,902,000
1870	22,501,000
1880	25,714,000
1890	28,764,000
1900	32,249,000

Table 2: Number of Farmers in England and Wales, 1841–1901*

1841	252,192
1851	249,431
1861	249,735
1871	249,907
1881	223,943
1891	223,610
1901	224,299

* Figures up to and including 1871 are misleading because the census returns included retired farmers up to this date. The actual numbers seem to have altered very little.

Table 3: Numbers of Labourers in England and Wales 1841–1901

	Males	Females
1841	922,719	37,663*
1851	1,232,576	143,475
1861	1,206,280	90,525
1871	1,014,428	58,656
1881	924,871	40,346
1891	841,884	24,150
1901	715,138	12,002

* The number of female labourers in 1841 was certainly much higher than that given by the census of that year which did not include married women. But 1851 was probably the peak census year.

Table 4: Child Workers in Agriculture 1851–81*

	Males under 15	Females under 15
1851	105.7 thousand	13.2 thousand
1861	119.0 „	6.1 „
1871	98.0 „	4.2 „
1881	68.0 „	2.1 „

* These figures are taken from Charles Booth's article, 'Occupation of the People of the United Kingdom 1801–81', in the *Journal of the Statistical Society* for June 1885.

2 Country Writing 1840-1900

Throughout the century the stereotype of a happy and innocent countryside where all the vicars were hard-working and all the girls virtuous remained very popular with urban readers, although it was ludicrous to anybody who knew the real facts. The sentimental poetry of Mary Burrows is typical of this school of thought:

> Scatter'd around the verdant village green
> The peasants'* humble cottages are seen;
> Some almost hidden by the clust'ring flowers,
> The produce of their evening's leisure hours.
> Within these small abodes the eye may see
> The neat and careful hand of industry.[1]

– and so on. This overlooks the fact that the village green had generally been enclosed more than a century before, that most cottages were small and filthy, and that the occupants had to live with the threat of eviction – what Hardy called 'the Damocles sword of the poor'.[2] The Dorset dialect poet William Barnes†

---

* The word 'peasants' was often used in the nineteenth century to describe agricultural labourers. In the sense of serfs or small landed proprietors it had long since ceased to have any relevance in England. The 'peasants' here were actually hired labourers – a proletariat.

† William Barnes (1801–86), the rector of Winterborne-Came in Dorset, was originally a farmer's son who worked in the local solicitor's office as a boy and taught himself 'an astonishing number of languages and dialects. A more notable instance of self-help has seldom been recorded', Hardy said in his obituary notice in *The Athenaeum*. He published several collections of poems in the Dorset dialect, which, as Hardy said, 'far from being, as popularly supposed, a corruption of correct English . . . is a distinct branch of Teutonic speech'. Hardy, who knew him and greatly admired his poetry, thought nevertheless that it was lacking in realism. 'He held himself artistically aloof from the ugly side of things – or perhaps shunned it unconsciously; and we escape in his pictures the sordid miseries that are laid bare in Crabbe . . . He does not probe life so deeply as the

writes in *The Hwomestead a-Vell into Hand* about a family
which is due to be turned out when the last of three lives drops:

> But after me, of all my kind,
> Not wone can hold them on;
> Vor we can't get a life put in
> Vor mine, when I'm a-gone.

And he recognises that this sort of thing is happening everywhere; the houses usually being pulled down when the people
have been evicted:

> Of eight good hwomes, where I can mind
> Vo'k liv'd upon their land, John,
> But dree be now a-left behind;
> The rest ha' vell in hand, John,
> An' all the happy souls they ved
> Be scatter'd vur an' wide.
> An' zome o' on be a-wanten bread,
> Zome, better off, ha' died . . .

> An' I could lead ye now all round
> The parish, if I would, John,
> An' show ye still the very ground
> Where vive good housen stood, John.
> In broken orcha'ds near the spot,
> A vew wold trees do stand;
> But dew do vall where vo'k woonce zot
> About the burnen brand
> In housen warm,
> A-kept vrom harm
> By elems that did break the storm.[5]

Compare this with the turnip-hoer's remark in the first chapter
of *The Mayor of Casterbridge*, 'There were five houses cleared
away last year, and three this; and the volk nowhere to go'. Or

other parson-poet'. Most of his poems are simple love-lyrics and the note
of social criticism in *The Hwomestead a-Vell into Hand* or another poem,
The Common a-Took in is untypical. 'His rustics are, as a rule, happy
people'.[3] Francis Kilvert quoted him as saying that his work was inspired
'by love for and kindly sympathy with . . . the dear scenes and friends of
his youth'.[4]

with the description in *The Woodlanders* of Giles's visit to the site of his old home after it has been pulled down:

> He noticed that the familiar brown-thatched pinion of his paternal roof had vanished from its site, and that the walls were levelled, according to the landlord's principle at this date of getting rid of cottages wherever possible . . . Even in the gloom he could trace where the different rooms had stood; could mark the shape of the kitchen chimney-corner in which he had roasted apples and potatoes in his boyhood, cast his bullets, and burnt his initials on articles that did and did not belong to him. The apple trees still remained to show where the garden had been, the oldest of them even now retaining the crippled slant to north-east given them by the great November gale of 1824, which carried a brig bodily over the Chesil Bank . . . Apples bobbed against his head, and in the grass beneath he crunched scores of them as he walked. There was nobody to gather them now.

This prose and poetry make it clear that there was another tradition of country writing, one which dealt realistically with the facts of destruction and destitution and which had no time for the pleasant fictions of the 'Arcadian school'. But sometimes we find the same writer wavering uneasily between the description of country life as it actually was and the idealised conception of what it ought to have been. The Howitts are among the best examples of this.

William Howitt

William Howitt (1792–1879) and his wife Mary (1799–1888), although they are almost forgotten now, were in their own day very popular writers. Jointly and separately they produced an enormous number of novels, poems, translations and non-fictional works – of which the most relevant here are William's *Rural Life of England* and *Year-book of the Country*. The Howitts, who both came from Quaker homes, were involved in several humanitarian movements. Their attitude to social problems was the same as the Christian Socialists; they sympathised deeply with the people's sufferings but dreaded a violent revolution. Mary Howitt was a commonplace, rather sentimental writer, but

William had a lively vigorous style and a streak of real talent, though the good part of his work is almost swamped by the bad.

*The Rural Life of England*⁶ is a vast, shapeless book, which can hardly be said to fulfil its object of rendering 'a perfect portraiture of English country life . . . as seen in all classes and all parts of the country'. And yet, here and there, sometimes almost by accident, it does give us several revealing glimpses of the English countryside, two years before Hardy was born.

In many ways Howitt idealised the *status quo*. His account begins:

> Let every man who has a sufficiency for the enjoyment of life, thank heaven most fervently that he lives in this country and age.

Yet the whole book is not like this – indeed the phrase 'every man who has a sufficiency' may already have hinted at what is to come. He writes in the most rhetorical way about the civilisation of rural England:

> The poetry and the picturesque of rural life . . . the delicious cottages and gardens . . . the scores of sweet old-fashioned hamlets, where a humble sociality and primitive simplicity yet remain . . . all those charms and amenities of country life, which have inspired poets and patriots with strains and with deeds that have crowned England with half her glory.

But Howitt's rhapsodies over 'the extraordinary blessings and privileges of rural life', his cheery assurance that everything is for the best in the best of all possible words, are continually being interrupted by unpleasant facts. Beside this kind of rhetoric, and embedded among long descriptions of forests and wild cattle, country houses and May Day celebrations, we find pages of sharp and relevant social criticism which are very startling in the context.

He describes the typical labourer like a creature from another planet:

> There he is, as simple, as ignorant, and as laborious a creature as one of the wagon-horses that he drives. The mechanic sees his weekly newspaper over his pipe and pot; but the clod-hopper, the chopstick, the hawbuck, the hind, the Johnny-raw, or by whatever name, in whatever district, he may be called, is everywhere the same . . . he sees no newspaper, and

if he did, he could not read it . . . He knows there is such a
place as the next town . . . and that is all he knows of the
globe and its concerns, beyond his own fields.

Howitt suggested popular education to improve this state of
things and advocated other reforms, such as security of tenure and
the abolition of the workhouse. He was a natural optimist, convinced that everything would be all right if all classes would
work together for the common good. When he had to report
examples of how, in fact, the ruling classes did no such thing,
but made fat profits out of exploiting the labourers, it was always
in a tone of indignant surprise.

One would naturally have supposed that in a *Christian*
country there would have been a desire to provide for those
who had nothing . . . The rule has always been exactly the
reverse.

In rural Surrey he found that there were 'two nations', each
ignorant of the life of the other:

The aristocracy shut themselves up in their houses and parks,
and are rarely seen beyond them . . . They know nothing and
therefore can feel nothing for the toiling class . . . The working classes grow up with the sense that they are regarded only
as necessary implements of agriculture.

Howitt found that this social gulf was less wide in 'more
trading, manufacturing and mixed districts', and also that
'education progresses more in the northern and manufacturing
districts than in the southern and agricultural ones'. Although
he was distressed by the growth of industrialism, he realised that
it might possibly have some good effects.

Howitt's *Year Book*⁷ is shorter than the earlier work and
contains much less solid material – and it too is very rambling
and disorganised. But there is plenty of interesting material,
particularly the sketch of the old squire who hates everything
that smells of progress:

The poor are a very good sort of people; nay, he has a thorough
and hereditary liking for the poor . . . so long as they go to
church, and don't happen to be asleep there when he is awake
himself; and don't come upon the parish, or send bastards
there; so long as they take off their hats with all due reverence,

and open gates wheri they see him coming. But if they pre-
sume to go to the Methodists' meeting, or to a Radical club,
or complain of the price of bread, which is a grievous sin
against the agricultural interest; or to poach, which is all
crimes in one – if they fall into any of these sins, oh, then,
they are poor devils indeed! . . . How joyfully, spite of all
pleas and protestations of innocence, does he commit them to
the treadmill, or the county gaol.

The old gentleman sees his position threatened, not only by
the undeserving poor but also by the new race of 'upstarts' who
are obliterating all traditional distinctions of rank. 'I can assure
you, men are living in halls and abbeys in these parts, who began
their lives in butchers' shops and cobblers' stalls.' Worst of all,
one of his own tenants, a wheelwright's son, has recently 'grown
into a man of substance under the squire's own nose'. He can
only fume about this:

> 'Only to think', says he, 'that this fellow's father hadn't even
> wood enough to make a wheelbarrow till my family helped
> him; and I have seen this scoundrel himself scraping manure
> in the high roads, before he went to the village school in the
> morning, with his toes peeping out of his shoes, and his shirt
> hanging like a rabbit's tail out of his ragged trousers, and now
> the puppy talks of "my carriage" and "my footman"!'

This is a vivid and amusing picture of the old-fashioned
village tyrant who is rapidly being superseded by modern developments. But there is no guarantee that what is coming will be
any better. The squire's son is an elegant young man, who lives
mostly in London or abroad and has no interest in village life at
all. When he starts to talk about the future, Howitt can only
produce platitudes:

> The peasant is educating into a man . . . but the higher classes
> of society must learn to meet him, not by condescension, but
> by a true amalgamation of interests and ideas . . . In such a
> future shaping of social life, it is clear that our Old Squire can
> be made nothing of.

He is fairly certain that the past is dead, but he can only hope
piously that in the future the upper classes will mend their ways.

Alexander Somerville

Alexander Somerville (1811–85) became, against his will, a hero
of the Left for a short time during the Reform Bill agitation.
Brought up in great poverty as a carter's son in Scotland, he
worked in the fields for a time and then joined the Army because
it offered an easier life. At this time the soldiers were being trained
to break up peaceful Reform demonstrations. Somerville wrote
anonymously to a newspaper, saying that they would refuse to
do this. He was given a hundred lashes, and almost overnight
found himself a popular hero. But he refused to co-operate with
the extreme radicals. He was always a dour individualist, and
what evidence we have suggests that he moved to the Right as
he grew older. There is plenty of political dynamite in his earlier
works, but fundamentally Somerville was an eccentric, a conservative radical like William Cobbett, a man in whom blatant
right-wing prejudices and real fury at social injustice were inextricably mixed.

During the 1840s he was commissioned by the Anti-Corn Law
League to travel round England and write articles on what he
saw in the agricultural districts. These articles, which were
collected under the title of *The Whistler at the Plough*,[8] were the
most comprehensive and the most biting survey since Cobbett's
Rural Rides. But, unlike Cobbett, Somerville was writing as the
hired partisan of a cause, and his articles were a sustained
attempt to convince the farmers that Free Trade was in their
own best interests and that they must modernise their techniques.

Somerville began with the advantage of knowing what he was
talking about:

I once toiled in summer and harvest days with scythe and
reaping-hook, with bended back and sweaty brow; in winter
days clearing out the watery ditches with feet immersed, or
picking the frozen turnips to the snow-bedded sheep.

But his experiences since that time had separated him widely
from the ordinary labourers. He attacked them for resisting
machinery and enclosures, because this held up the process of
modernisation. He wanted to see them better off, but he believed
that the interests of all classes were identical:

I would like to see the farm labourers lifted up, not that I would like to see a farmer or a landlord brought down . . . while this would elevate the working population, it would add to the wealth of those who are already rich.

The usual answer to this sort of statement was that 'every improvement that takes place is for the rich, and not for the poor'. A labourer whom he met breaking flints outside the Earl of Shaftesbury's estate abused him in no uncertain terms:

'I see you ha' got a good coat on your back, and a face that don't look like an empty belly; there be no hunger looking out atween your ribs I'll swear. You either be a farmer or somebody else that lives on somebody else. May be you be a lord for aught I know on; or a squire; or a parson – dang it – you be a parson perhaps! One thing I see, you ben't one of them as works fourteen hours a day, to feed lords, and squires, and parsons, and farmers . . . Ah! it be enough to drive men mad; it ha' made men think on things they never would ha' thought on.'

For all his rather brash optimism, Somerville's observation of things as they were was completely clear-sighted. 'The labourer', he wrote, 'has, during the present century, retrograded in condition in every respect'. In the beautiful Thames valley he had seen workhouses 'crowded with the unemployed poor' while

the half-employed, and less than half-fed labourers were crawling about, asking, in return to every question asked of them, for 'something to get a drop of beer', adding that 'times be so terrible bad that they couldn't get half enough of work to do', that they couldn't 'get bread enough no how'.

The best parts of Somerville's work were his faithful recordings of his conversations with ordinary labourers. In Hampshire a man with several children told him:

'We never have no clothing, not new – not to speak on as clothes . . . I eat this bit of bread and drink some of that water in the ditch, and when it be done I be done with dinner . . . I ha'nt every day a bit of bread for breakfast. I be many a day out in the fields without breaking my fast till midday, and then, an I have a bit of bread and a sup of water, I be better than them as have none . . . Nettles, when in season, be good vegetable eating. We have a bit of lard or butter an we can; an cannot, why the salt must do.'

A labourer near Salisbury, who had been transported to the West Indies for poaching and found he had had a better life as a convict than as a free man, told him:

'We had another boy, but he died two weeks aback; as fine a boy as you could wish to see he wur, and as much thought on by his mother and I, but we ben't sorry he be gone. I hopes he be happy in heaven. He ate a smart deal, and many a time, like all on us, went with a hungry belly. Ah! we may love our children never so much, but they be better gone; one hungry belly makes a difference where there ben't enough to eat.'

And near Abingdon Somerville had a long talk with a plough-boy of fifteen who earned three shillings a week, never had a fire and hardly ever touched meat or vegetables:

'What have I for breakfast? Why, bread and lard.'
'And what for dinner?'
'Bread and lard.'
'What for supper, the same?'
'Ees, the same for supper – bread and lard.'

He slept in the loft, where the sheets were changed only once a year. Somerville asked him, 'Don't you find your bed disagree-able?', to which the boy replied:

'Do I! I bees too sleepy. I never knows nought of it, only that I has to get up afore I be awake, and never get into it afore I be a'most asleep. I be up at four, and ben't done work afore eight at night.'

Marx and Engels

The authors of *The Communist Manifesto* never imagined that the problems of agriculture and the agricultural worker could be studied in isolation from the rest of society. Engels, in *The Condition of the Working Class in England*,[9] headed his final chapter about the workers *The Proletariat on the Land*. He described the original destruction of the peasant class and how the former peasant 'was now simply a wage-earner'. The old patriarchal relations had broken down in the countryside and been replaced by a system of supply and demand.

The farm-workers are nearly all day-labourers and are employed only when they are wanted. Consequently they are often without any work for weeks on end – particularly in the winter . . . Wages have fallen and the poor rates have increased enormously . . . The agricultural districts have been the seat of *permanent* pauperism, while the factory districts have been the seat of *fluctuating* pauperism.

As a result 'what was once the most stable working-class group has now been drawn into the revolutionary movement'. In the 1840s there were innumerable cases of incendiarism.*

What do my readers think of this state of affairs in the peaceful, idyllic English countryside? Is this social war or is it not?

Engels thought that there could be no peaceful cure for the troubles of the countryside because they arose from the basic contradictions in capitalist society:

The manufacturers tell their workers that all their troubles will be over when the Corn Laws are repealed. The landlords and the majority of the farmers promise the farm labourers a heaven on earth if only the Corn Laws are preserved. But neither group of capitalists has succeeded in persuading the workers to accept their own favourite panacea.

Karl Marx, writing some twenty years later,[10] described the Corn Law controversy as a 'quarrel between the two factions of the ruling class about the question, which of the two exploited the labourers more shamefully'. He continued:

The repeal of the Corn Laws gave a marvellous impulse to English agriculture . . . All kinds of new machinery, more intensive cultivation generally, characterised this epoch . . . The area under cultivation increased, from 1846 to 1856, by 464,119 acres, without reckoning the great area in the Eastern Counties which was transformed from rabbit warrens and poor pastures into magnificent corn fields. It has already been seen

* In his short story *The Withered Arm* Hardy shows a young boy being hanged because he was present when a rick was set on fire.

that, at the same time, the total number of persons employed in agriculture fell.

He described how the great 'improvements' in English agriculture were making the labourers' conditions ever more wretched. Several thousands were being literally driven off the land, while those who remained were crowded into hovels, overworked in summer and half-starved in winter:

The continual emigration to the towns, the continual formation of surplus population in the country through the concentration of farms, conversion of arable land into pasture, machinery etc., and the continual eviction of the agricultural population by the destruction of their cottages, go hand in hand . . . The continuous superseding of the agricultural labourers, in spite of their diminishing number and the increasing mass of their products, gives birth to their pauperism . . . The minimum of wages becomes a law of nature to them . . . There are always too many agricultural labourers for the ordinary, and always too few for the exceptional or temporary needs of the cultivation of the soil . . . The temporary or local want of labour brings about no rise in wages, but a forcing of the women and children into the fields, and exploitation at an age constantly lowered. As soon as the exploitation of the women and children takes place on a larger scale, it becomes in turn a means of making a surplus-population of the male agricultural labourer and of keeping down his wage.

Marx described in detail 'a beautiful fruit of this vicious circle – the so-called gang-system', which flourished in Lincolnshire, where the country had just been drained by the new steam-engines, 'What were once fens and sandbanks, bear now a luxuriant sea of corn and the highest of rents'. The 'gang' was a collection of women, adolescents and children who roamed about the countryside under the gang-master who hired them, doing any work that came to hand. They were not merely overworked but completely demoralised:

Coarse freedom, a noisy jollity, and obscenest impudence give attractions to the gang. Generally the gang-master pays up in a public house; then he returns home at the head of the procession reeling drunk, propped up right and left by a stalwart virago, while children and young persons bring up the rear, boisterous, and singing chaffing and bawdy songs . . . The getting with child of girls of 13 and 14 by their male companions of the same age, is common. The open villages which supply the contingent of the gang, become Sodoms and Gomorrahs, and have twice as high a rate of illegitimate births as the rest of the kingdom . . . Children, when opium does not give them the finishing stroke, are born recruits of the gang.*

The reason why this abominable system existed was that it was the way to get the greatest possible amount of labour out of women and children, who were much cheaper to hire than men. Marx found that the rich farmers were being enriched still more by the exploitation of these children, while their parents were forced to let them work in the gangs because they themselves were chronically under-employed. It was a repulsive paradox: 'The cleanly weeded land, and the uncleanly human weeds, of Lincolnshire, are pole and counterpole of capitalistic production.'

Rider Haggard

After these accounts had been written, conditions in the English countryside changed, partly because of the depression and the crisis for corn-growing farmers, partly because of the rise of trade unionism. The best account of this is still Joseph Arch's *Life*. By the nineties the worst abuses of the old system had disappeared. Women had almost completely stopped working out of doors, children had been withdrawn from the fields and sent to school, and there was no longer any danger of the labourers' being unemployed. Indeed the danger was the opposite; so many labourers were now leaving the land for the towns that the farmers were beginning to be terrified that there would soon be none left.

The dominant tone in Somerville, Marx, Engels, Arch and even to some extent Howitt is one of fierce moral indignation that the labourers should be treated as they were. By the end of the century this would have seemed outdated to many observers who felt that the labourers had benefited more than any other class from the great changes on the land. Their main feeling was one of panic in case agriculture collapsed.

* Compare this with Hardy's description of the drunken women returning from their night out at Chaseborough in *Tess*.

Sir Henry Rider Haggard (1856–1925) – better remembered today for his novels about Africa – was a lifelong farmer and served on several government commissions on agriculture. In the early years of the twentieth century he travelled through twenty-seven counties and produced a massive report, *Rural England*,[11] about their conditions. It was the first time such a task had been attempted since Caird, fifty years before. To present it he adopted 'a new system – that of the interview', and a large part of the book consists of his conversations with farmers and local dignitaries all over the country. Unlike Somerville he hardly ever spoke to the labourers, whom he found too shy to talk very much. Although Haggard was an honest writer who tried to be impartial, his work is seriously marred by the fact that it presents things only from the farmers' point of view.

The picture he drew of the situation in villages all over England was simple and drastic. Farmers being gradually squeezed out of existence, labourers in such short supply that they could dictate their own terms, and an ever-increasing exodus of the young and intelligent into the towns. He had seen parts of England becoming 'almost as lonesome as the veld of Africa'. A Wiltshire farmer told him, as he pointed to a young labourer, 'he is the last left to I, and he will be off soon'. Everywhere the story was the same – 'unless something unforeseen occurs, farming must come to an end for lack of labour'. Haggard summed up:

> It is now common for only the dullards, the vicious, or the wastrels to stay upon the land, because they are unfitted for any other life; and it is this indifferent remnant who will be the parents of the next generation of rural Englishmen.

He foresaw that this crisis would lead to 'the progressive deterioration of the race'.*

A Suffolk farmer said that people left the villages because of the better wages and amenities in towns, bad housing conditions and 'the injudicious way the farmers treated their men a few years ago'. Haggard found plenty of evidence about the last point. He was told by General Booth of the Salvation Army:

* Haggard's impressions of what was happening in the countryside at this time are quoted extensively in Douglas Brown's *Thomas Hardy*, and form the basis of his attitudes towards the novels.

I have been amongst the farmers and I have heard them talk to their horses and pat them on the neck and speak to them like a gentleman, and talk to Tom, Dick or Harry as if he were a beast.

He added that if the employers in the docks talked to their workmen like that there would be a strike. But by this time the agricultural labourers had found just as effective a weapon. They did not now go on strike very much but they had discovered the simple and crushing tactic of withdrawing their labour for good – which, said a Dorsetshire clergyman, was mainly due to 'the lingering influence of the teaching of Joseph Arch'.

The process by which they had emancipated themselves was described like this by one of Haggard's interviewees:

About sixty years ago numbers of the more enterprising farming hands, growing very dissatisfied with their scanty pay and wretched condition, emigrated to the colonies. There . . . they retaliated upon their late employers by flooding our markets with their produce and keeping down the prices of English meat and corn . . . As education spread and national wealth increased, the labourer no longer felt tied to the soil and afraid to leave his parish. High wages induced him to enter the towns . . . the farm hand easily converted himself into a bricklayer's assistant, a porter, or a van or 'bus driver.

A new feeling of freedom and independence had sprung up among the labourers. In Wiltshire one of them said, when he was on the point of leaving the land for ever, 'We are masters now. I would sooner go to penal servitude than work for a farmer'.

Many farmers blamed the exodus on the growth of popular education – a subject which comes up in Haggard's account over and over again. Country children who had previously left school at the age of nine and gone straight into rook-scaring or other odd jobs now went on studying until they were about twelve and were no longer interested in working on the land when they left school. The farmers lost, not only the traditional supply of child workers, but also the young people whose higher level of knowledge encouraged them to find more rewarding work in the towns. A small occupier in Herefordshire suggested that an act should be passed to abolish education. Haggard seems to have felt that this was going a bit too far, but he quotes other, almost as extreme views without comment. A large landowner in Devonshire 'believed that education turns English working-class folk into upstarts, and makes them think that if only they are educated they need not labour', and a common complaint was that 'it would be better if the children were thoroughly instructed in reading, writing and arithmetic, and all the etceteras left alone'. Haggard's own opinion was broadly similar:

> Education has certainly done much to depopulate the rural districts, for if a lad cannot read and write and do a sum he is of no use in a town, and what he otherwise learns at school has no reference and no value to country life and farm labour.

It is, in fact, the traditional ruling-class attitude that the children of the poor should be taught only such things as are directly useful to them in their working lives, and that education for its own sake should be reserved for their betters. On other subjects Haggard was less reactionary. Unlike most farmers, he was sympathetic to the campaign for smallholdings which he thought would slow down the migration. Another remedy which he often heard urged was the abolition of Free Trade. Haggard shared the farmers' hostility – 'it has brought the land and agriculture of England very near to the brink of ruin' – but he realised that public opinion would never tolerate a return to Protection and a rise in the price of bread. He could foresee only a major disaster, and he bitterly blamed successive English governments for their indifference to agriculture.

> To them the great questions of the prosperity of agriculture and of that which is dependent on it, the holding of the rural population to the fields and villages where their forefathers have dwelt for centuries, are things of small account. They will not face the fundamental facts that it is well that we should grow all the food we can within the limits of our own shores, and that of this we could grow a much larger quantity than we do today; that men are more than money and deteriorate when crowded into towns, and that without a continually renewed supply of men and women, healthy in mind and body, the greatness of the nation must dwindle.

While he was investigating conditions in Dorset, he wrote to Hardy and asked him for his opinions. Haggard knew and greatly admired Hardy's work, including his article 'The Dorsetshire Labourer',* from which he quoted in the same chapter. The novelist's views, he said, 'will, I am sure, command universal attention and respect'.

Hardy began by describing the labourers' great poverty up to the fifties, but went on to say that things were 'widely different now ... Their present life is almost without exception one of comfort, if the most ordinary thrift be observed':

But changes at which we must all rejoice have brought other changes which are not so attractive. The labourers have become more and more migratory, the younger families in especial ... I cannot recall a single instance of a labourer who still lives on the farm on which he was born.

As a result there was 'no continuity of environment in their lives', and 'village tradition – a vast amount of unwritten folk-lore, local chronicle, local topography and nomenclature – is absolutely sinking, has nearly sunk, into eternal oblivion'. Accordingly

If you ask one of the workfolk ... the names of surrounding hills, streams, the character and circumstances of people buried in particular graves, at what spots parish personages lie interned, questions on local fairies, ghosts, etc., they can give no answer; yet I can recall the time when the places of burial, even of the poor and tombless, were all remembered.

Hardy thought that the constant migrations of labourers within Dorset were partly due to their wish for adventure, but that this was not the most important reason:

The prime cause of the removal is, unquestionably, insecurity of tenure. If they do not escape this in the towns, it is not fraught with such trying consequences to them as in a village ... Why such migrations to cities did not largely take place till within the last forty years or so is, I think, in respect of farm labourers, that they had neither the means nor the knowledge in old times that they have now. And they had not the inclination, owing to the stability of villagers of the other class, such as mechanics and small traders, who are the backbone of village life.

* To be discussed in Part Two, Chapter 1.

He concluded the letter:

> As to the future, and the ultimate result from such a state of things, it hardly becomes me to attempt to prophesy here. That remedies exist for them, and are easily applicable, you will readily gather from what I have stated above.

Haggard commented, 'I think I am not wrong in concluding that Mr Hardy believes the best way to retain labourers and their families on the land is to give them some opportunity of securing as owners or occupiers an interest in the land.'

Haggard also believed this but, unlike Hardy, he looked at developments mainly from the farmers' point of view. It seemed to him that they were suffering badly from the new order of things whereas the labourers were doing quite well out of it. 'Employment is plentiful; wages, by comparison, are high... food and other necessaries are very cheap.' Yet 'in face of these advantages... the rural labourer has never been more discontented.' He was more educated, more mobile, more restless, and with a keen memory of the miserable past. During the seventeenth century, Haggard explained:

> the smallholders were bought out, and sank into a condition of great misery, being forced to live like swine, and as labourers to take whatever wage was flung to them. Doubtless they wished to depart in those days, but there was nowhere to go, and no means of going. So they stayed until some thirty years since their eyes were opened.

Essentially a fair-minded man, Haggard recognised that the proletarianisation of the English peasants, and the centuries of exploitation which followed it, had made the labourers desperate to leave for what they envisaged as a life of freedom. Those who did remain on the land were the epitome of the despised and rejected – the lowest of the low:

> The farm labourer is looked down upon, especially by young women of his own class, and consequently looks down upon himself. He is at the very bottom of the social scale.

There is not much difference between this judgement and Howitt's, sixty years earlier – 'there is no part of the population for which so little has been done, and of which so little is thought.'

This was why all those with any pride or intelligence seemed to be flocking away from the land. They did not worry much about what was awaiting them, although Haggard and many others warned them that they would have a miserable life in the cities. They only knew that they had had enough of being exploited by farmers and parsons; so they went in their hundreds of thousands to swell the ranks of the industrial working classes, and to be exploited in a new way. It was really derisory to speak of the labourers, or for them to speak of themselves, as masters of the situation, when they had the choice only between two kinds of wage-slavery. Haggard described the fate of one of them in his conclusion:

> A while ago I met a man, evidently an agricultural labourer, walking down the Strand and literally weeping. It appeared on investigation that he had come up with his family from some rural district in the hope of 'bettering himself'. The result was that at the time of our meeting he and they were learning by sharp experience the meaning of the word starvation.

This was the result of a long process which had stretched over two generations – the transformation of the 'clodhopper' of 1840 into the rootless, half-educated, overtly rebellious manual labourer who in 1900 had been completely absorbed into the industrial town. During these sixty years rural England had changed just as drastically. Instead of being divided into small villages where people spent their whole lives and where one class was completely dominated by another it was emptying rapidly and experiencing a new internal mobility – and the class struggle had reached a virtual stalemate. This process had its tragedies in many thousands; there must have been innumerable labourers like the one Haggard met in the Strand. Over all this loomed the larger question of what future there could be for English agriculture. But the village magnates, generally speaking, refused to consider the only possible solution, which would have been to stop treating people as wage-labourers and to give them a genuine stake in the land. 'Remedies exist', Hardy had written, but in 1900 nobody seemed inclined to put them into effect.

3 Richard Jefferies

Early Works

On 14 November 1872, a long letter appeared in *The Times* about the condition of the labourers in Wiltshire. The subject was a topical one, for the Agricultural Labourers' Union had been founded only nine months earlier and labourers all over the south-west were going on strike for more pay. The letter, which was signed Richard Jefferies, was obviously written by a partisan of the farmers, but the author was not a farmer himself. He was a young and impoverished journalist whose work had only been printed in local papers so far.

The letter claimed that 'the agitators can gain no hold upon a county where, as a mass, the labourers are well paid'. Wages were 'very good', cottages 'infinitely better than they were', and 'agricultural women are moral, far more so than th~~e of the town'. The only thing wrong with the labourers wa their ingratitude:

> I can confidently say that there is no class of persons in England who receive so many attentions and benefits from their superiors as the agricultural labourers.

This letter sparked off a lively correspondence and Jefferies responded with two more. The first, published on 23 November, praised 'the noble clergy of the Church of England' for their work with allotments. The second, which came out four days later, said that 'the farmer cannot . . . do more than he has done for the labourer . . . A harder-working class of men does not exist than the Wiltshire farmers.'[1]

All these letters were grossly misleading. The 'agitators' did make an impact on Wiltshire, where they forced up wages by about a shilling a week, and this was long overdue. Throughout the century Wiltshire competed with Dorset and some eastern counties for the honour of having the worst-paid labourers in all

England. In the 1840s, wages were six or seven shillings, and
about eleven shillings fifty years later. There was a constant
underemployment problem because of the large surplus and a
very high proportion of the people (one-sixth in 1846–7) were
dependent on parish relief. 'The story of Hodge in 19th century
Wiltshire', a modern commentator writes, 'is not a happy one.
Ireland was not the only place in the British Isles where the
potato prevented a population from starving.'[2]

In spite of an important dairy-farming industry in the north,
Wiltshire was primarily a corn-and-sheep county, and 'when
depression came in the 1870s, south Wiltshire was as hard hit as
any part of East Anglia'.[3] After this the sheep were largely replaced by cattle, and much arable land was converted to pasture.
The dairy farmers sent a large supply of milk to London by
railway and this soon became a flourishing trade. Apart from
the growing industrial centre of Swindon, the county remained
primarily agricultural and therefore vulnerable to large-scale
emigration. The net population dwindled between 1841 and
1851 and remained almost stationary after that.

It will be remembered that Alexander Somerville found some
of his worst cases of destitution among the Wiltshire labourers.
It was outside Salisbury that one of them told him 'we may love
our children never so much, but they be better gone'. In another
article he described a conversation he had with some Wiltshire
labourers outside a church, where a sermon had been preached
on behalf of missionaries:

> I inquired if the clergyman who had preached was the one
> who usually ministered there? The answer of one of the
> men . . . was, 'Yes, blast him! – he be our own parson sure
> enough – he be always a begging; he be always, sin' ever I
> knowed him' . . . 'Ah!' says a woman . . . 'and look at wages
> a comin down, look at them rich wagerbonds as the parsons
> hunt and dine and drink with! So help me God we bes more
> fitter to be taken into the union and starved, than pay for
> parsons to go abroad.' 'Why don't they', said another, 'send
> them parsons as be chantering every day in Salisbury Cathedral
> to nobody but the bare stones, and be so rich as to have so
> much land all over, why don't they go?' '*They* don't go', said
> the old man who spoke first, 'because they be rich, they wants

the money to send away the poor uns; I know what they want; I been knowing them too long not to know that.'[4]

They said that they only went to church because they were afraid of losing their jobs if they stayed away.

Jefferies, the son of a small farmer, was born in 1848 in the village of Coate near Swindon and worked for the local newspaper as a young man. Until he died prematurely of tuberculosis in 1887 he wrote many hundreds of articles (from Surbiton, where circumstances compelled him to live) describing the countryside and its people. His beautiful descriptive essays, of which 'The Pageant of Summer' is the most famous, and his spiritual autobiography, *The Story of my Heart*, help us to understand the position from which he criticised rural life. Nature to him was the source of everything good, without which human beings could be neither moral nor happy, and this feeling accentuated the contrast between the beauty of the countryside and the degradation of the labourers' everyday lives.

Whether he was sincere in his letters to *The Times*, or whether he was only saying what the majority of readers wanted to hear, cannot now be guessed. But at about the same time he wrote a short story, *A True Tale of the Wiltshire Labourer*, which remained unpublished till after his death. It is the story of a country girl who is deserted by her husband (the clergyman turns him off his allotment) and reduced to utter misery. The farmer who extorts the rent tries to seduce her; she catches 'that low aguish fever, the curse of the poor', and eventually dies in childbirth, 'totally worn out at nineteen'.[5]

The essays Jefferies wrote in the early seventies, which are mostly collected in *The Toilers of the Field*, give a clear picture of his growing dissatisfaction with the conditions of village life. He writes about the farmers' stolid conservatism; the squalor concealed by 'that Arcadian beauty which is supposed to prevail in the country'; the demoralising influence of the alehouse; the children who are perpetually 'kicked, punched and thrashed':

There is little filial affection among these cottagers – how should there be? The boy is driven away from home as early as possible; the girl is made day by day to feel her fault in being a girl; to neither can the poor man give any small present, or any occasional treat.

'In the life of the English agricultural labourers', he concluded, 'there is absolutely no poetry, no colour'. What shocked him even more than their poverty was the condition this led to – 'the blunting of all the finer feelings, the total erasure of sensitiveness'.

He made several suggestions in these early essays for improving things: 'Village Organisation' calls for more local self-government; 'Unequal Agriculture' for more scientific farming. Jefferies hated large towns, but in 'The Story of Swindon'[6] he recognised that they might have a good effect on the countryside round them. Village people who came to work in Swindon

> carry back with them into the countryside the knowledge they insensibly acquire from their better-informed comrades, and exhibit an independent spirit. For a radius of six miles round the poorer class are better informed, quicker in perception, more ready with an answer to a question, than those who dwell farther back out of the track of modern life. Wages had materially risen long before the movement among the agricultural labourers took place.

In 1880 appeared his most solid work to date, *Hodge and his Masters*.[7] 'Hodge' was the popular name for the whole body of agricultural labourers in England. Hardy, in *Tess of the d'Urbervilles*, criticised this concept – 'the pitiable dummy known as Hodge' – because he felt that it lumped together many thousands of human beings who were actually very different. Jefferies himself was well aware of this:

> There is perhaps no class of the community less uniform than the agricultural ... Varying an old saw, it might be said, so many farmers so many minds.

The twenty-eight short sketches which make up this collection study several different types in the village, but – and this is their great weakness – much more among 'the masters' than 'Hodge'. The theme which dominates them all is the great changes which are impending:

> There has grown up a general feeling in the villages and agricultural districts that the landed estates around them are no longer stable and enduring. A feeling of uncertainty is abroad, and no one is surprised to hear that some other place, or person, is going.

He describes a small tenant farmer who is compelled to move out because of the bad times, and another who sinks into being a bailiff on his own old farm:

> One would think he could never endure to work as a servant upon that farm of all others, nor to daily pass the scenes of his youth. For yonder ... stands the house where he dwelt so many, many years, where the events of his life came slowly to pass; where he was born; where his bride came home; where his children were born; and from whose door he went forth penniless.

Jefferies' sympathy with the small farmers, apparently hopelessly trapped by the crisis of the depression years, was very deep. Another threat to their way of life which he saw looming was the growth of sophistication, especially among the farmers' daughters, which made them dissatisfied with life in the country. In one essay he discusses a girl who is in very much the same situation as Grace in *The Woodlanders* when she comes home from school:

> She does not note the subtle tint of bronze that has begun to steal over the wheat, nor the dark discoloured hay, witness of rough weather, still lying in the meadows. Her face ... does not light up with any enthusiasm as well-remembered spots come into sight.

Although the result is disastrous – a 'continuous drain of women out of agriculture' – Jefferies refuses to condemn the advance of urban culture:

> You cannot blame these girls ... for thinking of something higher, more refined and elevating than the cheese-tub or the kitchen. It is natural, and it is right, that they should wish to rise above that old, dull, dead level in which their mothers and grandmothers worked from youth to age. The world has gone on since then – it is a world of education, books and wider sympathies. In all this they must and ought to share.

Education, he foresaw, would be the cause of a great awakening among the labourers – possibly of a radical movement which he did not at this time support. He prophesied the growth of a whole generation like Jude the Obscure:

Here, in the agricultural labourer class, are many hundred thousand young men ... educating themselves in moral, social and political opinion.

Jefferies usually regards the labourers, in these essays, from a middle-class point of view. He abuses them for their indifference to religion, and attacks 'agitators' as unrepresentative of the people. All this is fairly conventional stuff. But' the concluding essay, 'Hodge's Last Masters', strikes a new and much more tender note. It concerns an aged labourer who dies in the workhouse, having been evicted against his will. Jefferies often denounced the Poor Laws in essays and novels; here he only comments:

Of every hundred pounds paid by the ratepayers how much is absorbed in the maintenance of the institution and its ramifications, and how very little reaches poor deserving Hodge!

He gives a brief history of the old man, who worked hard all his life and was finally left alone in the cottage where he had been born.

Those old familiar trees, the particular hedges he had worked among so many years, the very turf of the meadows over which he had walked so many times ... all these things had become part of his life. There was no hope or joy left to him, but he wanted to stay among them to the end.

In the workhouse – where 'there are many persons but no individuals' – he is miserable.

He missed his plum trees and apples, and the tall pear, and the lowly elder hedge. He looked round raising his head with difficulty, and he could not see the sign-post, nor the familiar red-bricked farmhouse.

In the very last paragraph of a book which generally gives an unsympathetic picture of the agricultural labourer, Jefferies sums up with a restrained and moving tribute to the millions of anonymous poor:

The end came very slowly; he ceased to exist by imperceptible degrees, like an oak tree. He remained for days in a semiconscious state, neither moving nor speaking. It happened at last. In the grey of the winter dawn, as the stars paled and the whitened grass was stiffened with hoar-frost, and the rime coated every branch of the tall elms, as the milker came from the pen and the young ploughboy whistled down the road to his work, the spirit of the aged man departed.

What amount of production did that old man's life of labour represent? What value must be put upon the service of the son that fought in India, of the son that worked in Australia; of the daughter in New Zealand, whose children will help to build up a new nation? These things surely have their value. Hodge died, and the very grave-digger grumbled as he delved through the earth hard-bound in the iron frost, for it jarred his hand and might break his spade. The low mound will soon be level, and the place of his burial shall not be known.

Novels

It took Jefferies a long time to learn to write novels. *The Scarlet Shawl*[8] and *Restless Human Hearts*,[9] both published when he was in his twenties, are practically unreadable. Both of them contrast corrupt London life with the purifying influence of nature. His third novel, *World's End*, shows a distinct improvement. The hero is a kind of Jude the Obscure, self-educated and isolated in a country hamlet. Like Jefferies he is vaguely pantheist:

He saw – he felt Nature. The wind . . . spoke to him in a mystic language. The great sun, in unclouded splendour slowly passing over the wide, endless hills, told him a part of the secret.[10]

The boy is bullied by his uncle, a farmer 'totally incapable of comprehending that all men are not absorbed in sheep and turnips' who wants him to work on the land, and is totally out of place in 'the harsh and rude life at World's End, among the weather-beaten and rough-speaking rustics'. Jefferies combines a deep reverence for nature with a strong dislike of contemporary rural life and the kind of people it produced. A sub-plot deals with a bullying farmer who sets fire to his own ricks for the insurance money and puts the blame on one of his labourers who is a Union member. Jefferies refers briefly to 'the great agricultural labourers' movement of the eastern counties', and denounces the farmers' habit of treating the labourer as 'a cheap machine'. Here, in contrast to much of his early work, he is unequivocally on the labourers' side.

Greene Ferne Farm[11] consists of two rather slight love stories tagged on to a detailed description of contemporary village life. A fairly serious conflict develops on the estate of Andrew Fisher, an aged and miserly farmer whose insensitivity to nature is directly connected with his insensitivity to people.

Hard as his own nether millstone was the heart of Andrew Fisher. The green buds of spring, the flowers of summer . . . all the beauty and glory of nigh on a century touched him not.

Towards the end of the book there is an impressive scene when the women workers file past his window on their way back from the fields in the glorious red sunset, bowing to him as they pass:

Do you suppose these women moved in rhythmic measures to Bacchanalian song and pastoral pipe? . . . Do you suppose their brows were wreathed with the honeysuckle's second autumn bloom, with streaked convolvulus and bronzed ears of wheat? Their backs were bowed beneath great bundles of gleanings, or faggots of dead sticks carefully sought for fuel, and they carried weary infants, restless and fretful. Their forms had lost all semblance to the graceful curve of women; their faces were hard, wrinkled and angular, drawn with pain and labour . . . All things green and lovely were spread around them . . . but the magic of it touched them not, for their hearts were pinched with poverty.

As so often in Jefferies, the beauty of nature is directly contrasted with the degradation of man. It turns out later that Fisher was dead at the time – 'the wearyful women as they passed the window had curtsied to the dead' – and his house is robbed by the people he had exploited. The red sunset is compared to the Day of Judgement; nature seems to be mutely protesting against man's inhumanity to man. This is the first work in which Jefferies presents rural exploitation in all its harshness, although he could not yet build a whole novel out of this fact.

The Dewy Morn[12] represents a considerable development from the earlier works. Felise, an unspoiled child of nature – 'she thought of nothing but the sun and wind, the flowers and the running stream' – is in love with Martial Barnard, a struggling tenant farmer on the estate of a rich Tory M.P. called Cornleigh Cornleigh. Robert Godwin, Cornleigh's steward, loves Felise and is bitterly jealous of Martial. Godwin is a harsh, tyrannical man; like Andrew Fisher, his indifference to nature is the corollary of his indifference to human beings – 'Robert Godwin never walked by the sea, nor gathered a flower'.

Felise's maid, Mary, is engaged to Abner Brown, a young labourer whose aged parents are threatened with eviction to the workhouse. Without a home they cannot get married and Mary becomes pregnant. This is a double disaster, because if her condition is discovered her own parents will also be evicted, under the rules of the Cornleigh estate. She tries to drown herself, and dies in childbirth; Abner is arrested for her murder because he is poor.

Felise and Martial, who have tried to help them, come together at last. Godwin commits suicide. Martial denounces the landlords at a public meeting and then moves to London with Felise to become an engineer.

It is fairly clear from this outline that a good deal of radical social criticism and searching social analysis is mingled with elements of the conventional, melodramatic Victorian plot. The labourers are 'ungrateful, speaking ill of those who wish them well, incapable of understanding goodness of heart':

> These morals are born of generations of cruel poverty, and they are perpetuated by the brutal modern system which leaves for the worn-out labourer or labourer's wife no refuge but the workhouse or the grave.

But whereas they are the victims of a cruel system, the landed aristocracy (whom Jefferies had idealised in *Hodge*) are its perpetuators. Cornleigh Cornleigh is a spineless creature, dominated by his religious wife who, together with the local clergyman, introduces the eviction statute against unmarried mothers – 'The House thus kept the population short of cottages, and then punished those who transgressed for want of a home of their own'. Cornleigh is angling for a knighthood after the next election, but his seat has become unsafe since the Ballot Act, which 'if the labourers obtained votes, would put the axe to the root of the tree of Cornleigh'.

Jefferies' bitterest scorn is reserved for the charitable rich people who organise a scheme to give the labourers free pictures:

> To suppose that any man is likely to be the better because a picture is graciously hung on his walls above the heads of squalling children, and over the table scarcely supplied with bread, is indeed a monstrous perversion of common sense... There can be no art in a people who know that at any moment they may be thrust out of doors.

His ideal of genuine art was something much more deeply rooted in the life of the people:

> Is not art rather in the man than on the wall? Once now and then I have seen into the cottages of farm labourers (who had the good fortune to possess security of tenure) and found old oak furniture; curious grotesque crockery, generally much coloured – the favourite colour red... And out of doors they had planted trees; without love of trees, I doubt if there by any art. Of art itself in itself they had had no thought, not one had ever tried to draw or paint. They had coloured their strips of flower-garden or bordering with bright yellow flowers; that was all the paint they knew.
>
> Yet I think this home-life in itself was something like true art... Altogether a realistic picture painted in actual dark oak, actual brass, actual red china, and actual yellow flowers.

Art cannot be cut off from ordinary life; it is not something static, as the wealthy philistines in *The Dewy Morn* imagine. It is the life-force which creates art; in a sense, certain kinds of life *are* works of art. Felise represents the principle behind art at its purest, unsatisfactory character though she is.

As for the condition of English agriculture, Jefferies is deeply pessimistic. Martial, in his passionate closing speech which incorporates Jefferies' own attitudes, denounces not only the landlords and the Church for their exorbitant rents and tithes but also the farmers for submitting to them. The farmers howl him down, showing just how abject they are. His conclusion is:

> There never will be any more prosperity in English agriculture till the entire system is revised, till a man can cultivate the land free from vexatious hindrances, medieval hindrances, superstitious hindrances, and burdens such as tithes... till

there be nothing to contend against but the seasons and the honest competition of the United States.

But as Jefferies cannot show this happening, the conventional happy ending is qualified by an awareness that the system in rural England corrupts everyone whom it touches. Only a few people are strong enough to escape this corruption, and they are eventually driven away from the land.

After London[13] is a novel outside the mainstream of Jefferies' work. It is an adventure story set in the future, when most of England has relapsed into barbarism and London, the city that Jefferies hated, has been reduced to a poisonous swamp. Felix, the hero, escapes from the restricted existence of an aristocrat to the free life of the woods. Fulfilment, as in all Jefferies' works, lies in contact with natural, vigorous forces, outside the artificiality of modern civilisation.

His last novel, *Amaryllis at the Fair*[14] has no real plot; the original and more appropriate title was *Scenes from Country Life*. Amaryllis is the daughter of Farmer Iden, who is a species of Jude the Obscure. Under his ordinary countryman's exterior, unsuspected by most people, 'a great mind was working under the most unhappy conditions'. It is said that he was based on Jefferies' father, who remained a small farmer all his life although his son felt that he would have been capable of much better things.

Iden understands every aspect of country life – 'trees and grass, and all that the earth bears', but the long years of petty struggling have coarsened him, the farm is not a success and his family is always in debt. Jefferies is extremely bitter about society's indifference to talent. 'Nothing so hard as to succeed by merit . . . nothing so incredibly impossible.'

Amaryllis tries to help by selling sketches, but although they are good they are turned down. She eventually falls in love with her cousin Amadis, who is ill and can offer her no security. 'Nothing ever happens in the fitness of things', and we leave her apparently heading for the same fate as her mother, who has been worn down into a shrew.

Here was Amaryllis, full of poetic feeling and half a painter at heart, full of generous sentiment – what a nature to be ground down in the sordidness of married poverty!

Part of the book describes her uncle, a journalist who sketches wild flowers in the corrupt atmosphere of London. His life, too, is a brave attempt to hang on to his own values in a hostile or indifferent community; 'Have you ever seen London in the early winter morning, when the frost lies along the kerb, just melting as the fires are lit; cold, grey, bitter, stony London?' But the organisation of rural society – as distinct from nature – does not contrast favourably:

> Only those who have lived in the country and had some practical experience could fully comprehend the hopelessness of working a small farm, unless you are of a wholly sordid nature.

There is a particularly scathing portrait of some rich Tory landowners, the Pamments, who are sealed up 'hermetically' in their great estates – 'you could hardly throw a stone over the walls if you tried'.

For all its inconclusiveness, this last novel, written when Jefferies was dying, has an atmosphere of sadness and holds out little hope for the future. A natural genius like Iden is ignored and misunderstood because he has no chance to fulfil himself in the society of the village, and is limited by it:

> Why was he so poor? Why did he work in the rain under a sack? Why did he gossip at the stile with the small-brained hamlet idlers?

And a similar eventual fate seems to await Amaryllis:

> How unnatural it seems that a girl like this, that young and fresh and full of generous feelings as she was, her whole mind should perforce be taken up with the question of money; an unnatural and evil state of things.
>
> It seems to me very wicked that it should be so.

This is perhaps the novel in which Jefferies comes nearest to greatness, for the melodramatic elements of the earlier ones have dissappeared leaving him free to write in the way that came naturally. The impact on a sensitive adolescent of her parents' squabbles, and the endless small frustrations of life in the village, are described with an extraordinary psychological truth. The

girl's freshness and enthusiasm for life not only make us sym-
pathise with her position; they also make us wonder whether she
will not have to survive, like Jefferies himself, through finding
beauty in ordinary things:

> A baked apple, he said, was the most wholesome thing in the
> world; it corrected the stomach, prevented acidity, improved
> digestion, and gave tone to all the food that had been eaten
> before . . . Just look at an apple on a tree, said Iden. Look at
> a Blenheim orange, the mixture of colours, the gold, and
> bronze, and ruddy tints . . .

Unfortunately *The Dewy Morn* has been out of print for years,
and none of the other novels are read much today. Those who do
read them are immediately struck by Jefferies' similarities to
Hardy. Edward Garnett in his introduction to the 1911 edition
of *Amaryllis* compared it favourably with *The Mayor of Casterbridge* and said that it was 'one of the very few latter-day novels
of English country life that are worth putting on one's shelf, and
that to make room for it he would turn out certain highly-praised
novels by Hardy'. Q. D. Leavis* thought that 'in Jefferies' novels
the best parts are better and more mature than the best parts of
most of Hardy's'.[15] Douglas Brown wrote:

> *The Dewy Morn* and *Amaryllis at the Fair*, his two most
> impressive novels, should have their permanent place alongside
> Hardy's novels on our shelves. Of rural truth we shall discover
> less in Hardy's Wessex than in Jefferies' Wiltshire, for Jefferies
> had the more penetrating knowledge of the whole range of
> agricultural life, the more passionate sympathy with the
> labourers, by far the surer grasp of rural economies, and the
> more astonishing sensibility towards the natural environment.
> The insight, the candour, the modesty and the sensuousness of
> his prose, and the strange audacity of some strokes of invention
> in his narratives, lay bare a sort of poverty in all but the finest
> pages of Hardy.[16]

These are exaggerated judgements, a reaction against the
scandalous neglect from which Jefferies has never really emerged.
The truth is that he was not a natural novelist; his talent was for
descriptive and moral essays about life in the countryside and he

* In one of the very few really good critical essays on Jefferies.

never fully mastered the techniques of creating characters and a plot. In his early career he tried to write successful conventional novels, and failed badly; in his last years he turned back to the kind of writing he understood best and produced two really good, although uneven works. It is not in the melodrama, but in the philosophy of a loving response to nature which shapes his finest novels that we find the real, valuable and enduring centre of Jefferies' work.

Late Essays

Writing in *Longman's Magazine* in November 1883, a few months after Hardy's essay 'The Dorsetshire Labourer' had appeared in the same paper, Jefferies said that the labourers of Wiltshire were primarily conspicuous for their 'education and discontent'. As in Dorset, they changed their jobs from year to year in the hope of higher wages. 'The total population is probably the same, but half of it is nomad.' The only way to cope with this, Jefferies argued, was to give the labourers security, in the shape of their own cottages and allotments with no strings attached. In 'After the County Franchise (1884)' he takes up the same theme. Although the labourers had been given the vote in 1883, this was only a step towards total emancipation:

> Made a man of by education – not only of books, but the unconscious education of progressive times – the labourer and his son and daughter have thoughts of independence ... The rule of parson and squire, tenant and guardian, is repellent to them in these days. They would rather go away ... The sentiment of independence must be called into existence before the labourer ... will willingly settle in the village. That sense of independence can only arise when the village governs itself by its own council, irrespective of parson, squire, tenant or guardian ... Towards that end the power to vote is almost certain to drift slowly.

He wrote enthusiastically in the long essay 'Country Literature',[17] 'Four hundred years after the first printed book was sent out by Caxton the country has begun to read.' Nothing could be more untrue, he argued, than the common impression that labourers were stupid. In fact there was a real hunger for information, and the people read every scrap of print they could get. He formed a detailed plan for setting up good libraries in each village to bring them the books they demanded, 'The intelligence of the villagers naturally demands the best literature.'

'One of the New Voters',[18] perhaps the best essay Jefferies ever wrote, depicts a group of reapers toiling, until they grow sick and faint, in an open field under the blazing August sun. They drive themselves for fourteen hours a day because it is the peak earning period – 'the fire in the sky meant money'. The hero, or rather anti-hero, is a young labourer, Roger, who sleeps in the cow-house during harvest and makes himself sick by drinking enormous quantities of vile beer. 'Upon this abominable mess the golden harvest of English fields is gathered in.'

Roger is in a state of almost savage degradation because he has never been treated as anything more than a working animal:

His life was work without skill or thought, the work of the horse, of the crane that lifts stones and timber . . . Why should he note the colour of the butterfly, the bright light of the sun, the hue of the wheat? This loveliness gave him no cheese for breakfast . . . To many of us the harvest – the summer – is a time of joy in light and colour; to him it was a time for adding yet another crust of hardness to the thick skin of his hands.

In the evening he and the others go to the alehouse and get drunk; Jefferies explains why they need to do this:

Just as his body needed food and drink, so did his mind require recreation, and that chiefly consists of conversation. The drinking and the smoking are in truth but the attributes of the labourer's public-house evening. It is conversation that draws him thither . . . Their conversation, not your conversation, . . . talk in which neither you nor any one of your condition could really join. To us there would seem nothing at all in that conversation, vapid and subjectless, to them it means much. We have not been through the same circumstances: our day has been differently spent, and the same words have therefore a varying value . . . Not being an animal, though his life and work were animal, he went with his friends to talk.

Having made himself ill through drink and overwork, Roger's strength and youth are being wasted:

I am simply describing the realities of rural life behind the scenes. The golden harvest is the first scene; the golden wheat, glorious under the summer sun. Bright poppies flower in its depths and convolvulus climb the stalks. Butterflies float slowly over the yellow surface as they might over a lake of colour . . . Behind these beautiful aspects comes the reality of human labour – hours upon hours of heat and strain; there comes the reality of a rude life, and in the end little enough of gain. The wheat is beautiful, but human life is labour.

He came back to this point in another essay, when he described his conversation with the mother of a family which was emigrating:

For ten days, while the voyage lasted, she would have nothing to do, but could rest. She had never had such a holiday in all her life. How hard must be the life which makes such a trifling circumstances as a week's rest appear so heavenly![19]

As the end of his short life approached Jefferies became more and more radical. 'Primrose Gold in our Villages' (1887) describes the organisation of a Conservative club at the grass-roots. 'A powerful caucus is being established everywhere throughout the country', Jefferies wrote. Small tradesmen who conformed, went to church and voted Tory were patronised by the local élite, those who did not were left out in the cold – 'this is not boycotting, it is Primrosing':

If you are pliant and flexible and don't mind being petted you have nice things put in your way . . . If you are not pliant, you are not harrowed, but you are not watered, and it is best to get out of the local village.

'Thoughts on the Labour Question' and 'The Divine Right of Capital',[20] apparently some of the last things Jefferies wrote, are an amazing denunciation – never printed in his lifetime – of the class system in Victorian England. He contrasts the wealthy capitalists with the workers who keep them in luxury:

Hunger and thirst drive them; these are the fearful scourges, the whips worse than the knout, which lie at the back of Capital and give it its power.

Jefferies' conception of history, revealed by these essays, is virtually Marxist, and shows how completely he had changed in the long years of struggle and suffering since he wrote the Coate letters to *The Times*:

The history of the last hundred years, not the mere base chronicle of the movements of kings and queens, of armies, but the cause of the heavings and throbbings of the nations, has been written in blood by the workman's tool. The future, growing as inevitably out of the present as the tree from the acorn, will be shaped by the voices sounding from the bench, the mine and the plough.

4 The Country Novel before Hardy

The chief limitation of the country novel in the mid-nineteenth century is summed up admirably in an anonymous notice of *Silas Marner* in 1861:

> The words of George Eliot come on us as a new revelation of what life in quiet country parishes really is and has been. How hard it is to draw the poor may easily be seen if we turn to the ordinary tales of country life that are written in such abundance by ladies. There the poor are always looked at from the point of view of the rich. They are so many subjects for experimenting on, for reclaiming, improving, being anxious about, and relieving. They have no existence apart from the presence of a curate and a district visitor. They live in order to take tracts and broth.

This way of looking at the poor had virtually dehumanised them. They remained 'a distinct race. What they think of and do when they are not being improved and helped, remains a blank.' George Eliot was, therefore, doing something completely new when she wrote about this 'unknown, and to most people unknowable section of society',[1] as people with an independent existence and value of their own.

Whether George Eliot was in fact as original as the reviewer claimed is a complex question. But his analysis of the country novel before her time was, broadly speaking, correct. The poor were usually noticed as objects of charity or not at all. It was possible for works to appear with titles like *Town and Country* (a novel by Frances Trollope which draws a simple moral contrast between a country vicarage and Regency London),[2] or *The Village Comedy*,[3] which did not say a word about the majority of human beings who made up the rural population. The focus of interest – as we can see from a title like *A Country Gentleman and his Family*[4] – was the squirearchy who inhabited the local 'great house'. The adventures and love affairs of these people formed a staple part of respectable Victorian fiction. In these novels the countryside was seen as a picturesque background and the people who worked in it as natural inferiors who could be patronised if they were 'deserving'. Typical examples are Cuthbert Bede's *Our New Rector*[5] – where the hero shows his moral worth by calling on his poor parishioners before the rich ones – John Mills' *The Old English Gentleman*[6] and Holme Lee's *A Poor Squire*.[7] The poor – as servants or dependents of the great house – are shown as having the greatest affection and reverence for their superiors. R. D. Blackmore, the author of *Lorna Doone*, wrote several novels about the countryside which share the same attitudes. In his *Cripps the Carrier*[8] the bigoted old Tory, Squire Oglander, is a benevolent and 'lovable' character, and people only laugh when he threatens jokingly to send them to the workhouse. Paternalist attitudes were sometimes pushed to an extreme, as in Thomas Dolby's *Floreston*. The hero of this novel is an enlightened landlord who rescues the villagers from the workhouse and gives them decent wages. But they have to give him a security for their good behaviour:

> such security to be considered as extending to wilful neglect of Divine Worship, to drunkenness, or other immoralities, to dirtiness (except while actually employed in duties that should make it unavoidable), raggedness and the utterance of any blasphemous or obscene expression.[9]

These are the degenerate examples of a genre that had been lifted to greatness by Jane Austen at the beginning of the century. Her works are the classic examples of the country-house novel. In *Emma* the only characters who really matter are the small group of families who form the polite society of Highbury. The poor, never seen directly, are represented by some wretched cottagers to whom Emma is charitable; also by poultry-stealers and some rather aggressive gypsies. Later in the century new social questions began to enter fiction – questions which Jane Austen had not found it necessary to ask. The relationship between classes became the central issue of the time. In certain novels of the 1840s and onwards, the violence which was so marginal in *Emma* becomes pervasive and takes the form of rioting, machine-smashing and rick-burning. The image of a mob of starving and rebellious labourers haunts the literature of the countryside, from Disraeli to *Felix Holt*, and the impact of this mob action on the consciousness of educated and relatively enlightened observers is a central theme in the country novel before Hardy.

'Charlotte Elizabeth'

Charlotte Elizabeth Tonna (1790–1846) was a militant Evangelical novelist whose best-known work is an attack on industrialism and impiety. *Helen Fleetwood*[10] is an impressive assault on the factory system – it mostly takes place in a large town – but its conception of rural society is a good deal more blurred.

Helen – 'a girl of delicate mind, such as is often found in our sequestered villages' – and her friends are turned out of their cottages, like so many of Hardy's characters, when the last of three lives drops and the property reverts to the landlords. The workhouse committee is eager to get them out of the parish, and they are deluded into moving to an industrial town to find work. But the town is a dreadful disappointment; the children either die or become corrupted by factory morals and only a few of them manage to struggle back to the village and find peace.

By contrast with the horrors of city life, the countryside seems all happiness and innocence:

> There are districts in the land still retaining much of the primitive character of English rusticity – places where the blight has not come, where the demoralising swarm of railway excavators has never alighted, nor the firebrand of political rancour scattered its darkening smoke, nor the hell-born reptile of Socialism trailed his venomous slime.

We are shown the labourers celebrating a harvest-home, with the squire and parson taking a kindly interest in their welfare. It all seems a very simple contrast. Yet the author seems to have forgotten that in the very first chapters of the novel she had shown the injustice deeply embedded in rural life itself – the scarcity of cottages, the reluctance of parish administration to help the destitute, the ever-looming threat of 'that truly national edifice, the workhouse'. These are what orginally cause the tragedy, by uprooting Helen's family and forcing them into the town, but once the novel has got under way, they are almost forgotten. Mrs Tonna knows that certain evils exist in the countryside, but does not feel that they are really dangerous. Her main concern is to preach the Gospel and uphold traditional ways of life, reserving her attacks for such modern phenomena as Socialism, railways and free thought. What emerges from this novel is a nostalgia for the past, and the simple and characteristic wish that industrialism should be wiped from the face of the earth.

Benjamin Disraeli

The novels of Benjamin Disraeli are also essentially propagandist, this time for the Young England philosophy. In *Coningsby* and *Sybil* we can trace many of the ideas of that important tradition in which opposition to contemporary society was expressed through an idealisation of feudalism. An admiration for medieval life and religion, and for the old aristocracy and landed interest, is combined with a rather cloudy sympathy for the oppressed 'English People'. But there are few vivid or concrete presentations of the ordinary people with whom Disraeli is theoretically so concerned; instead they are fitted into romantic, comic or sinister stereotypes.

In *Coningsby* Eustace Lyle, 'a Christian gentleman of high degree', is presented as the ideal nobleman. 'All classes are mingled in . . . joyous equality' on his estate, where he dispenses alms to the deserving poor with great ceremony because 'I wish the people constantly and visibly to comprehend that property is their protector and friend'.[11]*

The same hankering for a vanished feudal order can be seen in Disraeli's next novel, *Sybil*,[13] although he is trying here to deal with a modern industrial phenomenon, Chartism. The book frequently attacks the short-sighted selfishness of the landowning class, which is seen as betraying its trust. Lord Marney, the hero's brother, gives prizes to the most 'deserving' labourers on his

---

* Charles Kingsley attacked this scene as 'amusingly inconsistent, however well-meant'. It was treating the labourers 'as if they had been middle-age serfs or vagabonds, and not citizens of modern England'.[12]

estate and yet viciously punishes poachers; the people retaliate by setting fire to his ricks. The labourers' condition is utterly miserable:

> After cultivating the broad fields of merry England, the bold British peasant returned to encounter the worst of diseases, with a frame the least qualified to oppose them; a frame that, subdued by toil, was never sustained by animal food, drenched by the tempest, could not change its dripping rags; and was indebted for its scanty fuel to the windfalls of the woods.

The indignation is real enough, but its function is to give substance to a particular version of history and politics. Disraeli contrasts the labourers' degradation with their alleged happiness in the Middle Ages, dating their miseries from the Reformation and the break-up of the monasteries. His romantic ideal is embodied in the ruined abbey; personified by Walter Gerard and his daughter who are descended from the last of the abbots. Gerard is an exceedingly unlikely figure for a Chartist leader. He is the modern representative of a once noble family (his counterpart in Hardy is Sir John Durbeyfield) who regards himself as a dispossessed aristocrat and will not 'sink to be a labourer on the soil that had once been our own'. Unlike the Durbeyfields, he has a legal claim on the family estate, which falls into Sybil's hands at the end of the book. The 'real' aristocracy is distinguished from modern upstarts (whose pedigrees are manufactured) by the fact that ordinary people give it their love and support. Here is a description of Sybil visiting a model estate:

> Some beautiful children rushed out of a cottage and flew to Sybil, crying out, 'the queen, the queen' . . . 'My subjects', said Sybil, laughing, as she greeted them all.

Her superiority to ordinary people could hardly be more clearly emphasised. Sybil is no working girl, however much she may claim to represent the oppressed. She is an ethereal, angelic being, pure as the driven snow and living several removes away from ordinary life. Apart from transforming society, her great ambition is 'to see the people once more kneel before our blessed Lady'. Her personality and values are completely opposed to everything that is modern:

Think you not it would be a fairer lot to bide this night at some kind monastery, than to be hastening now to that least picturesque of all creations, a railway station?*

The archaism of her language perfectly matches her feelings, as we see from another extract in which the revolutionary, Stephen Morley, reproaches her for her relationship with Egremont:

'Unmannerly churl!' exclaimed Sybil . . . her eye flashing lightning, her distended nostril quivering with scorn.

'Oh, yes, I am a churl,' said Morley; 'I know I am a churl. Were I a noble, the daughter of the people would perhaps condescend to treat me with less contempt.'

Sybil's language here betrays her real feelings for ordinary people; all those below her, unless they consent to be her 'subjects', are 'churls'. Her eventual succession to a title and her marriage to Egremont (whose progressive sympathies don't prevent him from leading an anti-Chartist army) are no surprise. In the end Disraeli disowns Chartism, which he associates with a mob of rioters, 'burning mills, destroying all they could put their hands on, man, woman and child'. Egremont and Sybil collapse into a state of supine bliss – 'The Earl and Countess of Marney departed for Italy, where they passed nearly a year' – and the English people are left to solve their problems as best they can. Disraeli seems to have persuaded himself that with the marriage of his two principal characters (which represents the union of two great estates, not 'two nations') all the problems which had been raised in his book could be shelved. His Tory Democracy emerges in the end, despite its superficial concern with the poor, as a sham.

There is an interesting conversation near the beginning of the novel between Egremont and one of the labourers on his brother's estate. They are talking about the recent outbreaks of incendiarism:

'And what do you think of the fire?' said Egremont to the hind.

* Compare Sue in *Jude the Obscure*, 'I'd rather sit in the railway station . . . That's the centre of the town life now. The Cathedral has had its day!'

'I think 'tis hard times for the poor, sir.'

'But rick-burning will not make the times easier, my good man.'

The man made no reply, but with a dogged look led away the horse to the stable.

The breakdown of communication between the rulers and the ruled is absolute. The 'two nations' of Disraeli's subtitle remain.

Charles Kingsley

Marx described Christian Socialism in *The Communist Manifesto* as 'the holy water with which the priest consecrates the heart-burnings of the aristocrat',[14] and it would be true to say that the Christian Socialist novels of Charles Kingsley deal primarily with the tormented conscience of rich people faced with the class war. In many ways his novels are very similar to Disraeli's. The aristocracy, the country's natural leaders, are in a state of indecision about how to cope with the rebellious and suffering people; Christianity which is pro-charity but anti-revolution shows them the way. Christian Socialism shares many of the attitudes of Tory Democracy but places a greater emphasis on religion and shows more real understanding of conditions among the agricultural and industrial poor.

In *Yeast* the labourers are seen entirely from the viewpoint of educated observers. All the characters belong to the landed gentry except the gamekeeper, Tregarva, who tries to teach Lancelot the principles of social justice, and even he is a very ambiguous figure as gamekeepers were regarded by the hungry labourers as their worst enemies. On one occasion he catches a poacher – 'a dripping scarecrow of rags and bones' – and exhorts him to lead an honest life; the man points out that if he cannot poach he will starve. Lancelot tries to solve the problem by giving him some money, but this is obviously inadequate. Kingsley knows that charity is not the answer to the system, but neither will he admit that anybody, however wretched, has the right to break the commandments to escape from his misery. He resolves the dilemma by showing the labourers as hopelessly degenerate beings – Lancelot wonders if they are 'even animals of the same species' as their social superiors. The apparent radicalism of showing how the people have been degraded by the system merges into the more questionable feeling that they have totally lost their humanity. The ambiguity personified by the humanitarian gamekeeper persists right through the book.

On one level *Yeast* is a scathing indictment of the English landowning classes. This indictment covers not only cruelty, but also indifference; Lancelot's friend Bracebridge is shocked into committing suicide because he has ruined a country girl, but retribution can also come as the result of an indirect sin. Argemone, dying of the fever she has picked up in the labourers' hovels, says that 'the curse of the Lavingtons had truly come upon her. To perish by the people whom they made.' Her only crime was ignorance, but this is bad enough:

'Have I not wantoned in down and perfume while they, by whose labour my luxuries were bought, were pining among scents and sounds – one day of which would have driven me mad!'

The 'picturesque villages' are 'the perennial hotbeds of fever and ague, of squalid penury, sottish profligacy, dull discontent'. This poison (as in *Bleak House* and Kingsley's later novel *Alton Locke*) spreads upwards to every layer of society, infecting all those who were indifferent to their responsibilties to the working class.

By the time Kingsley wrote *Alton Locke*[15] his attitude had slightly changed. This was a novel written directly about Chartism, and his purpose was to show that working-class protest was futile if it was not sanctified by Christianity. Alton is a self-educated Jude the Obscure, 'cleverer than ninety-nine gentlemen out of a hundred', but snubbed by the gentlemen-scholars of Cambridge University which, like Christminster, has forgotten its original purpose of educating the poor. Like Jude, too, he does not completely belong to either town or country. As a Cockney child he dreams of 'the gay green country, the land of fruits and flowers, for which I have yearned all my life in vain'. But Kingsley's attitude to rural England is much less simple than this might suggest. When Alton goes down to the country to organise the labourers it is very different from his expectations:

I arrived in the midst of a dreary, treeless country, whose broad brown and grey fields were only broken by an occasional line of dark, doleful firs, at a knot of thatched hovels, all sinking and leaning every way but the right, the windows patched with paper, the doorways stopped with filth, which surrounded a beer-shop.

On meeting the crowd of labourers he notices their 'crushed, dogged air, which was infinitely painful, and bespoke a grade of misery more habitual and more degrading than that of the excitable and passionate artisan'. The people get up one after another to talk about the wretchedness of their condition. Alton tries to calm them down, but only infuriates them more and eventually they rush off to sack the nearest farmhouse. This is possibly the first appearance in fiction of the hero as an inadvertent mob-leader – a vaguely sympathetic outsider who gets caught up in, and blamed for, the violence he is actually trying to control. When the mob begins looting and burning Alton reacts with outrage – 'I almost excused the rich for overlooking the real sufferers, in indignation at the rascals'.

The labourers, passive victims in *Yeast*, have here become active and class-conscious rebels, but they are still being treated as objects rather than subjects. They are still an anonymous mass, from whom Kingsley cannot help recoiling because (unlike the semi-educated London workers) they seem to him almost inhuman. His ideal is the enlightened Christian aristocrat, Lord Ellerton, with his 'magnificent philanthropic schemes, and his deep sense of the high duties of a landlord'. We are back with the paternalism and the idea of a natural hierarchy on which Disraeli had relied.

Yet there is more forcefulness and more honesty in *Alton Locke* than in *Sybil*, and when Kingsley, who claimed a familiar knowledge of the poor in both town and country, allowed them to speak for themselves as he would have actually heard them, he achieved a much more real and moving effect than when he was preaching through the mouths of educated nonentities. Listen to the widow with seven children, who gets up to speak at the popular meeting:

Early and late I hoed turnips, and early and late I rep, and left the children at home to mind each other; and one on 'em

fell into the fire, and is gone to heaven, blessed angel! and
two more it pleased the Lord to take in the fever; and the next,
I hope, will soon be out of this miserable sinful world!

Kingsley was a poor theoretician but an honest observer. This
is the authentic voice of the labourer whom Somerville met
outside Salisbury, 'We ben't sorry he be gone. I hopes he be
happy in heaven'.

The Howitts

The fiction of William and Mary Howitt, like their other work, is
very uneven both in attitude and in quality. Mary's unaided
works are extremely weak, but their fiction becomes much more
interesting when William takes part. His short stories of country
life are distinctly better than his full-length novels; *John Darby-
shire, a Country Quaker* and *The Country Manty-Mekker* are
comic masterpieces on a small scale. Both of them can be found in
a collection, *The Hall and the Hamlet*[16] in which Howitt explains
his social attitude thus:

The hall may, and must, do much to elevate the hamlet, and
the hamlet, in a more enlightened and prosperous condition,
can add much to the interest of living at the hall.

It is the familiar theme that all classes must work together to
help each other. At present, as Howitt argues in a passage which
is very similar to Hardy's criticism in *Tess* of the concept of
'Hodge', the labourers are merely despised:

The English peasant is generally reckoned a very simple,
monotonous animal, and most people, when they have called
him a clown, or a country hob, think they have described him.

But in fact he is 'a rather multifarious creature . . . a very
Protean personage. He has rich fallows in his soul, if anyone
thought them worth turning'. The tragedy is that nobody does so
at present, and the countryman feels that he is 'a mere serf . . .
a mere machine'.

Howitt shows the evil consequences of this condition in another short masterpiece, *Sampson Hooks and his man Joe Ling*, a sketch of a village tyrant and his methods. Hooks is a soft-spoken landowner who ingratiates himself with his neighbours until he has cheated them out of all their land:

> The crofts and cottages were gone, and the footpaths were all gone, yet not a legal complaint could be exhibited against the virtuous and compassionate Sampson Hooks, nor even against the faithful Joe Ling. Could any man say that they were not really most innocent, falsely-accused, fair-dealing, conscientious, though clever, successful men, as men with money in their pockets usually are?

All this is admirable, as are the detailed descriptions of the ways in which Hooks twists the law to his purposes, but the second half of the story is much less convincing. Hooks over-reaches himself by going outside the law, is exposed and soon afterwards dies. One cannot help feeling that Howitt is manipulating probabilities, in order to make sure that the villain gets punished. Hooks' success is believable; his failure is simply contrived. The story ends finely, however, when the people try to tear his body out of its coffin:

> The villagers, to whom he had not left one single foot of their paternal soil, vowed that he should not have one foot of churchyard earth to rest in.

In *Stories of English and Foreign Life*[17] the Howitts show class conflict in the countryside assuming a more violent form. The central character of *The Hunt* is a brutal squire, a sort of Alec d'Urberville, who 'ruined every country girl he came near'. He repeatedly tries to assault the daughters of two respectable families on his estate, who, as his yearly tenants, are practically helpless. 'To resent such an outrage as it ought to be resented, would ensure an instant notice to quit.'

Despite the provocation, the Quaker Howitts are determined to show the futility of answering violence with violence. The brother of one of the girls finds the squire asleep in a wood and is tempted to shoot him, but 'the innocence of my own soul was worth to me a thousand vengeances'.

Like so many of the persecuted poor in Victorian fiction, the two families emigrate and are happy ever afterwards. But when, instead of withdrawing from the struggle, the labourers try to fight back, their punishment is terrible. In *The Poacher's Progress* a young labourer, forced to take up poaching to support his children, deteriorates morally under the strain and is eventually killed in a skirmish with the gamekeeper. The author's final comment is that with decent treatment he 'might have lived a respectable and comparatively happy man'.

The Meldrum Family tells a very similar story in more detail. James Meldrum is a respectable Methodist labourer in a village which is idyllic and happy because it has not yet been modernised. But he is turned out when the new squire, a vicious young man, brings in machinery which makes him redundant. Going to live with his children in a squalid lodging in Reading, from which he has to walk several miles to work, he is almost broken down by the toil. Morally, too, the family goes downhill; the daughter becomes a prostitute and Meldrum an atheist. He decides that he owes nothing to the society which has so ill-used him. 'There was poaching and there was theft.'

Like Alton Locke, he goes to a public meeting, attended by hundreds of ragged and starving labourers, and impulsively delivers an inflammatory speech which makes him even more of an outlaw. He roams the countryside stealing food and tries to escape on an emigrant ship but is identified and jumps overboard:

> Thus terminated the strange career of James Meldrum. Who could have imagined such a beginning and such an ending? Who shall say what are the crimes that they give origin to when they drive peaceable men desperate, and close the avenues of life against them? . . . Under a better system the better nature of the man had been maintained.

In this passage crime is traced decisively back to its social roots and the authors come close to suggesting that Meldrum was scarcely responsible for his actions. But in fact their tone continually oscillates between sympathy for Meldrum's sufferings and horror at his reaction. As an example of how he should have behaved he is contrasted with a Christian young woman, violated by the wicked squire, who still manages to lead a happy and virtuous life. Another weakness in the story is its blanket hostility to industrialism, and its idealisation of the labourers' past:

> There *were* good old times for them. It is no fable... In the old-fashioned equality of village society he was at ease . . . The parson had a friendly word for him when they met, and the farmer was a sort of old patriarch that was respected, but yet familiarly addressed.

This conception of the good society is essentially paternalistic, with an emphasis on the natural superiority of the rich to the poor. This helps to explain why the Howitts so dreaded the possibility of a working-class rebellion; society must only be reformed from above. This point is made very clearly in two of William's later novels, written after the collapse of the Chartist movement. *The Man of the People*[18] depicts a virtuous young aristocrat who gets involved in radical politics but is horrified by any suggestion of violence or atheism. In the climax of the book he tries to calm a mob of labourers and is arrested as a ringleader, but released when the authorities find out that he has a title. *Woodburn Grange*[19] shows an old-fashioned bullying squire being replaced by a benevolent manufacturer who buys up his land. Howitt had become more optimistic about the future, now that the labourers were growing more prosperous, and had overcome his hankering for the pre-industrial past. The moral which he draws from this last novel is, however, predictable: 'The laws of property should be maintained in consistency with the laws of God'.

Elizabeth Gaskell

The 'industrial' novels of Elizabeth Gaskell are, of course, in the centre of the Christian radical tradition, to which, in their different ways, Kingsley and the Howitts belonged. In *Mary Barton* (1848) the countryside is seen as a place of lost peace and innocence by contrast with Manchester, and in *North and South* (1855) the emphasis has shifted only slightly. Helstone seems to be a typical Arcadian village, with roses round the cottage doors and the wealthier classes doing all they can to help the poor. But when Margaret goes back there near the end of the story she finds that the contrast with city life is less sharp than she had imagined. She hears the story of an old woman who has roasted a cat 'according to one of the savage county superstitions',[20] which we hear more about in *The Return of the Native*. Only education can stamp out cruel customs like this.

But in between these two novels came *Cranford*,[21] in which country life is studied directly, and here the tensions and bitterness of the 'industrial novels' vanish. Cranford is a small-scale Casterbridge, a metropolis for the surrounding villages and yet still so close to the countryside that 'the fragrant smell of the neighbouring hayfields' can be felt in the principal street. With the rough lives of ordinary labourers, of course, it has nothing to do; the society consists mainly of elderly gentlewomen, a few ranks above the farmers and tradesmen, who condemn any departure from etiquette as 'vulgar'. Even the 'yeoman' Holbrook (who is little lower than a small squire) is not sufficiently refined to satisfy this group's strict requirements. The Jenkyns family is proud of its aristocratic connections, and the whole town defers to the Honourable Mrs Jamieson (although she is 'dull, and inert and pompous and tiresome') because of her rank. Mrs Gaskell writes as a detached observer, inviting the reader to laugh at the snobbery and absurd taboos which are at the heart of Cranford life. But the laughter is gentle, for Cranford is seen as an essentially pre-industrial community, belonging in spirit to an earlier and kindlier age. The railways are a simple destructive force ('Captain Brown is killed by those nasty cruel railroads') and equally negative is the industrial civilisation which we glimpse through the medium of the Town and County Bank.

The collapse of this bank forms the moral climax of the story. Miss Matty as a shareholder feels partly responsible, and expresses this sense of responsibility by giving five pounds to a poor farmer in exchange for a worthless banknote. She cannot explain the reason for her quixotic behaviour, but in fact it is inherent in the code of her social group, which accepts as a condition of its own status that it should look after the poorer classes when they are in trouble. The same semi-feudal convention is observed by her servant Martha who insists on staying with her for no wages when she loses her money. The crisis brings out the community's best qualities; everybody rallies round and the ladies of Cranford contribute enough money to set Miss Matty up in a little shop. The way she manages this shop, is, of course, quite un-businesslike, although nobody takes advantage of it, and the narrator's father objects that 'such simplicity might be very well in Cranford, but would never do in the world'. This, however, is followed by the comment:

> I fancy the world must be very bad, for with all my father's suspicion of everyone with whom he has dealings, and in spite of all his many precautions, he lost upwards of a thousand pounds by roguery only last year.

The values of Cranford – which we have been given every encouragement to smile at – are thus shown to be far more truly human than those of 'the world' – which means the ruthless and grasping industrialism that Mrs Gaskell described with such passion elsewhere. These values shine through the superficial absurdity when the climax of the book has been reached. Mrs Gaskell does not wish, any more than the average Victorian writer, to abolish classes, but her ideal of the class system is not Mrs Jamieson's pecking order but a society based on mutual help and respect. Yet this seems impossible anywhere in the world outside Cranford, and the novel is outside the mainstream of her work; it is an elegy for the quiet country town she had known in her childhood which was coming to seem an anachronism in the year 1853.

Hollingford in *Wives and Daughters*[22] is a meaner Cranford, with the same snobberies and rigid etiquette but not the same kindliness. There is a heavier emphasis on the continual gossip and backbiting which goes on in a small town; the community is ready to spread a slander about an innocent girl and only desists when Lady Harriet extends her patronage to her. The deference which the whole village shows to the aristocratic Cumnor family is laughed at, as are old Squire Hamley's obstinate prejudices. Yet the aristocrats, especially Lady Harriet, are shown as bene-volent people, and the Squire, for all his faults, is depicted with respect and affection. Mrs Gaskell's vision extends wider than Hollingford, but her sympathetic characters are those who are rooted most deeply in its traditions. Molly, the straightforward country girl, is contrasted very favourably with the cosmopolitan Cynthia. Similarly, Roger Hamley, who is interested in natural history and the working of his father's estate, is a much more reliable person than his sophisticated brother Osborne. The contrast between Osborne and his father is very like that between the old and young squires in Howitt's *Country Book*, a contrast which brings together and illuminates two ways of life. It resembles Howitt's sketch even down to the detail of the ancestral trees, which the old man fears will be destroyed when the young one inherits. Squire Hamley 'loved the trees he had played under as a boy as if they were living creatures', and his attitude shows how much closer to nature he is than his elder son. But there is no real threat, in this novel, of change. Osborne dies and we cannot doubt that Roger will manage the estate in a responsible way.

The attitude to the Hamleys is practically feudal. The oldness of their family is stressed – 'there was Hamleys of Hamley afore the time of the pagans' – as are their 'primitive manners and customs', and the 'dignity' of the old man's 'quiet conservatism'. It is typified by the cottager who asks to see the squire when he is dying, because of the feeling of 'feudal loyalty, which made it seem to the dying man as if it would be a comfort to shake the hand, and look once more into the eyes of the lord and master whom he had served and whose ancestors his own forebears had served for so many generations'. As he expresses it himself: 'Your father came for to see my father as he lay a-dying'. The relationship between the two classes is static in time.

Hollingford is described as a place where 'a very pretty amount of feudal feeling still lingered' and in this, her last novel, it really does seem as if Mrs Gaskell had relapsed into an admiration for feudalism and an unawareness of many problems which she had explored in some depth in her earlier works. The action is set in the years before the Reform Bill – the years of her own childhood – which George Eliot was later to remember in much the same spirit.

Anthony Trollope

Anthony Trollope resembled Hardy in creating a fictitious tract of countryside (he called it Barsetshire) where the action of many of his major novels take place. He gives a general description of it in the opening of *Doctor Thorne*:[23]

There is a county in the west of England not so full of life,
indeed, nor so widely spoken of as some of its manufacturing
leviathan brethren in the north, but which is, nevertheless,
very dear to those who know it well. Its green pastures, its
waving wheat, its deep and shady and – let us add – dirty
lanes, its paths and stiles, its tawny-coloured, well-built rural
churches, its avenues of beeches, and frequent Tudor mansions, its constant county hunt, its social graces, and the general
air of clanship which pervades it, has made it to its own inhabitants a favoured land of Goshen. It is purely agricultural;
agricultural in its produce, agricultural in its poor, and agricultural in its pleasures.

This gives the conventional impression that Barsetshire (located
somewhere in the traditionally agricultural western region of
England – Barchester is said to be Salisbury) is, despite a little
dirt, a much pleasanter place to live in than the industrial north.
The scenery is described in the same breath as the county hunt
and social graces, for Barsetshire to Trollope means primarily a
society which could only exist in a rural area. On the next page
we hear about the 'clerical aristocracy . . . a society sufficiently
powerful to be counted as something by the county squirearchy.
In other respects the greatness of Barsetshire depends wholly on
the landed powers.'
The characters who tend to matter in Trollope are aristocratic
landowners, clerical dignitaries (or younger clerics scheming for
promotion) and a sprinkling of professional men. Their servants
are sometimes shown but hardly ever the farmers and labourers.
Orley Farm in the novel of that name is merely an estate to be
squabbled over, not a place where people live and work. His
nearest approach to a mere general realism is in *The Last
Chronicle of Barset*, where he shows the poverty of the curate,
Mr Crawley, and the still greater hardships of the brickmakers
among whom he works. Yet Mr Crawley is one of the very few
male characters in Trollope who is not worldly (religion is recognised as supplying another standard) and the poor 'exist only to
take tracts and broth'. There is an essential conservatism about
all Trollope's work; the moral of *The Warden* is that any attempt
to reform long-standing abuses will only do damage. It is not,
however, an old-fashioned rural conservatism. The conscious-

ness of his leading characters is urban and sophisticated to a degree.

Doctor Thorne, set in the 1850s, is the story of Greshamsbury Park, 'a fine old English gentleman's seat', which is threatened with being sold. The tradition which country seats of this kind represented is valued highly by Trollope:

> May such symbols long remain among us; they are still lovely and fit to be loved . . . They explain more fully, more truly than any written history can do, how Englishmen have become what they are. England is not yet a commercial country in the sense in which that epithet is used for her; and let us still hope that she will not soon become so. She might surely as well be called feudal England, or chivalrous England.

By the year 1854, however, the chivalrous classes are in a bad way. The estate is heavily mortgaged, through election expenses and extravagant living, and Frank Gresham, the heir, is expected to redeem the family fortunes by marrying somebody rich. The fact that he wants to marry the penniless Mary Thorne provides the central tension of the novel until it is discovered (by that familiar magic of the conventional Victorian plot) that she is an heiress. This removes the necessity for a moral choice; Frank can have his cake and eat it, and when we next hear of him, in *Framley Parsonage*, he is well on the way to becoming a Tory M.P.

There is an obvious symbolism in the Gresham family's getting control of the fortune of the plebeian Roger Scatcherd, who has made his money by railway contracting. Scatcherd has certain homely virtues but his title and honours are obviously ridiculous, and anyway he drinks. His son Louis is a cruel caricature of an upstart *nouveau riche*. So 'the race of Scatcherd becomes extinct' and Mary, who is a lady by habits and upbringing, comes into possession of their thousands. Equilibrium is thus restored, and Greshamsbury Park remains in the hands of its owners. But this solution does not strike one as particularly honest. It is dictated not by realistic considerations but by Trollope's desire to see the old landed gentry preserved in an age which was making them obsolete; to give his heroes plenty of money without making them do anything unpleasant to get it, to have things both ways.

George Eliot

George Eliot, as we have seen, was not really the first English novelist to write in depth about the emotions and working lives of ordinary country people. The Howitts and others had preceded her. But it was not only that her novels seemed exceptionally realistic and detailed. It was also that they did not carry (as in Disraeli or Kingsley and even in the Howitts) any overt or detachable social philosophy. Ordinary country life could then be seen as at last being written about as it 'really is'.

This admiration of George Eliot's rural realism become so widespread that when *Far from the Madding Crowd* appeared the *Spectator* suggested that she might have written it; somewhat to Hardy's surprise:

> So far as he had read that great thinker − one of the greatest living, he thought, though not a born story-teller by any means − she had never touched the life of the fields; her country-people having seemed to him too, more like small townsfolk than rustics; and as evidencing a woman's wit cast in country dialogue rather than real country humour.[24]

In fact only two of George Eliot's novels, *Adam Bede* and *Silas Marner*, are really about village life. *The Mill on the Floss* and *Middlemarch* are set mainly in small country towns, and *Felix Holt* and *Daniel Deronda* centre round the country house. In the country novels, the life of the cities is seen as something vaguely frightening and of ambiguous moral quality. In contrast with cities, country life is mainly shown as healthy and good. Yet George Eliot's formal intentions were always realistic, as we can see from an essay she wrote for the *Westminster Review* in 1856:

> The notion that peasants are joyous . . . that the cottage matrons are usually buxom, and village children necessarily rosy and merry, are prejudices difficult to dislodge from the artistic mind, which looks for its subjects into literature instead of life. The painter is still under the influence of idyllic literature, which has always expressed the imagination of the cultivated and town-bred, rather than the truth of rustic life . . . But no one who has seen much of actual ploughmen thinks

them jocund; no one who is well acquainted with the English peasantry, can pronounce them merry . . . Haymaking time is a time for joking, especially if there are women among the labourers; but the coarse laugh that bursts out every now and then, and expresses the triumphant taunt, is as far as possible from your conception of idyllic merriment . . . To make men moral, something more is requisite than to turn them out to grass.[25]

But the mood she describes here is not often depicted in her novels, which can more accurately be seen as celebrating the rural past which was also her childhood. A central theme in nearly all her work is the contrast between agricultural and industrial England, between two ways of life. Most of her novels are set at the time of the Reform Bill, or even earlier – that is in George Eliot's childhood years when railways and industrial towns still seemed new and strange things. This contrast is made explicit in the author's introduction to *Felix Holt*,[26] describing the Midlands in the 1830s. On one side is 'the district of protuberant optimists, sure that old England was the best of all possible countries . . . the district of clean little market-towns without manufactures, of fat livings, an aristocratic clergy, and low poor-rates'; on the other the ugly manufacturing towns, where the workmen are usually radicals and dissenters and are 'not convinced that old England was as good as possible'. In fact she is showing us the birth of industrialism and free thought (the two things are intimately connected), which were eventually to disturb not only the rural but the whole social order. And in comparing these two sentences we cannot be entirely sure which spirit the author prefers. She knows about the intellectual limitations of life in the countryside, but the cities appear to cause more human suffering. A further sentence is less ambiguous:

Yet there were the grey steeples too, and the churchyards, with their grassy mounds and venerable headstones, sleeping in the sunlight; there were broad fields and homesteads, and fine old woods . . . allowing only peeps at the park or mansion which they shut in from the working-day world.

In this passage rural England seems to be reposing in perpetual sunlit tranquillity. The key word is 'venerable', for the landscape has always been there and the churches and mansions are seen in their picturesque aspect as buildings, overlooking their social significance. This nostalgia for the idea of a timeless, traditional and conservative England runs through all George Eliot's works. Yet the development of contemporary England, and her own radical questioning intelligence, prevented her from seeing this civilisation in too simple terms. In most cases she shows it being broken up from within, through some personal weakness or through the loss of fortune by lawsuits or mortgage. Maggie Tulliver has to leave the idyllic world of her childhood for one which confronts her with definite and exposed moral choices. As in George Eliot's own history, the often necessary transition from rural life and traditional thought can be ambivalent and profoundly disturbing.

In *Mr Gilfil's Love Story*[27] Sir Christopher Cheverel represents the aristocratic tradition at its best. Yet this tradition also produces the worthless Captain Wybrow, and serves as a mask for his faults. Contrasted with him is the hard-working clergyman Gilfil who eventually devotes himself to the poor of his parish (although they are somewhat stylised objects for displaying his virtue who 'exist only to take tracts and broth'). *Adam Bede*[28] is distinctly more complex. The squirearchy here is seen as in many ways oppressive. Old Squire Donnithorne is a tyrant, and the semi-feudal relationship between landlord and tenant provides the framework for Hetty's seduction by his grandson. The tenants and the labourers are not able to escape these pressures, but they can and do fight back vigorously, as when Mrs Poyser turns the squire out of her kitchen and when Adam knocks Arthur down. The characters with whom George Eliot mainly identifies – it is an interesting connection and a pointer to Hardy – are the semi-independent class of small tenant farmers and skilled craftsmen. These people are self-educated and self-respecting, taking their religion seriously (by contrast with Mr Irwine's cultivated laxness) and influenced in several cases by the spiritual force of Methodism which originated in the industrial towns. Martin Poyser is the typical conservative farmer who cannot understand or tolerate deviations from traditional norms. Adam, the skilled craftsman, has the same tendency towards rigidity but is softened by Dinah, who represents the new Methodist creed. All of them accept the class system as perfectly natural (Adam is 'very susceptible to the influence of rank, and quite ready to give an extra amount of respect to everyone who had more advantages than himself') but this respect will be given only for as long as the upper classes behave decently according to their code. When they find out the truth about Arthur's behaviour, both Adam and the Poysers reject his authority instinctively and at once.

In spite of the factors which menace stability, there seems to be nothing harsh or unpleasant about work in the countryside. Adam in the carpenter's shop is described in almost lyrical terms:

> The afternoon sun was warm on the five workmen ... A scent of pinewood from a tent-like pile of planks outside the open door mingled itself with the scent of the elderbushes which were spreading their summer snow close to the open window opposite; the slanting sunbeams shone through the transparent shavings that flew before the steady plane, and lit up the fine grain of the oak panelling.

The dairy where Hetty works is described even more enthusiastically:

> It was a scene to sicken for with a sort of calenture in hot and dusty streets – such coolness, such purity, such fragrance of new-pressed cheese, of firm butter, of wooden vessels perpetually bathed in pure water; such soft colouring of red earthenware and creamy surfaces, brown wood and polished tin, grey limestone and rich orange-red rust . . . But one got only a confused notion of these details when they surround a distractingly pretty girl of seventeen, standing on little pattens and rounding her dimpled arms to lift a pound of butter out of the scale.

This is practically 'a rural painting in the Dutch school', as Hardy called *Under the Greenwood Tree*. The figures are seen mainly in terms of their background. Human labour has been transformed into a visual art by means of the word-painting technique which George Eliot continually applies to the landscape itself. In the 'pleasant uplands' and 'brook-watered villages' near Hayslope work is easy and delightful, unlike that of the factories and mills. It seems like part of the natural order, or the procession of seasons:

Michaelmas was come, with its fragrant basketfuls of purple damsons, and its paler purple daisies, and its lads and lasses leaving or seeking service, and winding along between the yellow hedges, with their bundles under their arms.

The human workers on the land have been reduced to an aspect of scenery. The mellow landscape painting leaves little room for any individuality in this book.

George Eliot's next novel, *The Mill on the Floss*[29] deals with a distinctly more complex society. The mill is the centre of a small farm, held for generations by the Tulliver family but capable of being lost through a lawsuit, and Mr Tulliver's social position is somewhere in between those of his brothers-in-law, the gentleman-farmer Pullet and the 'unlucky agriculturist' Moss who lives in a region of 'foul land and neglected fences', the property of 'a poor non-resident landlord', where people sink into apathy or console themselves by going to the pub. Life at Dorlcote Mill is very different from this, and seems idyllic to Tom and Maggie as children, but the pressures of a harsh external world eventually break in and the idyll is smashed.

This shifting, varied and vulnerable society is very similar to that of early Hardy. It relates, significantly, not to the extreme and often dramatised classes of landowners and labourers, but to the important middle class of the countryside: the tenants and dealers, sometimes prospering, sometimes failing. The recognition and exploration of this intermediate class is one of the vital sources of George Eliot's realism, but also, perhaps, of her uncertainties. In their attachment to the past, in which they had found a place, but in their frequent incomprehension of the present and fear of change in the future, this class expresses most vividly a crisis of values in rural society as a whole.

The other characters in *Mill on the Floss* are country bankers and small manufacturers, for St Ogg's is a trading town, dealing in oil and exporting 'the well-crushed cheese and the soft fleeces' which neighbouring farmers supply. Its position in the countryside is only semi-autonomous; it is menaced by floods, 'bad harvests, and the mysterious fluctuations of trade'. In fact it is a country metropolis, where 'the farmers' wives and daughters . . . came to do their shopping on market-days', larger than Cranford and more sophisticated than Casterbridge, but very like them in its inward-looking and back-biting atmosphere, which is felt at its most claustrophobic in the conversations of Maggie's mother and aunts; a connected rural and urban middle-class family network. The town is so self-satisfied, so hostile to anybody who tries to transcend its limitations, that Maggie's good name (like Molly's in *Wives and Daughters*) is almost casually destroyed. George Eliot at once recognises what is valuable in this society and feels that it is impossible for the idealist, with whom she identifies, to breathe in so limited an atmosphere.

Silas Marner[30] is more like *Adam Bede* in its emphatic contrast between town and countryside, and between the ardent dissenting religion of educated working men and the villagers' passive and somewhat superstitious adherence to the established church. But whereas in *Adam Bede* the Methodist working-girl Dinah brings a spirit of humanity to the village which it badly needs, Silas is broken and demoralised by the intolerance of his sect and by becoming a slave to his loom. He is only redeemed by becoming absorbed in the life and customs of Raveloe, the remote village 'aloof from the currents of industrial energy and Puritan earnestness', which represents 'old-fashioned country life'.

Not that the village is wholly idealised. The upper-class characters are unsympathetic; Squire Cass and his family all behave badly in various ways and Eppie's eventual decision to stay with Silas instead of being recognised as the squire's daughter is an affirmation of solidarity with the labouring class:

I wasn't brought up to be a lady, and I can't turn my mind to it. I like the working-folk, and their houses, and their ways . . . I'm promised to marry a working-man as'll live with father, and help me to take care of him.

Yet there seems to be no special poverty in the village; indeed the dominant impression is of an idle comfortableness:

Orchards looking lazy with neglected plenty; the large church in the wide churchyard, which men gazed at lounging at their own doors at service-time; the purple-faced farmers jogging along the lanes or turning in at the Rainbow; homesteads, where men supped heavily or slept in the light of the evening hearth, and where women seemed to be laying up a stock of linen for the life to come.

If any hardship exists, the upper classes (represented at their best by Nancy) are always ready to be charitable; there is never any question of real destitution. Of course – we see it exemplified in this passage – the limitations and complacencies of village life are made clear enough. The local religion, for example, is much less educated and serious than that of Silas, but it is a good deal more tolerant. In the end Silas clings to this life as a refuge from the old one which has bruised him so deeply. When he returns to his native town, he finds himself totally alienated; his landmarks swept away and replaced by a factory. Indeed this is the most anti-industrial novel George Eliot ever wrote. Silas is disinherited almost from birth, cast out by a community which was never worth belonging to anyway, and enslaved for long years to money and a machine. The contrasts are quite explicit. Immediately after Silas's fruitless return to the town comes the description of Eppie's wedding amid flowers and sunlight and the final unequivocally blissful conclusion:

> 'O father', said Eppie, 'what a pretty home ours is! I think nobody could be happier than we are'.

Felix Holt is a study of radicalism in a country house and in a small town. Several of the earlier patterns can be traced in it. Esther, like Eppie, gives up her chances of wealth to marry a poor man, and the landed classes, both Transomes and Debarrys, are morally inferior to the dissenting clergyman, Rufus Lyon, and the skilled artisan Felix Holt. But the radicalism is blunted, for Felix attacks the workers much more than the ruling classes and, in the now familiar scene when he finds himself the reluctant leader of a riot, is only concerned with restoring law and order. The poor who had been so carefully and lovingly depicted in the earlier novels have now turned into an undifferentiated and sinister mob.

Middlemarch[31] is set in a provincial town and the country estates – Tipton, Freshitt and Lowick – scattered round it. These estates are inhabited by conventional Tory squires like Sir James Chettam, and the inept Mr Brooke who flirts briefly with radicalism – a theme which is studied here much more deeply and fully than in *Felix Holt*. Dorothea Brooke feels that her only vocation in a limited society like this is to help people, but she is trapped by marrying Casaubon who dismisses her charitable work as a hobby – 'as other women expected to occupy themselves with their dress and embroidery'. Her only way out, in the end, is to marry the radical politician Ladislaw who has seen through Brooke's pretensions and who has no family or economic ties with the society. Lydgate's idealism is similarly broken down by the meanness and narrowness of Middlemarch life. In order to carry out his ambitious medical projects he has to keep compromising with the solid array of business men who control the town – Bulstrode the banker, whose money has been acquired by such dubious methods, and the manufacturer Vincy:

> One of those who suck the life out of the wretched handloom weavers in Tipton and Freshitt. That is how his family look so fair and sleek.

The fine flower of the Vincys is Rosamond, who ends by sucking the life out of Lydgate – 'a plant which had flourished wonderfully on a murdered man's brains'. Her brother Fred very nearly does the same thing to the Garth family. He almost destroys himself and ruins them by his 'great expectations' of becoming a fine gentleman and owning land (something which all the leading Middlemarch families are anxious to do) but is saved by deciding to do a useful job as an assistant to Caleb Garth.

The Garths are very close to the author's sympathies as self-respecting, hardworking, responsible people who have a definite moral code yet whose financial security rests on a knife-edge. But Caleb, too, as an agent of the landowners, is forced into an ambiguous moral position when the labourers riot over a railway which is being built on their land. An old man addresses him in an offensively radical tone to which he can find no reply:

> I'n seen lots o' things turn up sin I war a young un – the war an' the peace, and the canells, and the oald King George, an' the Regen', an' the new King George, an' the new un as has got a new ne-ame – an' it's been all aloike to the poor man. What's the canell's been t'him? They'n brought him neyther me-at nor be-acon, nor wage to lay by, if he didn't save it wi' clemmin' his own inside. Times ha' got wusser for him sin' I war a young un. An' so it'll be wi' the railroads.

They'll on'y leave the poor man furder behind... But yo're for the big folks, Muster Garth, ye are.

A similar contradiction is shown in the figure of Mr Brooke, who is adopted as a parliamentary candidate by the leading men in Middlemarch who support the Reform Bill (Bulstrode, and the textile manufacturers Plymdale and Vincy) because he is a landed gentleman of good family. But 'the weavers and tanners of Middlemarch ... had never thought of Mr Brooke as a neighbour, and were not more attached to him than if he had been sent in a box from London'. He is justly ridiculed as 'a man who shrieks at corruption, and keeps his farms at rack-rent'. The crowning indignity comes when he is 'insulted on his own land' by a drunken farmer who feels that he has been thoroughly exploited by him. Describing Dagley's farmhouse George Eliot obliquely questions many of the commonplaces of rural description which she herself had used in her earlier works:

The mouldering garden-wall with hollyhocks peeping over it was a perfect study of highly-mingled subdued colour, and there was an aged goat (kept doubtless on interesting superstitious grounds) lying against the open back-kitchen door. The mossy thatch of the cow-shed, the broken grey barn-doors, the pauper labourers in ragged breeches who had nearly finished unloading a waggon of corn ... would have made a sort of picture which we have all paused over as a 'charming bit', touching other sensibilities than those which are stirred by the depression of the agricultural interest.

Mr Brooke, when he approaches this scene in the spirit of kindly patronage with which many readers might approach George Eliot's (and Hardy's) novels, is naturally startled to be met by a stream of abuse – and to be told that the purpose of the Reform Bill which he is supporting is 'to send you an' your likes a-scuttlin''; and wi' pretty strong-smellin' things too'. On the farmer, who is very poor and nearly illiterate, George Eliot comments:

Some ... may wonder at the midnight darkness of Mr Dagley, but nothing was easier in those times than for an hereditary farmer of his grade to be ignorant, in spite somehow of having

a rector in the twin parish who was a gentleman to the backbone, a curate nearer at hand who preached more learnedly
than the rector, a landlord who had gone into everything,
especially fine art and social improvement, and all the lights
of Middlemarch only three miles away.

There is no romanticism here. The culture which the educated
class takes for granted, the light and learning of Middlemarch, is
built out of the 'midnight darkness' of villages where handloom
weavers are bled white by the rich manufacturers, and labourers
and small farmers struggle for a living and keep up their spirits
with vague dreams of change. Yet George Eliot expresses this
frustrated or exploited humanity, not so much through the
excluded majority – who are seen at a distance – as through the
frustration of exceptional individuals like Dorothea and Lydgate,
whose energies are diffused in the struggle to do good to humanity
as a whole. But what perhaps needs most emphasis is that the old
facile contrast between rural innocence and urban corruption has
been transcended. A new system is emerging in which 'municipal
town and rural parish gradually make fresh threads of connexion'.
The landed gentry and the rising manufacturers now need each
other and, despite their many differences, have to work together.
The world of Middlemarch which is both town and country – the
two ways of life are increasingly connected – thus illustrates
George Eliot's mature and essentially modern response to the
human crises of a whole civilisation.

Daniel Deronda[32] is mainly outside the scope of this chapter.
The country-house element is still there, but George Eliot has
drawn back to a more selective (though more cosmopolitan)
interplay of sensibilities and ideas; village people do not exist
even to take tracts and broth, and the human renewal will take
place quite elsewhere. The interests of the landed gentry, in
property but also in marriage and leisure activities (hunting and
archery tournaments) are very intently observed. But the English
countryside itself has dwindled to a landscape, not a place where
people live and work but a mere panorama:

the distant villages, the church towers, the scattered homesteads, the gradual rise of surging woods, and the green
breadth of undulating park which made the beautiful face of
the earth in that part of Wessex.

Wessex; this was the name which Hardy had given his country in *Far from the Madding Crowd* only a short time before. George Eliot uses the name, but she was writing about quite another country, as we shall see when we study Hardy's own work.

5 The Theme of Seduction

The seduction of village girls was a theme deeply rooted in rural tradition, going back as far as the very earliest ballads, yet in accordance with varying attitudes towards rural civilisation it was possible to treat this theme in widely differing ways. The Lancashire poet Edwin Waugh (1817–90) expressed the most traditional, romantic attitude:

> The woods were gay and green again;
> The sun was smiling on;
> But the charmer of the rural glen
> For evermore was gone:
> Now, mouldering near the churchyard way,
> All stricken in her pride,
> The white rose of the valley lay,
> With an infant by her side.[1]

The Royal Commission of 1868 was altogether more prosaic about 'the bad moral effects' on young girls of 'employment in field labour'.[2] A witness from Cambridgeshire said:

From an early age they became accustomed to the use of foul language, such sense of decency as they may have when they first go out is entirely broken down and a roughness of manner and a dislike of restraint are engendered which entirely unfits them for domestic service or for their duties in the future as wives and mothers.[3]

We have seen that Jefferies often notes this 'roughness of manner' in labouring women. In an early essay he wrote

Stern necessity leads to a coarseness and indelicacy which hardens the mind and deadens the natural modesty even of the best girls ... and if a little can be said in favour of the poor girls, not a word can be said in favour of the agricultural men, who are immoral almost without exception.[4]

The purpose of this chapter is to compare three serious novels which centre on the village-seduction theme. All three submit, to a certain extent, to novelistic conventions, the heroine dies rather than enduring a life of dishonour. But all of them are to a greater or lesser degree realistic; a realism culminating in Hardy's *Tess*.

Adam Bede

George Eliot's first novel centres on a village girl's seduction by the young squire. Strangely enough (in view of the facts) the community is astonished and scandalised by his behaviour; nothing like this ever seems to have happened in the village before. Hayslope is an idealised portrait; the action is set in the beginning of the century and we get a strong impression that the English village at that date was a happy and stable community. The people are healthy and cheerful – 'well-to-do farmers, with their apple-cheeked families ... clean old women, mostly farm-labourers' wives'. This is in Loamshire, a rich agricultural district which is sharply contrasted with the next county, Stonyshire:

> The country grew barer and barer; no more rolling woods, no more wide-branching trees and frequent homesteads ... but grey stone walls intersecting the meagre pastures, and dismal wide-scattered grey stone houses on broken lands where mines had been and were no longer.

This is a region of growing industrial cities, with their accompaniment of poverty, overcrowding, joblessness and dissent. Dinah, the Methodist working-girl, is an outsider in the comfortable world of Hayslope. In contrast with the easy-going local religion, she preaches an extreme doctrine of sin, suffering and redemption. When she speaks on the village green the people cannot understand her, and she feels impelled to leave them and go back to Stonyshire:

> I've noticed, that in these villages where the people lead a quiet life among the green pastures and the still waters, tilling the ground and tending the cattle, there's a strange deadness to the Word, as different as can be from the great towns ... the soul gets more hungry when the body is ill at ease.

Loamshire people, in fact, are essentially narrow as we see when the genial farmer Martin Poyser is talking about the French wars:

> Th' war's a fine thing for the country, an' how'll you keep up prices wi' out it? An' them French are a wicked sort of folk . . . what can you do better nor fight 'em?

This complacency is brought out even more strongly in their reaction to the novel's main event, the seduction of Poyser's niece.

Hetty Sorrel is not quite the innocent country girl of popular legend. She appears sweet and childlike, but is actually the moral opposite to Dinah – 'Hetty's dreams were all of luxuries' – nothing else. Like Jefferies' inadequate characters, she is indifferent to the community, her family and nature:

> There are some plants that have hardly any roots . . . Hetty would have been glad to hear that she should never see a child again; they were worse than the nasty little lambs that the shepherd was always bringing in to be taken special care of . . . The round downy chicks peeping out from under their mother's wing never touched Hetty with any pleasure, that was not the sort of prettiness she cared about, but she did care about the prettiness of the new things she would buy for herself . . . with the money they fetched.

If Hetty is no stereotyped figure of innocence, neither is Arthur Donnithorne the conventional wicked squire. On the contrary he is a nice young man who is very aware of his public responsibilities:

> He was nothing, if not good-natured; and all his pictures of the future, when he should come into the estate, were made up of a prosperous, contented tenantry, adoring their landlord, who would be the model of an English gentleman.

Arthur's grandfather is a grasping squire of the old type, hated by the farmers (he threatens to evict the Poyser family). Arthur, however, at his twenty-first birthday feast, promises the farmers a new deal:

> When the course of events shall place the estate in my hands, it will be my first desire . . . to be looked on by all my deserving tenants as their best friend.

Hetty's uncle proposes 'our young Squire's health' in the most glowing terms. We are made to feel that there is a bond of affection and trust between the classes (though there is also a gulf between them which can never be bridged by marriage) which Arthur perversely and wilfully breaks. Like Tess, Hetty through her seduction is eventually driven to murder, and Arthur's behaviour has the effect which his grandfather's harshness could not have had, of making her relations determined to leave the village for ever:

I wonna stay upo' that man's land a day longer nor I'm forced to . . . a man as has brought shame on respectable folks . . . an' pretended to be such a friend to everybody.

Arthur is forced to look at his own conduct directly when Adam, who formerly respected him as much as anybody, confronts him with what he has done:

You think little o' doing what may damage other folks, so as you get your bit o' trifling, as means nothing.

And in the end, after Hetty has died in exile, and Arthur has returned, ill and broken-spirited, from years in the army, he is forced to admit, 'There's a sort of wrong that can never be made up for'.

Hetty's family turn against her, after she has made them notorious:

The sense of family dishonour was too keen even in the kind-hearted Martin Poyser the younger, to leave room for any compassion towards Hetty. He and his father were simple-minded farmers, proud of their untarnished character, proud that they came of a family which had held up its head and paid its way as far back as its name was in the parish register; and Hetty had brought disgrace on them all.

In fact, their very strengths lead to intolerance and another form of the moral complacency we have noted; the nature of their moral code makes them reject anybody who violates it. Clearly, for George Eliot, this is not enough. The only person who shows any sympathy for Hetty is Dinah, who comes to her in the prison when 'the poor sinner is forsaken by all'. Dinah represents universal compassion, and under her influence Adam is able to forgive even Hetty's seducer, for Arthur has become aware through suffering of his weakness and lack of responsibility. Everyone in the novel has to suffer, in order to learn to feel the sympathetic identification with others which, for George Eliot, was the most important of all virtues. *Adam Bede* is her most uncompromisingly moral work, yet at the same time it subtly undermines the traditional moral positions. Arthur and Hetty are pathetic rather than sinful; the Poysers (and even Adam) who have a strong code of behaviour are hard and self-righteous. The pleasant village community which seemed so positive at first is therefore, in the long run essentially limited. It has to be redeemed through the influence of Dinah, who represents the whole vast experience of suffering learned in the industrial towns.

A Village Tragedy

Margaret Woods (1856–1945) was born Margaret Bradley, the cousin of a famous family of Victorian intellectuals. Her father was the Dean of Westminster, her husband (also a clergyman) became the President of an Oxford college. Despite this her novels showed a preference for dealing with ordinary people; *The Vagabonds* (1894) and *Weeping Ferry* (1898) are both well worth reading. But her first work, *A Village Tragedy*[5], was her best and most popular. It is one of the extremely rare country novels which focus directly on ordinary people; one critic called it a record of 'sheer tragedy ... the poignant, merciless, dumb suffering which breaks in pieces the humble lives of villagers'.[6]

The story begins when Annie, a girl of fifteen, is brought home from London by her uncle, James Pontin, a farmer in Oxfordshire. The child grows up feeling thoroughly out of place in the village:

> The hill folk are a rough lot, far from Arcadian in their words or ways, and full of a suspicious wonder at strangers; and Annie felt the want of companions.

Her uncle and aunt are 'two narrow and preoccupied hearts' who can feel no affection for her. Her aunt is particularly coarse – 'she loved the human creature in proportion as it approached the animal'. The author's comments have a note of superiority which show that we must not expect sensitive or sympathetic feelings from people like them:

Mrs Pontin heaved a sigh over the husband of her youth, as she began mixing the potato-peelings with meal, for a lady pig in a delicate state of health.

We can see here that we are expected to laugh, as no doubt contemporary London readers would have done, at these ridiculous people. However comic we may find the Poysers in *Adam Bede*, George Eliot gives us nothing like this. Mrs Poyser is comic as an individual; Mrs Pontin purely and simply as a farmer's wife; nor is there any such obvious attempt in the earlier novel to direct our response.

The worst aspects of village life are personified in Albert, an idiot boy of whom Annie is terrified:

His unwieldly head rolled loosely on his shoulders; he had a blind eye – a white, viscous-looking eye – and a great shapeless mouth, that was always wet, and generally munching some unclean food ... The pigs seemed quite to have adopted him into their family ... it was difficult to tell which of the occasional snorts and squeals which expressed the emotions of the party were human and which porcine.

In this passage we can feel the writer's own shrinking distaste, her instinctive reaction that the boy is so nearly an animal that he is outside the range of normal human sympathy. So far as Albert is concerned, the 'sensitive' Annie has a much cruder response than the coarse Mrs Pontin. Her aunt accepts him naturally as a person and as part of the community, whereas Annie wants him to be locked up.

Annie's only friend is a young labourer called Jesse, a workhouse boy abandoned by his parents. They are drawn together because both are foreigners in the village:

His attachment to her was chiefly the clinging of one lonely human creature to another, though there was in it a grain of romance, arising from the consciousness that he was not her equal. Though treated as a farm servant, Mr Pontin's niece was socially above the former workhouse boy and actual carter, besides being really his superior in manners and intelligence.

The novel's emotional range is thus clearly defined. It is a severely limited range – limited by the writer's conviction that deep emotions are not possible among the people she is describing. Annie is much finer and quicker than anyone else she comes into contact with, but since she has to live in the village she must adapt to it as well as she can. Her case is quite different from Hetty's, who allows herself to love the squire and who wants to escape from a life of hard work. Hetty yields because of her dreams of refinement and luxury – dreams which are inconceivable in *A Village Tragedy*. Annie yields because she has almost no choice. She is without illusions. Her courtship is consciously presented as being on a very low emotional level. When Jesse gives her some roses:

'They be just about the same colour as your face, Annie', he said, and grinned a dreary grin of embarrassment.

But, for Annie, his roses are the only alternative to her aunt's blows and bullying. The Pontins forbid her to associate with him, as her social inferior, but she is literally driven into his arms by their treatment. Because of Albert she is turned out on a rainy night and goes to Jesse for shelter; her uncle and aunt jump to the wrong conclusion and disown her.

This whole episode is treated in terms of extreme melodrama. The novelist seems to be underlining the point that the behaviour of Albert and Mrs Pontin is so brutal, so far beneath civilised human standards, that there is nothing Annie can do except try to escape. Here is her description of Albert's actions:

He jerked himself into a crouching posture, and seized her dress with his dirty, long-nailed, claw-like hands, his great mouth seeming to divide his head in half as it yawned up at her in an insane grin . . . Gibbering inarticulately he thrust the pink cotton flounce between his teeth, and began gradually sucking and chewing inch after inch into his mouth, like a brown bloated reptile slowly absorbing its prey.

Mrs Pontin in a rage is described as follows:

Her face was dark red and puffy, the swollen veins were standing out on her neck and forehead, her double chin and large purple lips quivered as she gasped and slobbered inarticulately

... With a roar like that of a wild beast she sent the girl staggering back to the opposite wall.

Passages like this are rather startling in a novel which is usually low-toned emotionally, but their point is to emphasise that in Annie's unendurable situation she has no alternative but to accept Jesse's protection. When her uncle turns her out there is a great storm, heightening the sense of crisis, and she struggles desperately to reject Jesse 'because I must be an honest girl'. But she knows this is only a formula:

All was rough and cold and cheerless ... The arms that held her were strong and warm, the eyes that looked into hers were full of love and anguish and entreaty.

The temptation is too great for human nature to stand.

They want to get married at once, but believe mistakenly that they are too young. When Annie becomes pregnant she is deeply upset about her position:

There were several couples in the village who had had children before they were man and wife, but once married no one troubled to rake that up against them ... But Annie came from a higher social stratum, where morals are less careless ... The irregularity of her position branded her, in her own eyes, with a shame that marriage itself could not wholly obliterate.

Apart from this, they are nearly destitute and Annie becomes desperate 'thinking about the bill at the shop, and the baby coming into a world where it would find nothing to clothe it but a scarlet cotton pinafore'. She goes to the vicar's wife, who refuses to help her because she is not 'respectable'. But her niece, Mary, a kindly nurse, does what she can for Annie and tells her it will be perfectly legal to get married at once. Mary is not well integrated into the scheme of the novel. Like Dinah in *Adam Bede*, she is too much a visitor from another world, a supernatural stranger who can set all problems right. This is confirmed by Annie's reaction to her:

'I don't believe you're a lady', she said; 'I believe you're an angel'.

The trouble is that Mary can be an angel only because she is a lady, for nobody living inside the narrow oppressive world of the village could develop her qualities of detachment and strength.

Jesse goes to Oxford to buy the wedding-ring, but on the way back he is fatally injured by a train. Annie is now expecting the baby at any moment. He makes her put on the ring, 'No one can't say now as I didn't mean to make an honest woman of you'. There is another thing that obsesses him:

You mustn't let my child go to the work'us, whatever you do . . . Starve it, I say, sooner than send it to the work'us.

This is a version of poor people's instinctive terror of public 'charity', which never left them throughout the nineteenth century. Annie shares this terror; she cannot accept the idea of the workhouse, but there is no other future for her and her child. The curate who tries to comfort her is useless:

He was but a lad fresh from Oxford, without experience of a deeper sorrow than a plough in the schools . . . What could he say or do, brought face to face with the workings of a remorseless Fate?

He reminds us of the narrow Oxford scholars in *Jude the Obscure* and in fact the whole situation, with the emphasis on 'the workings of a remorseless Fate' is strongly reminiscent of Hardy. It is exactly the situation which keeps recurring in his novels, that of a marriage thwarted at the last moment by some unforeseeable accident. Annie senses the irony bitterly:

'Yes, it's my wedding-ring', she said, stretching out her left hand, 'and I've as good a right to wear it as anyone who's been married in church. It was Jesse's wish as I should wear it . . . It's bad enough for me to be left without him; it's cruel if it's happening today instead of tomorrow is to make a difference to me and my child as long as we live'.

She thinks that it would be worse for the child to be a girl, to grow up and suffer like herself: 'A woman's life was a poor affair for the most part . . . she did not think the little girls of the lower classes would lose much if Judgement Day came before they had taken their turn'.

But the child is a girl, and she is reduced to a state of total, passive despair:

'Poor little thing!' said Annie again. 'It would be happier for her to die, wouldn't it? Life's so hard for us poor folks'.

Although the village is, in these matters, distinctly more tolerant than Hayslope (the novel was written thirty years later and in an atmosphere of much greater realism), Annie's future as an unmarried mother is as bleak as Hetty's:

Her child would be taken from her, brought up in the dreary prison of the workhouse school, and turned out into the world despised, friendless, fatherless and motherless, Motherless, because she herself would be a stranger to him, either in the Union or toiling somewhere as the drudge of a coarse mistress, who would overlook the blot on her character, if she were allowed to pay her less on account of it. All her shame came back upon her mind with crushing weight, mingled with impotent exasperation against the cruel fate which had bound its burden irrevocably upon her at the very moment when it seemed about to be lifted off. It felt heavier now there was no longer any living creature besides herself who knew and understood all the circumstances of her step aside from the path of respectability. Our notions of our own personalities are so largely gained by the reflections of ourselves we see mirrored in the eyes of others, that Annie's self-respect was involuntarily injured by the consciousness that now in the whole world there were no longer any eyes which could reflect back to her an unsullied Annie; the victim not of passion, but of injustice and ill-fortune.

The false judgements of society are beginning to be internalised in her own mind. The references to the destructive workings of fate, which are so often found in contemporary writers, probably resulted not so much from an abstract general conception (though in the popular versions of 'social Darwinism' this was undoubtedly there) as from the blind, instinctive feelings of thousands of the Victorian poor that there was nothing they could do to escape from the system. For it was the system as a whole that was at fault, not an incidental aspect of the society but the society itself, which crushed any tentative plans they might have formed for happiness and respectability. Some writers tried to account for the fact of human misery by the Christian doctrine of redemption through suffering; others rejected this, but still could not see beyond the concept of a cruel necessity, an inexorable fate. Ultimately both doctrines came down to the same thing; it was useless for the lower classes to struggle against their degradation, because they would only be crushed.

This, we should remember, was the reality in which the frequently grotesque incidents of Hardy's novels were based. It was necessary to invent far-fetched and unconvincing reasons for a tragic outcome in each individual case, so that the apparently hopeless misery of a whole society should not be falsified. Margaret Woods does the same thing. Annie has tried to resist, indeed to transcend, her environment, therefore she is destroyed by it. The incident of Jesse's fatal accident on the eve of the wedding may be unconvincing and melodramatic. But it was necessary to be unrealistic in order to be realistic on a wider scale, for if an individual were shown escaping from the cruel mechanism of society, the sufferings of millions of other people in that society would be implicitly passed over – or it would appear that the society was capable of being changed for the better, and this was just what some of the most honest writers could never believe.

The final incidents of the novel are heavy with symbolism. Early one morning, a few days after the birth of Annie's child, the young doctor sees Albert playing with what turns out to be the baby. He follows him, and comes upon the corpse of Annie:

> She had slipped on a skirt over her nightgown, a pair of shoes and a shawl, and had evidently, from the position of her left arm and hand, been carrying the baby. By some supreme exertion of the will she had struggled so far with it, probably intending to lay herself and her child under the deep waters of the pond, when suddenly her strength had failed her and the end had come. Albert must have found or followed her, and carried the child away from its mother's body.

At this point Albert again creeps up, takes the ring from the dead girl's hand and throws it 'with a cry of rage and spite' into the pond:

> For a moment it turned and glittered in the air, then with a faint splash it disappeared, and a tiny circle of ripples, widening till they touched the grassy bank, disturbed the dark surface of the pond.

The contrast between aspiration and reality, the bright ring and the dark water, is presented in the clearest terms. Albert, the symbol of animal imbecility, reappears at the tragic climax of the novel to emphasise the destruction of Annie's hopes for happiness, or at least for recognition as a decent woman, which the ring represents. Nature appears as a blind, brutish force, remorselessly sucking down human beings' efforts towards a better life. Everything Annie has struggled for is hopeless. The lowest, most physical forces are certain to win.

A Village Tragedy does not deserve to be forgotten as completely as it now is, although it is limited both in achievement and in awareness. Annie is deliberately shown as a person whose emotional responses are poor and restricted, for though she is capable of seeing beyond the village she is also limited by it. Hetty is a limited character too (more so than her community). Margaret Woods and George Eliot both seem to be creating characters well within their own emotional range, and whom they can easily keep at a distance. It was not until Hardy wrote *Tess* that an educated author was able to identify, unreservedly, with an uneducated village girl.

Tess of the d'Urbervilles

Tess Durbeyfield, over and above her qualities as a person, is portrayed as a representative of her class and her sex. She is 'a figure which is part of the landscape; a fieldwoman pure and simple'. When he is describing the women reapers Hardy explains what this means:

> A field-man is a personality afield; a field-woman is a portion of the field; she has somehow lost her own margin, imbibed the essence of her surrounding, and assimilated herself with it.

The method by which the heroine is thus merged and identified both with the landscape in which she works and the other women who work with her reinforces our impression of her as an essentially passive and suffering figure. Tess is doubly vulnerable because she belongs to the working class and because she is a girl. She is liable to be reduced, not only to the status of an unskilled labourer, but also to that of a mere sexual object, in a society which she has no means of resisting. Hardy's heroes, like Clym and Jude and Henchard, are able to struggle actively with their destiny, form plans for opposing it, try to hew out a recognised place in the world. The women in his novels have no such outlet, and this makes their situation potentially more tragic. They are limited to a very few, easily recognisable social roles, and they are always subject to sexual domination and destruction from men.

Nothing in the novel caused more offence to critics than Hardy's description of Tess in the subtitle as 'a pure woman'. The *Quarterly Review* thought that this was 'a strain upon the English language'.[7] *The Independent* complained that the novel was 'a pretty kettle of fish for pure people to eat' and that it menaced 'the moral fibre of young readers'.[8] There were plenty of similar reactions, condemning Hardy as immoral because he called a girl who had lost her virginity 'pure'. Hardy replied that these critics were being too literal-minded:

> I still maintain that her innate purity remained intact to the very last; though I frankly own that a certain outward purity left her on her last fall. I regarded her then as being in the hands of circumstances, not morally responsible, a mere corpse drifting with the current.[9]

She remains pure, despite her involvement in adultery, and finally murder, because her destiny is not freely chosen but forced upon her by the circumstances which Hardy calls Fate. What this means is that in her particular social situation it was inevitable that her innocence should be destroyed. In the beginning when we see her in the May Day procession she seems to embody the traditional, Arcadian view of the countryside which the novel is later to undermine:

> The whole troop wore white garments . . . every woman and girl carried in her right hand a peeled willow wand, and in her left a bunch of white flowers.

But Tess's innocence is dependent on her family's circumstances and has to be bartered for a desperately-needed material profit. The Durbeyfield children are totally subject to ruin, if she does not help them:

> If the heads of the Durbeyfield household chose to sail into difficulty, disaster, starvation, disease, degradation, death, thither were these half-dozen little captives under hatches

compelled to sail with them – six helpless creatures, who had
never been asked if they wished for life on any terms, much less
if they wished for it on such hard conditions as were involved
in being of the shiftless house of Durbeyfield. Some people
would like to know whence the poet . . . gets his authority for
speaking of 'Nature's holy plan'.

Hardy is saying, with an incidental swipe at Wordsworth, that
if Nature does have a plan it is anything but holy. It is actively
malevolent, and most people would have been better off if they
had never been born. The same deep-rooted pessimism, the same
total disbelief that human life can lead to any permanent happiness, is shown in his famous comparison of the world to a blighted
apple on a healthy tree. But we can see that Hardy's fatalism is
inseparable from his social attitudes in the context of the quota-
tion, which is not about metaphysical forms of suffering but about
the actual misery of the Victorian labourers – 'starvation, disease,
degradation, death'. In order to avert these disasters, Tess is
packed off to work for the family's rich 'cousin'. Mrs Durbeyfield
knows what she is doing in sending the inexperienced girl into
Alec's clutches but she deludes herself that 'if he don't marry her
afore he will after'. Tess only realises when it is too late how
much she has been harmed by her mother's attempt to work out
a fantasy at her expense:

Why didn't you tell me there was danger in men-folk? Why
didn't you warn me? Ladies know what to fend hands against,
because they read novels . . . but I never had the chance o'
learning in that way, and you did not help me!

Tess has fallen an easy victim to Alec, as Hardy continually
stresses, not because she is abandoned but because she is innocent.
When she leaves home she is plunged into a corrupt atmosphere
which she is utterly unequipped to resist. Alec functions within
the community as a sexual despot:

The levity of some of the younger women in and about Trantridge was marked, and was perhaps symptomatic of the choice
spirit who ruled . . . in that vicinity.

Her associates are no longer unsophisticated girls in white
frocks but 'careless women' such as 'a dark virago, Car Darch,
dubbed Queen of Spades, till lately a favourite of d'Urberville's',

and 'Nancy her sister, nicknamed the Queen of Diamonds'. The latter has 'stood in the relations to d'Urberville that Car had also been suspected of'; Tess describes them, not unreasonably, as 'a whorage' in the crucial scene which culminates in her betrayal. Hardy published this scene separately under the title of *Saturday. Night in Arcady*. The picture of the women staggering drunkenly home from their weekly orgy, making a jealous scene with Tess over Alec 'because th' beest first favourite with He just now', and then roaring with laughter when she escapes with him 'out of the frying pan into the fire' shows just how far the Arcadian stereotype was removed from the facts. Alec's behaviour is not, like Arthur's, a disgraceful secret from the community but something which he openly flaunts and in which it abets him. The community itself delivers Tess into his hands.

These community attitudes make it possible for her (unlike Hetty Sorrel) to return home and even to suckle her child in the field. But she still feels with justification that everyone is observing her:

> The event which had made of her a social warning had also for the moment made her the most interesting personage in the village to many.

She says that she 'wishes the baby and her too were in the churchyard' and she baptises the dying child Sorrow, because there is no future for an illegitimate child, or an unmarried mother, in the society she has to live in. Yet Hardy emphasises that she can recover from her early degrading experiences, if she is allowed to do so – 'But for the world's opinion those experiences would have been simply a liberal education'. In fact she does recover when she goes to Talbothays, but this recovery cannot be permanent, because there she meets Angel Clare, who becomes in effect her second betrayer – 'the one man on earth who had loved her purely, and who had believed in her as pure'.

Angel is essentially different from everyone else in the dairy, cut off from the labourers because he is a gentleman, and largely for this reason he is, like Alec, a sexual magnet within his own sphere. This fact is not given overt sexual expression, because Talbothays is gentler than Trantridge and Angel considerably more scrupulous than Alec, but it is nevertheless true that he has 'the honour of all the dairymaids in his keeping'. These girls, all of whom love Angel, have a great importance in the structure of the novel because they represent the class from which Tess emerges. Socially they are in exactly the same position as she is, and their feelings are also very similar – not only their feelings for Angel, but their entire scheme of values. These values are given expression by Marian:

> You will think of us when you be his wife, Tess, and of how we told 'ee that we loved him, and how we tried not to hate you, and did not hate you, and could not hate you, because you were his choice, and we never hoped to be chose by him.

It is her feeling of responsibility to them which finally makes her tell Angel her secret:

> They were simple and innocent girls on whom the unhappiness of unrequited love had fallen; they had deserved better at the hands of Fate. She had deserved worse – yet she was the chosen one. It was wicked of her to take all without paying. She would pay to the uttermost farthing; she would tell there and then.

It is a fatal mistake, for, despite the past entanglement which Angel admits so light-heartedly, he is much too conventional a Victorian to forgive a similar lapse in his wife. Many critics have found this 'double standard' impossible to swallow, thus Arnold Kettle:

> Hardy can convince us that Angel is a prig and a hypocrite but he simply cannot convince us that the Angel he presents to us in the novel would be quite so morally obtuse as to see no affinity whatever between his confession and hers.[10]

I think this is underestimating the full depth and subtlety of Hardy's characterisation of Angel. He is not, in fact, unaware of the problems which Tess has raised; he cannot deny it when she points out, 'I have forgiven you for the same'. But the point which he keeps coming back to obsessively is that she is no longer the same person as the one he fell in love with. He has never seen her as she really is, only as an idealised figure, which he identifies in a superficial way with uncontaminated nature:

> 'What a fresh and virginal daughter of Nature that milkmaid is!' he said to himself.

And, after he has discovered his mistake, he complains:

I thought – any man would have thought – that by giving up
all ambition to win a wife with social standing, with fortune,
with knowledge of the world, I should secure rustic innocence
as surely as I should secure pink cheeks!

There is no need to comment on the self-centredness of this
speech, the self-pity, the acquisitive attitude to people which it
reveals so damningly – the only point we need notice here is that
it proves he has always regarded her as an abstraction. 'Rustic
innocence' – this is all he can see in her, and once it has gone
there is nothing left. He loves her, as Hardy says, 'perhaps rather
ideally and fancifully then with the impassioned thoroughness
of her feeling for him'. In other words, Tess loves him for himself, whereas he is only in love with a dream-image of her. Angel
has very much the same emotional structure, apparently tender
almost to softness but basically frigid, as Sue in *Jude the Obscure*.
He cultivates his emotions as things in themselves – if they were
stronger, they would not need cultivation – but in fact these
emotions are divided, inauthentic. Here he is talking about the
Church:

I love the church as one loves a parent. I shall always have the
warmest affection for her . . . but I cannot honestly be ordained
her minister . . . while she refuses to liberate her mind from
an untenable redemptive theolatry.

And this is his reaction to old aristocratic families, like the
d'Urbervilles:

Politically I am sceptical as to the virtue of their being old . . .
but lyrically, dramatically, and even historically, I am tenderly
attached to them.

He cannot commit himself to what he loves, and he is emotionally attracted by what he rejects intellectually. In fact, he is a
dilettante in his emotions – or rather he has *no* emotions worth
speaking of – and this means he is able to play about with other
people's feelings without himself getting hurt. He idealises Tess,
but his attitude is also one of unconscious patronage, and these
are two sides of the same coin. Demanding that his wife should
not share his vices really means that he is restricting her freedom
as he has no idea of restricting his own. His response to her, and

through her to the whole civilisation of rural England, is of the same kind as his response to the Church and the aristocracy – an unreal cloudy attachment to something he cannot truly accept. When he finds that Tess is the product not of a happy and innocent rural Arcadia but of a rough, brutal village existence where the men's jobs and the girls' virtue are at the mercy of local landowners, he blames her for his misapprehension instead of himself. 'Angel', as Hardy said, 'is a type of a certain class of the modern young man.'[11] He is in no sense a freak of nature. He is a typical representative of that Victorian society in which intellectuals complained about how much they would like to believe in God, if they only could, and which idealised woman and the home in the most fulsome language at a time when the number of prostitutes in England was greater than ever before.

We see Angel at his worst in his scene with Izz Huett, when he asks her to come to Brazil with him, still acting up to his unspoken conviction that it is all right for him to do what is all wrong for Tess. But, like Tess, Izz loses him through her own innate honesty, when she tells him that 'nobody could love 'ee more than Tess did'. At this Angel changes his mind and leaves her, telling her to 'forget my momentary levity'. Of course this is only another example of his irresponsibility in playing with feelings deeper than his own, and he has to realise that he has wounded Izz terribly. 'It was no levity to me.'

Meanwhile Tess is gradually reduced back to a field labourer. The necessity to support her family forces her to take on more and more hard and degrading work, and exposes her more and more to unwanted attentions from men. Her only means of escape is deliberately to deny her own sexuality – 'I'll always be ugly now, because Angel is not here'. She finishes up on the bleak farm at Flintcomb-Ash, working for a bullying farmer with Marian and Izz and the 'two Amazonian sisters' from d'Urberville's village, the Queen of Diamonds and the Queen of Spades. Hardy's purpose is to show that here, where the agricultural life of England is most brutal, all these girls, whatever their individual differences, are reduced to slaves of the system – both the technically chaste and the technically fallen, those who have kept their human integrity in spite of circumstances and those who have let themselves become brutalised. From now on, Tess is presented increasingly as the representative of an entire group.

Her attempt to make contact with Angel's family breaks down because she cannot bear the comparison between herself and Mercy Chant, the 'ladylike young woman' they wanted him to marry. But in fact the attitude of Angel's brothers only shows up their narrowness. 'The purity of Tess, warm and natural, is contrasted with that of Mercy Chant, cold and class-bound.'[12] Mercy can *afford* to be pure and pious and respectable because she has always been carefully shielded from the coarser sexual and social pressures. She is contrasted not only with Tess but also with Marian and Izz. All these girls, however different as people, discover a deep solidarity through their common experience of work on the land, of rejection and suffering. This enables them to help each other against the bullying farmer, and not to be driven apart by their common love for Angel. So when Tess is again threatened by Alec, the other two write to Angel and beg him to come back to her. Their action is not sentimentalised, but the letter reveals more unselfishness, and a more humane understanding of weakness, than Angel ever had:

A woman should not be try'd beyond her Strength, and continual dropping will wear away a Stone – ay, more, a Diamond.

Tess does everything she can to keep Alec at bay. She is convinced by this time that Angel will never come back, but she can resist Alec's offer of an easy life, so long as only she herself is concerned. We realise where she is vulnerable when she appeals to him, 'Don't mention my little brothers and sisters – don't make me break down quite!' Her family is turned out partly because of her – 'the village had to be kept pure'. When they can find nowhere to live, and the only available source of protection is Alec, Tess realises that she has to choose between herself and the children. Like Sonia in *Crime and Punishment*, it seems to her that her own self-respect is a small thing, compared with the suffering of these innocents. This is the sole reason why she gives in. And Hardy, who always maintained definitely that she was 'a pure woman', believed that she was right to do so, or rather that it was the only thing she could have done. This is at a crucial historical distance from Shakespeare, in *Measure for Measure*, having the 'pure' Isabella say 'more than our brother is our chastity'. Hardy believed that there were some situations in which one might have to sacrifice oneself in the deepest sense because, in a corrupt society, one could only remain pure at other people's expense.

By the time Angel comes back he has undergone a great change. He has been in Brazil, where he has seen real suffering; he has been ill, and, like Arthur Donnithorne, he has learned through suffering to judge himself more clearly than in the past. He returns to England ready to go back to Tess if she will accept him, but when he finds her she has been forced to become Alec's mistress. Angel admits, 'It is my fault'.

This experience is so shattering for Tess that it drives her over the border of sanity. She had never completely overcome the feeling that, in one sense, her connection with Alec was dissoluble only by death. Angel told her, after her confession:

How can we live together while that man lives? – he being your husband in nature, and not I. If he were dead it might be different.

And, trying to explain to him why she has murdered Alec, she says:

I owed it to you, and to myself, Angel. I feared long ago, when I struck him on the mouth with my glove, that I might do it some day for the trap he set for me in my simple youth, and his wrong to you through me. He has come between us and ruined us, and now he can never do it any more . . . Will you forgive me my sin against you, now I have killed him? I thought as I ran along that you would be sure to forgive me now I have done that. It came to me as a shining light that I should get you back that way.

The ordinary moral restraints have become inverted. It seems to Tess that by killing Alec she is really killing part of herself – the self that was rejected as unworthy of Angel, the past that she wants to blot out. But of course it is useless. She has not destroyed the image of herself which is received by society; she has only made herself worse in its eyes. Whatever she does, society will not let her fulfil her real nature, which is that of 'a pure woman'. By the end, she has realised the futility of her crime, and it is no longer possible for her to believe in herself as pure. Her last words to Angel, at Stonehenge when the police come, are poignant in their humility:

> It is as it should be . . . Angel, I am almost glad, yes, glad! This happiness could not have lasted. It was too much. I have had enough; and now I shall not live for you to despise me!

But it is clear enough by this time that it is not her, but society that we should really despise.

In the intervening generation the world of George Eliot, in which really guilty individuals can still escape the worst punishments, has darkened into the world of Hardy, in which an essentially innocent girl can be hanged. In this process the values of a whole society have been radically called into question. George Eliot saw the problem mainly in terms of individual moral choices, against a background which was relatively static. Margaret Woods in the next generation portrayed a society which was much more inclined to force people's actions and pressurise them into stereotypes alien to their real personality – but with less insistence on human strength and purity. Hardy *mourns* Tess, and this is new.

Part Two

Part Two

1 Hardy's Wessex

The 'Wessex novels' were so christened because Hardy revived the ancient name of Wessex to describe the south-western region of England in which they are almost entirely set. His reasons for this were explained in the 1895 Preface to *Far from the Madding Crowd*:

> The series of novels I projected being mainly of the kind called local, they seemed to require a territorial definition of some sort to lend unity to their scene. Finding that the area of a single county did not afford a canvas large enough for this purpose, and that there were objections to an invented name, I disinterred the old one. The region designated was known but vaguely, and I was often asked even by educated people where it lay. However, the press and the public . . . willingly joined me in the anachronism of imagining a Wessex population living under Queen Victoria; – a modern Wessex of railways, the penny post, mowing and reaping machines, union workhouses, lucifer matches, labourers who could read and write, and National school children. But I believe I am correct in stating that, until the existence of this contemporaneous Wessex in place of the usual counties was announced in the present story, in 1874, it had never been heard of in fiction and current speech.

The name soon passed into common currency. Hardy was rather surprised by its popularity:

> Since then the appellation which I had thought to reserve to the horizons and landscapes of a partly real, partly dream-country, has become more and more popular as a practical provincial definition; and the dream-country has by degrees solidified into a utilitarian region which people can go to, take a house in, and write to the papers from.

This tension in the relationship between Hardy's material and his imagination, the complexity of his idea of this 'partly real, partly dream-country', is essential to the understanding of his conception of Wessex. He was describing a region which he knew intimately and whose history and traditions were a major part of his consciousness, but he was, simultaneously, retaining his creative autonomy so that his descriptions are never entirely literal. The immediate relationship was summarised accurately by his friend Hermann Lea:

> We have it on his own assurance that the Wessex of the novels and poems is practically identical with the Wessex of history, and includes the counties of Berkshire, Wilts, Somerset, Hampshire, Dorset and Devon – either wholly or in part.[1]

In fact all the major novels except *Jude* are set primarily in Dorset. *Under the Greenwood Tree, Far from the Madding Crowd, The Return of the Native* and *The Mayor of Casterbridge* are all staged in the immediate Dorchester area. *The Woodlanders* is set wholly, and *Tess* partly, in the Vale of Blackmoor on the other side of the plateau, though the Talbothays scenes in *Tess* take place in the Frome Valley, near Dorchester and on the edge of Puddletown or 'Egdon' heath. *Jude* has a quite different setting, in Berkshire, about twenty miles south of Oxford, in 'an undulating upland adjoining the North Wessex downs'.

Hardy took great pains to preserve the local quality of the novels, and to make his descriptions of life in the region authentic:

> At the date represented in the various narratives things were like that in Wessex: the inhabitants lived in certain ways, engaged in certain occupations, kept alive certain customs, just as they are shown doing in these pages.[2]

Dorset: Land and Cultivation

The 'southern, sea-bordered shire of Dorset',[3] as Rider Haggard called it, differs from most English counties in that it 'shows no one soil so predominant as to constitute a county characteristic'.[4] The soils vary between deep rich loam, sandy loam with flints, chalk on the downs and rock on the islands of Purbeck and

Portland. The woods include several apple orchards in the west of the county. Caird in the middle of the century saw it as a region of

> breezy open downs and bare uplands . . . lofty downs still untouched by the plough. The white, flinty roads . . . can be distinguished for miles . . . winding over the long ascent of the smooth down, and again descending on the rich, bare, open country which surrounds Dorchester.[5]

Darby and Finn write that Dorset 'has sometimes been characterised as a county of three parts . . . the down, the vale, and the heath'.[6] 'The down' is a great ridge of undulating chalk uplands, which runs down the centre of the county between the fertile clay lowlands. Tess on the way to Flintcomb-Ash saw it as an 'irregular chalk table-land or plateau . . . which stretched between the valley of her birth and the valley of her love' (the valleys of the Stour and the Frome). The area contains large stretches of clay with flints where arable farming is possible, but the basic chalk formation is suitable primarily for grazing sheep.

The northern escarpment of these uplands looks down over the Vale of Blackmoor, a region of heavy soil drained by the Stour. Hardy in *Tess* called it a 'fertile and sheltered tract of country, in which the fields are never brown and the springs never dry'. In contrast to the bleak uplands:

> here, in the valley, the world seems to be constructed upon a smaller and more delicate scale; the fields are mere paddocks, so reduced that from this height their hedgerows appear a network of dark green threads overspreading the paler green of the grass . . . Arable lands are few and limited; with but slight exceptions the prospect is a broad rich mass of grass and trees.

This is an area of dairy farms and there are also several orchards around Sherborne, in the cider-producing region where *The Woodlanders* is set.

'The heath' was the large stretch of waste land which Hardy called Egdon in *The Return of the Native*, at that time 'a vast tract of unenclosed wild'. This was mostly light sand and quite useless for cultivation – 'not a plough had ever disturbed a grain of that stubborn soil'. On the edge of the heath is the Frome valley where there are several small dairy farms like that described as Talbothays in *Tess*.

Dorset has always been primarily agricultural, but there have been a few scattered industries – cider-making, the stone and marble-cutting trade around Portland and Purbeck, tourism in seaside towns like Weymouth and Poole. The railway only reached Dorchester in 1847 when Hardy was a small child.

The essentially mixed character of farming in the county led to several economic fluctuations in the difficult years after 1879. Caird, in 1852, included Dorset among the arable counties in his map but said that its main characteristic was sheep-breeding. By the end of the century great stretches of arable land had been converted to pasture in accordance with what was happening all over England. The *Victoria County History* summed up:

> So great has been the change that the farmer of 1800, were he alive now, would scarcely recognise his county. The number of sheep kept has dwindled, the corn area has become less, dairying is more general, the area of permanent and rotation pastures has increased, and many small minor industries ... have completely died out.[7]

The great increase in dairy-farming in the last quarter of the century was due partly to the labour shortage and the difficulties of small farmers, partly to the changing pattern of public demand. While the home corn trade was suffering, the market for milk and animal products was steadily growing larger. The *Victoria County History* says:

> It was after the disastrous year 1879 that farmers in Dorset commenced to pay greater attention to dairy supplies. That year reduced farmers' capital to such a degree that many of them found it imperative to turn their attention to a brand of agriculture which would yield them an immediate return for their outlay. In addition the growth of the larger towns and seaside resorts was instrumental in increasing the production of milk by the reason of the growing demand which the workers in the towns created ... It is impossible to give figures for early years showing the growth of the milk supply from Dorset, which goes to London, Bournemouth, Weymouth, and other seaside places within or near the county, but some idea may be gathered from the fact that during 1906 there were dispatched by the London and South Western Railway to London and elsewhere nearly 5,000,000 gallons of milk.[8]

The balance of agricultural production in Dorset had radically altered during the fifty years since Caird wrote. At the turn of the century Haggard found that the county was now 'chiefly noted for its dairy products', although 'a large acreage is given up to the production of cereals'. He also discovered that 'the corn and sheep farms had depreciated 50 per cent in value, but thé grass land only 10 or 15 per cent'.[9]

Dorset farmers had learned how to modernise themselves in the period of high farming, which among other things taught them the advantage of chemical fertilisers. The *Victoria County History* notes that, in 1908, 'no farmer of any size or repute is to be found who sticks to antediluvian methods of cultivation'.[10] The growth of modernisation was accelerated by the depression years which made farmers eager to adopt the machine as a labour-saving device. The cutting down of the agricultural labour force was a reciprocal process; labourers left the countryside to find better pay and steadier jobs, and farmers found that grazing cattle, as well as bringing in higher profits than corn growing, was also cheaper as it absorbed much less labour. The profits enabled them to pay the higher wages which the labourers could now demand from a position of strength.

However, the falling value of land, the difficulties of many small farmers and the continual draining away of labourers led observers around 1900 to a pessimistic view. Rider Haggard at the end of his survey came to a thoroughly gloomy conclusion – 'it is impossible to take a favourable view of the present prospects of the land, or of any class connected with it, in Dorsetshire'.

Dorset: The Agricultural Labourers 1840–1900

In 1844, Alexander Somerville, in his travels through what he called the 'ill-cultivated counties of the west',[11] wrote about 'the wretched villages of Dorsetshire . . . where the traveller sees the worst of houses and the poorest of labourers'.[12] Dorset was always known as a county where 'the labourer's lot was particularly bad'.[13] In the early fifties Caird wrote in his survey:

> The condition of the Dorsetshire labourer has passed into a proverb, not altogether just, as compared with the counties adjoining.[14]

The proverb may not have been altogether just, but the facts were bad enough.

Dorset was one of several counties involved in the 'last labourers' revolt' of 1830, when the demand for a decent living wage was brutally smashed. In 1834 six labourers who became known to history as the Tolpuddle Martyrs, from the small village near Dorchester where they lived, were transported for trying to form an agricultural trade union. Hardy was born six years later, in Higher Bockhampton only a few miles away. Growing up in a tiny isolated village, and in a home which was only a little more prosperous than those of the labourers, he had many opportunities as a boy to see what the social condition of Dorset was like. Before he grew up he saw two public hangings. When he was fourteen there was a cholera epidemic, in which many people died, in the Dorchester slums. In a letter to Haggard, when he was over sixty, he wrote:

> As to my opinion on the past of the agricultural labourer in this county, I think, indeed know, that down to 1850 or 1855 his condition was in general one of great hardship . . . As a child I knew by sight a sheep-keeping boy who, to my horror, shortly afterwards died of want, the contents of his stomach at the autopsy being raw turnip only. His father's wages were 6s a week.[15]

Of course this was an extreme example. But throughout the century Dorsetshire labourers' wages were at or near the bottom of the wages scale – in the forties they averaged 7s 6d a week, lower than any other county in England. The new Poor Law of 1834 ensured that anyone who failed to manage on this would be sent to the workhouse. The situation was made worse by the fact that there was a large labour surplus here as in most of the south-western counties, and, as Hardy said in the same letter, labourers 'had neither the means nor the knowledge' to emigrate at this time.

The average labourer lived in a cottage from which he could be evicted at the farmer's convenience, and which Somerville described as a 'crumbling hovel of clay and wood'.[16] The *Victoria County History* records that in 1842 'a family of eleven persons . . . lived in a cottage of only two rooms' and that 'a family of twenty-nine persons lived in one cottage'.[17] There was no access to the commons as enclosures in Dorset had been completed a century before.

Somerville, visiting Cranborne in 1842, spoke to two carters who as skilled men would have been earning a little more than the ordinary labourers. They told him that their jobs involved

> rising at four in the morning and coming home to dinner and supper at seven in the evening. They had been receiving eight shillings a week, but were now reduced to seven. I asked if they could afford bacon and vegetables to their dinner every day? and they said no, they could not when they had eight shillings, and they did not know how they would with seven.[18]

The country was so badly cultivated that Somerville thought it could have yielded ample work for all the unemployed men. But no one seemed interested in this, as all the classes on the land distrusted each other, 'and the result is, that we have foulness of soil and poverty of crop, and a population poor and uncultivated as either'.[19]

Employment in many parts of the county was regulated by hiring fairs, like that held in Dorchester every 14 February which Hardy described in *The Mayor of Casterbridge* and *Far from the Madding Crowd*. During his youth it had a strong flavour of the traditional and archaic:

> They came in smock-frocks and gaiters, the shepherds with their crooks, the carters with a zone of whipcord round their hats, thatchers with a straw tucked into the brim, and so on.[20]

The farmers at this time had a very large pool to select from:

> To see the Dorset labourer at his worst and saddest time, he should be viewed when attending a wet hiring fair at Candlemas, in search of a new master. His natural cheerfulness bravely struggles against the weather and the incertitude; but as the day passes on, and his clothes get wet through, and he is still unhired, there does appear a factitiousness in the smile which, with a self-repressing mannerliness hardly to be found among any other class, he yet has ready when he encounters and talks with friends who have been more fortunate.

Once a man was lucky enough to ·be hired, his earnings largely depended on how many members of his family were employed with him. Women's labour, as Hardy said, was 'highly in request, for a woman . . . like a boy, fills the place of a man at half the wages'. His comments on female labour are very interesting in relation to *Tess*:

Not a woman in the county but hates the threshing machine. The dust, the din, the sustained exertion demanded to keep up with the steam tyrant, are distasteful to all women but the coarsest. I am not sure whether, at the present time,* women are employed to feed the machine, but some years ago a woman had frequently to stand just above the whizzing wire drum, and feed from morning to night – a performance for which she was quite unfitted, and many were the manoeuvres to escape that responsible position. A thin saucer-eyed woman of fifty-five, who had been feeding the machine all day, declared on one occasion that in crossing a field on her way home in the fog after dusk, she was so dizzy from the work as to be unable to find the opposite gate, and there she walked round and round the field, bewildered and terrified, till three o'clock in the morning, before she could get out.

Children, before the coming of compulsory education, began work at the earliest possible age. As late as 1867 a Royal Commission reported that children younger than six were working in the fields in Dorset. In no other county did it find 'such low wages, nor on the other hand such small children at work'.[21]
According to the *Victoria County History*:

The habit existed in Dorset of hiring whole families; not only was the labourer expected to work, but his wife, or at least the daughters, were drawn in to full work, and the boys were taken away too early from school, and then kept on after they were grown up for the same purpose. Thus female labour was encouraged and the education and future prospects of the men neglected.[22]

In fact the county was one of the most backward in England, in the sense of being one of the poorest and least industrialised,

* Written in 1883.

and this partly accounts for the survival of many of the old customs and superstitions which Hardy records.

However, the spread of railways and the slow growth of popular education helped to emancipate the labourers from their psychological bondage to their locality, so that many of them tried to solve their problems by going elsewhere. The population of Dorset grew very slowly throughout the second half of the century; between 1841 and 1901 it increased by only about 15 per cent, while the population of the country as a whole had doubled. It has been calculated that between 1851 and 1861 Dorset had a 'migration proportion of about 76 per cent of the natural increase'.[23] In the seventies, after the Agricultural Workers' Union had given a further strong impetus to migration it was one of only nine counties in England which recorded an absolute population decline.

The so-called golden age of agriculture had brought real benefits only to the farmers and landowners. 'In 1868', according to the *Victoria County History*, 'when Dorset was at the height of agricultural prosperity, the condition of the labourer was by no means proportionately improved'. Wages had gone up by a few shillings since the forties, but then so had the cost of living, and wage rates in the south-western counties still lagged behind those everywhere else. When he was organising the Union in Dorset in 1872, Joseph Arch found that 'the condition of the labourer in that county was as bad as it very well could be'.[24]

The union had an unequal impact in various parts of Dorset. According to Dunbabin it 'scarcely affected the west – perhaps because the west had no hiring fairs to cause discontent, and no railways to spread it'.[25] In the east it was much stronger, especially in the countryside round Blandford where labourers successfully struck for more pay. Hardy calculated in 'The Dorsetshire Labourer' that the movement had resulted in 'an average rise of three shillings a week in wages nearly all over the county', and also noted that 'if a farmer can afford to pay thirty per cent more wages in times of agricultural depression than he paid in times of agricultural prosperity . . . the labourer must have been greatly wronged in those prosperous times'.

Despite the Union's collapse, emigration went on even faster than before for the rest of the century. Population movements in Dorset took place on a larger scale than could be measured by statistics, owing to internal migration within the county. One of Haggard's interviewees said that:

> in Dorsetshire, as elsewhere, the scarcity of agricultural labourers was an undoubted fact, although he thought that there were still a fair number of them floating about the county; that actual scarcity was made to appear greater than it is by the fact that the labourers did not remain in the service of the same farmer, as many of them changed their situations every year.[26]

He ascribed this to the influence of Arch who had constantly advised them not to bind themselves for more than a year. The labourers' new mobility was an essential part of their emancipation. Hardy commented:

> Dorset labourers now look upon an annual removal as the most natural thing in the world, and it becomes with the younger families a pleasant excitement. Change is also a certain sort of education. Many advantages accrue to the labourers from the varied experiences it brings . . . The sojourning existence of the town masses is more and more the existence of the rural masses, with its corresponding benefits and disadvantages.

Under these pressures, the old-style hiring fair rapidly lost most of its social significance. The *Victoria County History* says:

> The hiring fair tends to become a picturesque survival – it is fast dying out as the modern, more educated labourer can find work through advertisements, instead of being dependent on the chances of one day.[27]

And Hardy, in his letter to Haggard in the spring of 1902, wrote:

> I am told that at the annual hiring fair just past, the old positions were absolutely reversed, the farmers walking about and importuning the labourers to come and be hired, instead of, as formerly, the labourers anxiously entreating the stolid farmers to take them on at any pittance.

During and after the seventies real wages in the countryside rose steadily though they remained much less than those of industrial workers and were still, according to the 1898 survey quoted by Ernle, lower in Dorset than practically anywhere else. But the men had more independence and a better education than ever before, food was cheaper, some cottages were being improved and by the nineties the employment of female labour was almost a thing of the past. Observers calculated that they had suffered less than any other class from the agricultural depression. Trying to sum up what had happened, Hardy wrote:

That seclusion and immutability, which was so bad for their pockets, was an unrivalled fosterer of their personal charm in the eyes of those whose experience had been less limited. But the artistic merit of their old condition is scarcely a reason why they should have continued in it when other communities were marching on so vigorously towards uniformity and mental equality. It is only the old story that progress and picturesqueness do not harmonise. They are losing their individuality, but they are widening the range of their ideas, and gaining in freedom. It is too much to expect them to remain stagnant and old-fashioned for the pleasure of romantic spectators.

The real tragedy for the villages was the virtual destruction of the intermediate class of small tradesmen and craftsmen – the class to which Hardy's parents had belonged – who had always in the past been the most energetic and talented group. They either lost their trade through the decline of the village market or were forced out, as Hardy claimed in *Tess*, by the farmers who disliked their independence:

Cottagers who were not directly employed on the land were looked upon with disfavour, and the banishment of some starved the trade of others, who were thus obliged to follow. These families, who had formed the backbone of village life in the past, who were the depositaries of the village traditions, had to seek refuge in the large centres; the process, humorously designated by statisticians as 'the tendency of the rural population towards the large towns', being really the tendency of water to flow uphill when forced by machinery.

In 'The Dorsetshire Labourer', where he described the displacement of this group in very similar language, he added:

The poignant regret of those who are thus obliged to forsake the old nest can only be realised by people who have witnessed it – concealed as it often is under a mask of indifference. It is anomalous that landowners who are showing unprecedented activity in the erection of comfortable cottages for their farm labourers, should see no reason for benefiting in the same way these unattached natives of the villages who are nobody's care . . . Every one of these banished people imbibes a sworn enmity to the existing order of things, and not a few of them, far from being merely honest Radicals, degenerate into Anarchists, waiters on chance, to whom danger to the State . . . is a welcomed opportunity . . . But the question of the Dorset cottager here merges in that of all the houseless and landless poor, and the vast topic of the Rights of Man, to consider which is beyond the scope of a purely descriptive article.

2 Economic and Social Relationships in the Wessex Novels

The last chapter attempted to describe the structure and development of rural society in nineteenth-century Dorset, as the material out of which Hardy's novels were written. This chapter will explore in more detail the relationship between this material and the novels themselves. Its main purpose is to outline the various types of farming and related economic activity in Hardy's novels, and the economic and social relationships between the main characters. The main thing to remember is that, although several of the novels show work on the land as a shaping background factor, Hardy only occasionally presents the relationship between labourers and farmers directly. His real preoccupation is with the 'interesting and better-informed class' which he describes in some detail in *Tess* – the independent, intermediate class to which all his major characters tend to belong. His own family – his father was a stonemason – had belonged to this group. It was more responsive to the pressures of education and industrialism than the ordinary labourers, and more likely to have an indigenous culture. It was also more mobile socially in both directions. Its members might lose everything, through the constant fluctuations in rural society, and be reduced to the most menial forms of labour, but they could also hope to rise out of their class through marriage or education or indeed through sheer energy, as the Mayor of Casterbridge does. The society which Hardy presents in his novels is not feudal, not a rigid caste system which denies all mobility, but a developing capitalist society, in which it is possible for families and individuals either to sink or to rise from their original status, and in which accident plays a large part. The relatively slow and old-fashioned nature of rural Wessex, as compared with the contemporary industrial centres where the same thing was happening much faster, should not confuse our understanding of this process.

Under the Greenwood Tree

The first of Hardy's novels set in rural England has practically nothing to say about work on the land. Mellstock is obviously a farming community but none of the characters are farmers except Shiner, who occupies a respected place in the community on that account. Dick is considered much less eligible as a suitor for Fancy because he is the son of a 'tranter' or carrier, which is only one rung above a labourer. But his family is reasonably well off – we hear in *Tess* that they 'used to do a good deal of business as tranters' and Dick looks forward to becoming 'the regular manager of a branch o' father's business which we think of starting elsewhere'. This business 'has very much increased lately', and the Dewys are clearly on the way up.

Dick's maternal grandfather is 'by trade a mason' and the members of the choir, though described as 'all of them working villagers of the parish of Mellstock' appear to be skilled workers or tradesmen, not labourers. There is Robert Penny, a 'boot and shoe-maker' and Elias Spinks, who 'was considered to be a scholar, having once kept a night-school'. It is this intermediate class of skilled and trained men who keep the old village tradition of church music alive. All of them defer to the vicar, Maybold, who is the leading person in the community but is also in a sense outside it, having few ideas in common with his parishioners.

Fancy's social position is somewhere in between the Dewys and Maybold. She is a qualified schoolmistress and her father, who has risen from an ordinary keeper to be the 'head game-keeper, timber-steward, and general overlooker for this district' on the Earl of Wessex's estate, has saved money for her dowry and wants her to marry a gentleman. In Hardy's novels marriage is never isolated from social status, and the ambiguity in her position is a factor in her hesitations between Shiner, the vicar and Dick. It is not only a matter of which man she prefers, but also of which group she wishes to join.

Far from the Madding Crowd

This novel has a much more solid social base than any of the earlier novels – the whole action centres on the life and work of Bathsheba's farm. Gabriel Oak begins life as a shepherd, 'having from his childhood assisted his father in tending the flocks of large proprietors', then becomes a bailiff for a short time and then rises through his own efforts to lease a small sheep-farm. But when the sheep which represent his entire capital are destroyed he has to go on the labour-market again and offer himself as a candidate for any kind of work at the hiring fair. He is passed over here but manages to get a job as a shepherd on Bathsheba's farm, which is a mixed arable farm producing both corn and wool. Later he becomes her bailiff and later still takes up the tenancy of Boldwood's farm, marries Bathsheba and becomes an independent farmer again.

Boldwood is a gentleman-farmer, one of the leading figures in the district – 'his person was the nearest approach to aristocracy . . . the parish could boast of'. Only Troy, the wandering sergeant with professional and aristocratic connections, is outside this network of relationships. As Bathsheba's husband he tries briefly to manage the farm, but takes no real interest in the work.

The Return of the Native

Egdon Heath is too wild for any farming of a normal kind to be possible. There are, however, districts on the outskirts which are more fertile – the valleys of the Frome and other rivers – and these contrasts are illustrated dramatically in Hardy's description of the bonfires on November the fifth.

> Attentive observation of their brightness, colour, and length of existence would have revealed the quality of the material burnt; and through that, to some extent the natural produce of the district in which each bonfire was situate. The clear, kingly effulgence that had characterised the majority expressed a heath and furze country . . . the rapid flares and extinctions at other points of the compass showed the lightest of fuel – straw, beanstalks, and the usual waste from arable land. The most enduring of all – steady unaltering eyes like planets – signified wood . . . They occupied the remotest visible positions – sky-backed summits rising out of rich coppice and plantation districts to the north, where the soil was different, and heath foreign and strange.

Most people on the heath live by cutting turf or furze, or, like Olly Dowden, 'by making heath brooms, or besoms'. Diggory Venn is a dairyman's son who lapses into the uncouth trade of reddleman – travelling around the heath and the neighbouring districts to sell 'the bright pigment so largely used by shepherds in preparing sheep for the fair'. Eventually he leaves the heath and goes back to dairy farming, withdrawing with Thomasin to the fertile land on the edge of the heath, 'where the meads begin'. Apart from Clym, who works for a time as a furze-cutter, Diggory is the only major character to retain any connection with the land. Mrs Yeobright is the widow of a small farmer but 'she herself was a curate's daughter, who had once dreamt of doing better things'. She sends her son to Paris to join the diamond trade and resents it bitterly when he wants to work with his hands, or to teach. Wildeve is an engineer turned inn-keeper; Eustacia is the grand-daughter of a retired naval officer, and her roots are in Budmouth. All these people consider them-selves to belong to a higher class than those who work on the heath. Clym's attitude is less exclusive, but in the end he finds his vocation, not by working with these people, but by becoming a preacher.

The Mayor of Casterbridge

The county town of Casterbridge is virtually the centre of an agricultural community – 'Casterbridge lived by agriculture at one remove further from the fountain-head than the adjoining villages – no more'. In other words, it lives by the seasonal fluctuations of the corn trade, through which fortunes are made or broken. As Hardy states in the Preface:

> In the days recalled by the tale, the home Corn Trade, on which so much of the action turns, had an importance that can hardly be realised by those accustomed to the sixpenny loaf of the present date, and to the present indifference of the public to harvest weather.

Because of its smallness and the inherent uncertainty of the trade which it is based upon, Casterbridge is a world which allows a good deal of social mobility. Henchard comes to the town as an experienced hay-trusser – a 'skilled countryman as distinct from . . . the general labourer', but with no money or influence. However, in the course of years, he makes himself into one of the chief local traders – 'Never a big dealing in wheat, barley, oats, hay, roots, and such-like but Henchard's got a hand in it'. He rises to be a considerable employer of labour and Mayor of the town despite his obscure social origins; Lucetta, who sets herself up in the world by the traditional means of inheriting money, seems comparatively rather old-fashioned. The penniless Scotsman Farfrae – typically on his way to emigrate – rises to be a prosperous corn-dealer and pillar of the community by a very similar process. But in so doing he ruins Henchard, who goes back to hay-trussing and becomes 'a day-labourer in the farms and granaries he formerly had owned'. There is, however, no reason why he should remain in this state, except that he has lost his ambition. 'Externally there was nothing to hinder his making another start on the upward slope.' His former colleagues on the town council are even ready to 'afford him a new opening' by getting him a 'small seed and root business'. The society is still mobile and still offers limited opportunities to an energetic man.

The Woodlanders

The whole life and work of the community in *The Woodlanders* is connected with trees. The biggest employer in the district (though of course she has a steward to manage things for her) is Mrs Charmond, who owns most of the timber and orchards and has the power to turn people out of the cottages on her estate. Melbury is a 'timber, bark, and copse-ware merchant' whose wood is made up into 'faggots, hurdles, and other products'. Marty and her father work for him making 'spars, such as are used by thatchers'. Giles Winterborne is 'in the apple and cider trade' and originally has a working partnership with Melbury, though he is not so well off. He employs a few workmen, travels round the country 'with his portable mill and press to make cider' (a job which Marty takes over after his death), and takes contracts to plant trees for timber. Marty, 'who turned her hand to anything' does a wide range of odd jobs such as peeling bark, planting saplings and shaping the wood with her tools.

Both she and Giles originally belong to the semi-independent class of copyholders which Hardy singled out as the most interesting one in the village, but both are dispossessed by Mrs Charmond when John South dies. Marty sinks almost to the bottom of the social scale and Giles also becomes something very much like an ordinary labourer. This opens a social gulf between them and the prosperous Melburys as wide as that between the Melburys themselves and Fitzpiers or Mrs Charmond. These are the only two characters who feel out of place in the countryside, though Mrs Charmond has an economic connection with it as a landowner. Only Fitzpiers is completely outside the pattern of relationships based on the care of orchards and the manufacture of timber, as he is both a professional man and a dispossessed aristocrat.

Tess of the d'Urbervilles

The Durbeyfields, as a haggler's family, are originally self-employed. They have the tenure of a cottage during John Durbeyfield's lifetime, though after his death they are forced to move out. Their only capital is their horse, the 'bread-winner' of the family, and after it is killed they are in the same position as Oak when he loses his sheep. To support them Tess goes to work looking after poultry on Alec d'Urberville's 'little fancy farm'. d'Urberville belongs to a rich merchant family which has bought its way into the landed gentry, and his mother keeps the farm only as a hobby. The poultry are kept in a cottage, formerly occupied by 'certain dusty copyholders who now lay east and west in the churchyard', but 'indifferently turned into a fowl-house by Mrs Stoke d'Urberville as soon as the property fell into hand according to law'. This is an early reference to the squeezing out of the 'intermediate class'.

Back in Marlott, Tess works in the fields binding corn, and then gets a job on the dairy farm at Talbothays which supplies milk to London by train. Here she is on exactly the same footing as the other milkmaids (some of whom are also descended from aristocratic families) and the only person who has a superior status within the community is Angel, because he is a clergyman's son and 'learning how to be a rich and prosperous dairyman, landowner, agriculturist and breeder of cattle'. By marrying him she appears to be rising out of her class and giving up manual work. But after he deserts her she is gradually forced to rely on herself again, and by this time the more pleasant kinds of work are no longer available:

> Beginning with the dairy and poultry tendance that she liked best, she ended with the heavy and coarse pursuits which she liked least – work on arable land: work of such roughness, indeed, as she would never have deliberately volunteered for.

She has, in fact, 'to remove from the pasture to the stubble', which involves a qualitative change in the nature of her work. At Flintcomb-Ash she crawls about the fields grubbing up turnips, works at the backbreaking task of reed-drawing and feeds sheaves to the threshing-machine. In the process she is transformed from the apparently idyllic figure of a milkmaid which attracted Angel's sentimental regard into a wage-labourer of the least romantic kind. Her only way of escaping from this life is to become something even less romantic, a kept woman.

Jude the Obscure

Jude Fawley is brought up in the arable country of Berkshire. His great-aunt keeps a baker's shop and is therefore a member of a semi-independent class. He begins life by scaring rooks from the corn, as small boys in English villages had done for generations.* But his position yields him certain limited social opportunities; he can afford to get apprenticed to a mason and become a skilled stone-worker – one of the very few industrial crafts open in Wessex at that time. When he goes to Christminster he finds that his skill and education, so exceptional in the village, are of no use to him as he is only wanted to repair the college buildings. In fact he has become a member of the urban working-class and remains one for the rest of his life.

* Joseph Arch tells us, 'My first job was crow-scaring, and for this I received fourpence a day. This day was a twelve hours one, so it sometimes happened that I got more than was in the bargain, and that was a smart taste of the farmer's stick ... I can remember how he would come into the field suddenly, and walk quietly up behind me, and, if he caught me idling, I used to catch it hot.'

The only other person connected with agriculture is Arabella. Her father keeps pigs, which are 'bred and fattened in large numbers in certain parts of North Wessex'. In Christminster, however, she becomes a barmaid. Phillotson, who has also been rejected by the University, remains a struggling schoolmaster. Sue is 'an ecclesiastical worker in metal'. All these people are either ignored by the church and university system in Christminster or are pressed into its service as workers of the most mechanical kind. They are part of that vast array of 'manual toilers . . . unrecognised as part of the city' without whom 'the hard readers could not read nor the high thinkers live'. All their connections with the land have been broken by the time the real story begins, and when Jude does go back to his village it has scarcely any meaning for him. The change from the social world of *Under the Greenwood Tree* is complete. Hardy has moved from the enclosed and backward village community, through the socially mobile and varied (but still relatively enclosed) communities of the middle novels, to this final world, in which physical mobility is very important, but social mobility decisively blocked.

3 Under the Greenwood Tree

Hardy's first novel, *The Poor Man and the Lady, by the Poor Man*, was never published. He tells us that:

> The story was ... a sweeping dramatic satire of the squire-archy and nobility, London society, the vulgarity of the middle class, modern Christianity ... the tendency of the writing being socialistic, not to say revolutionary.[1]

The publisher Alexander Macmillan said that it 'meant mischief'[2] because of its very violent hostility to the upper classes, and George Meredith warned Hardy that 'if he printed so pronounced a thing he would be attacked on all sides by the conventional reviewers, and his future injured'.[2] The manuscript is now lost, but the title confirms other evidence that it was concerned with class differences between lovers and their emotional repercussions, which became a major theme in Hardy's more mature work. Meredith's advice, however, was to try a story with a more complicated plot. Hardy responded by producing *Desperate Remedies*, which was published in 1871.

This was a sensational melodrama, written, as Hardy explained in the 1889 Preface, 'when he was feeling his way to a method'. As literature it is a work of indifferent value, but it has a few interesting moments, as in the characterisation of the villain, Manston, who is applying for an architect's job:

> His letter is bold and frank in tone ... not honesty, but un-scrupulousness of conscience dictated it. It is written in an indifferent mood, as if he felt that he was humbugging us in his statement that he was the right man for such an office, that he tried hard to get it only as a matter of form which required that he should neglect no opportunity that came in his way.[3]

This indicates Hardy's other great preoccupation – the nature of people's work and their attitudes towards it, either whole-hearted or 'indifferent'. The great dividing line between Hardy's authentic and inauthentic characters is determined by their various approaches to work.

Manston is a rather extreme example as he is a villain of the deepest dye who eventually turns out to have murdered his wife. But the point is a serious one; Manston is not interested in his life's profession – Hardy's own profession as an architect – and therefore, as Hardy sees it, all his other activities are bound to a greater or lesser extent to be false. The quality of their work, and the quality of their relationships with other people, defines all the major characters he creates.

Under the Greenwood Tree contains both these themes, though they are not treated as yet in a serious way. Looking back on this earliest of his country novels, in the 1912 Preface, Hardy wrote:

In rereading the narrative after a long interval there occurs the inevitable reflection that the realities out of which it was spun were material for another kind of study of this little group of church musicians than is found in the chapters here penned so lightly, even so farcically and flippantly at times. But cir-cumstances would have rendered any aim at a deeper, more essential, more transcendent handling unadvisable at the date of writing.

Perhaps 'circumstances' meant the publishers who had to be pleased, or perhaps Hardy merely felt that he was not yet equal to writing a serious work. Accordingly, situations and themes which were later to become tragic are here only touched on slightly, and there is always a way of escape. Yet it is no longer possible to see this book as a mere charming rustic idyll. Hardy originally meant to call it ('more appropriately', he said in the 1912 Preface) *The Mellstock Quire*, instead of the rather romantic title we now have; and it is at least as much the choir's story as 'the attractive tale of Fancy and her three lovers'[3] to quote Douglas Brown. Fancy has a dual role, as sexual magnet and as the organist in whose favour the choir is disbanded, and in each role she betrays a distinct, if not fatal, human in-adequacy.

The choir is described in the 1896 Preface in great detail and with a warm reminiscent affection. Its function is not primarily religious, although the result of its disappearance has been 'to curtail and extinguish the interest of parishioners in church doings'. It is a group of minor artists, skilled craftsmen whose enthusiasm for their music leads them to make tremendous efforts, like trudging

> on foot every Sunday after a toilsome week through all weathers to the church, which often lay at a distance from their homes. They usually received so little in payment for their performances that their efforts were really a labour of love.

Their work is authentic, and therefore valuable, because it is a natural expression of this enthusiasm:

> Their music in those days was all in their own manuscript, copied in the evenings after work, and their music books were home-bound.

The choir also has an independent value as folk culture, as Hardy obviously feels when he comments on the mixture of ballads and hymns which could be found in these books:

> Some of these compositions . . . are good singing still, though they would hardly be admitted into such hymn-books as are popular in the churches of fashionable society.

It is really through the indirect influence of this 'fashionable society' that the choir is destroyed. The vicar, Maybold, who is completely out of touch with the people's feelings (they find his sermons 'a terrible muddle') considers organ-music 'most proper'. The crisis is precipitated because he and Shiner both have a sexual interest in Fancy and want to encourage her to play. It is for no better reason than this that the choir is destroyed, and the substitute seems to be distinctly inferior. When Fancy takes over, replacing their uninhibited warmth by correctness and fashion, the people's alienation from the church has begun:

> Having nothing to do with conducting the service for almost the first time in their lives, they all felt awkward, out of place,

abashed, and inconvenienced by their hands... They stood and watched the curls of hair trailing down the back of the successful rival, and the waving of her feather as she swayed her head. After a few timid notes and uncertain touches her playing became markedly correct... But, whether from prejudice or unbiased judgement, the venerable body of musicians could not help thinking that the simpler notes they had been wont to bring forth were more in keeping with the simplicity of their old church than the crowded chords and interludes it was her pleasure to produce.

Indeed Fancy is not particularly interested in organ-playing (her main concern on this occasion is with her appearance) or in her work as a teacher. Her vocation is to marry someone – a vocation reinforced by her temperament and upbringing. Whom she marries is a question to be determined by other considerations than love. This is made quite clear in Dick's conversation with her snobbish father:

'D'ye think Fancy picked up her good manners, the smooth turn of her tongue, her musical notes, and her knowledge of books, in a hole like this?'
'No.'
'D'ye know where?'
'No.'
'... Did ye know that... she went to the training-school, and that her name stood first among the Queen's scholars of her year?'
'I've heard so.'
'And that when she sat for her certificate as Government teacher, she was the highest of the first class?'
'Yes.'
'Well, and do ye know what I live in such a miserly way for... and why I make her work as a schoolmistress instead of living here?'
'No.'
'That if any gentleman, who sees her to be his equal in polish, should want to marry her, and she want to marry him, he shan't be superior to her in pocket. Now do ye think after this that you be good enough for her?'
'No.'

The keeper, like Melbury in *The Woodlanders*, has educated his daughter with the conscious intention of making her 'superior' to the people of her native place. He sees marriage as a means of rising in the world, and culture and education – with money – as determining factors in marriage. Confronted with all this, Dick is quite inarticulate and ends up 'wondering at his presumption'. Fancy is not responsible for her father's plans – in fact she eventually rejects them – but she shares his susceptibility to external good breeding and 'polish', and his relative indifference to love. Throughout their relationship Dick is made painfully conscious that she cares less about him than about herself and the impression she makes. Indeed she has a sneaking feeling that he is not good enough for her:

> I like Dick, and I love him, but how plain and sorry a man looks in the rain, with no umbrella, and wet through!

This feeling leads her on to accept Mr Maybold, who is as much above her socially as she is above Dick – he has 'struggled against my emotion continually, because I have thought that it was not well for me to love you'. After Maybold has found out about her duplicity she admits:

> It is my nature – perhaps all women's – to love refinement of mind and manners . . . to be ever fascinated with the idea of surroundings more elegant and pleasing than those which have been customary. And you praised me, and praise is life to me. It was alone my sensations at these things which prompted my reply. Ambition and vanity they would be called; perhaps they are so.

Fancy's name is symbolic (as names often are in Hardy). In contrast to Dick's warm and undivided feelings for her she has no deep emotions, but lets herself be attracted by one man and then another in proportion to how much they feed her vanity. In this respect she is very like Grace Melbury, a girl who holds a similar position within her community. Similar to *The Woodlanders* too, is the ambiguous 'happy ending', when Fancy is married to Dick. Somebody wonders 'which she thinks most about, Dick or her wedding rainment', and the novel ends on an ironic note:

'Fancy', he said, 'why we are so happy is because there is such full confidence between us... We'll have no secrets from each other, darling, will we ever? – no secret at all.'

'None from today', said Fancy ... and thought of a secret she would never tell.

Just as Dick's openness is contrasted with Fancy's insincerity, the old musicians' spontaneity and lack of sophistication are contrasted with the superior 'refinement' of Fancy and Maybold. Yet is it surely a mistake to suggest, as Brown does, that the story illustrates how 'the old, stable order is passing from agricultural life'. What we are shown is not a conflict between orders of civilisation but a highly complex adjustment of social relationships in which each group is only separated from the next by near-indiscernible shades. It is not true, as Brown says, that 'productive agricultural life provides the essential material'; the members of the choir, as we have seen, are mainly skilled artisans who are not directly engaged in agricultural work. Maybold, 'the lonely urban invader' whom Brown sees as responsible for the choir's destruction, is shown as much more sympathetic than the boorish Shiner, farmer and churchwarden, who represents the traditional ruling class of the village and who is equally keen to get rid of the choir. Yet it is true that the Mellstock choir is related to nature and the rhythm of the seasons in a much more creative and vital way than either the coarse or the sophisticated characters can understand. The very first paragraph establishes this intimate relationship between human beings and trees:

To dwellers in a wood almost every species of tree has its voice as well as its feature. At the passing of the breeze the fir-trees sob and moan no less distinctly than they rock; the holly whistles as it battles with itself; the ash hisses amid its quiverings; the beech rustles while its flat boughs rise and fall. And winter, which modifies the note of such trees as shed their leaves, does not destroy its individuality.

The trees are humanised through their significance for those who live among them. Dick, walking through 'the darkness of a plantation that whispered thus distinctively to his intelligence', is similar to Marty and Giles in *The Woodlanders* in the quality of his response. And in the last chapter the ancient 'Greenwood

Tree' is transformed from a natural into a social symbol; the birds and rabbits and insects which normally cluster around it are replaced by the village people who come there to celebrate the wedding with 'music, dancing, and the singing of songs'.

Still, this closing effect carries a wry irony, for while the story ends with music and dancing we know that the indigenous art of the village has nevertheless been supplanted. 'One is inclined to regret the displacement of these ecclesiastical bandsmen by an isolated organist', Hardy wrote in the 1896 Preface, and the 'isolated' carried several shades of meaning. Fancy is genuinely isolated from the community by her sophistication and self-regard, though hers is not the tragic isolation of the more mature works. Rather, the sources of conflict seem deliberately undeveloped, and a compromise adjustment has been reached. Fancy will behave herself in future, though she will not really change, and the village will gradually become used to the loss of the choir.

4 *Far from the Madding Crowd*

Far from the Madding Crowd is a much more substantial novel than its predecessors, and several themes which were only glanced at in *Under the Greenwood Tree* are now fully sustained. There is still a good deal of indifferent writing, and a tendency towards shallow philosophising, yet this is definitely the first of Hardy's major works.

Of all his novels, it is the most optimistic and positive. The tensions, far greater than those in *Under the Greenwood Tree*, are still contained and harmoniously resolved in the end. It was the novel which the Victorian critics wanted him to write over and over again, and referred back to nostalgically when they were deploring the 'pessimism' of *Jude* and *Tess*. But it is not a rustic idyll – although most people thought it was – or a simple romance about three men and a girl. The characters are defined in terms of their work more clearly than in any of the earlier novels: Gabriel and Bathsheba are skilled land-workers or overseers; Boldwood is a respectable gentleman-farmer; Troy is a drifting soldier who could have done much better things with his life. All of them are subordinated to the novel's central preoccupation – the care of the land and flocks, and the maintenance of the community in a condition of health. Individuals are characterised as good or bad directly through their contributions to these ends.

Hardy illustrates what this means in his description of sheepshearing in the old barn, which has endured for generations because it is necessary for 'the defence and salvation of the body by daily bread'. He comments:

> One could say about this barn, what could hardly be said of either the church or the castle, akin to it in age and style, that the purpose which had dictated its original erection was the same with that to which it was still applied. Unlike and

superior to either of those two typical remnants of mediaevalism, the old barn embodied practices which had suffered no
mutilation at the hands of time . . . For once mediaevalism and
modernism had a common standpoint.

The barn is 'timeless' not in a romantic or mystical sense but
because the human needs for food and shelter never change. The
workers in the barn are engaged in a 'timeless' activity because
they are meeting these needs:

In these Wessex nooks the busy outsider's ancient times are
only old; his old times are still new; his present is futurity.

The flashy Troy is contrasted with these workers in the most
direct language. 'With him the past was yesterday; the future,
tomorrow; never, the day after'. Completely absorbed in the
moment he is unaware of all permanent needs and emotions; his
activities are 'exercised on whatever object chance might place
in their way' and his feelings continually change. His energy
usually takes the form of casual destructiveness – we see him
aiming 'light cuts at the horse's ear with the end of the lash, as a
recreation' – and his profession is destructive too; he is a soldier.
After marrying Bathsheba he squanders the money which she
needs to keep up the farm and almost ruins her financially.
'Nothing has prospered in Weatherbury', a labourer comments,
'since he came here'. It is only superficially that he is fascinating,
in the 'scarlet and gilded form' in which Bathsheba sees him.
Shorn of his brilliant externals his human quality is poorer and
meaner than that of anyone else in the book.

However it is a mistake to see him, with Douglas Brown, as a
destructive urban figure invading a peaceful agricultural community. It is not nearly so simple as that. For one thing he is not
the only destructive force in the community (Boldwood is in
many ways equally negative) and also – as we shall see later –
the community badly needs a positive stimulus from the outside.
Troy's links are not so much with cities – he has grown up in
Casterbridge – as with the army and the aristocracy. He is an
earl's illegitimate son, in many ways a preliminary sketch for
Alec d'Urberville (his treatment of Fanny is much the same as
Alec's of Tess). Moreover, he represents none of the qualities of
education and modernisation which Brown associates with urban
influence. He does not try to modernise the farm, but neglects it,

and he has had a good education which he has thrown away. Hardy is not praising him when he describes how 'he wasted his gifted lot, and listed a soldier'. As Gabriel says, this 'shows his course to be down'ard'. He would have admired him far more if he had developed such abilities as he had.

If Troy is not a sophisticated urban invader, neither is Bathsheba just a simple country maiden who succumbs to his wiles. She is a vain girl, rather like Fancy Day, and she resembles her, too, in being better educated and on a higher social rung than the ordinary villagers. Her parents were townsfolk and she is a stranger to Weatherbury, where the people are surprised by her self-reliance. But, unlike Fancy Day, she is bitterly punished for her vanity and thoughtless flirtations. Having trifled with Boldwood's and Gabriel's feelings, she finds herself tied to Troy who is incapable of loving her or indeed anyone else. We have suspected this before, but we do not fully realise it until we are shown what he has done to Fanny, in her agony on the road to the Casterbridge workhouse, which is shunned by everyone except the most destitute poor.

Bathsheba has to suffer both for her cruelty to Fanny, although this was unconscious, and for betraying her own deepest instincts by marrying Troy. She is rejected by him, imagines herself to be rejected by Gabriel, and has to recognise her share of the responsibility for Boldwood's collapse. As a result, she is agonisingly purged of self-centredness:

> Taking no further interest in herself as a splendid woman; she acquired the indifferent feelings of an outsider in contemplating her probable fate as a singular wretch.

When she helps Gabriel to replant the flowers on the grave of the dead girl she had seen as a rival, 'with the superfluous magnanimity of a woman whose narrower instincts have brought down bitterness upon her instead of love', she has finally learned to be more like him in not thinking first of herself.

Gabriel is exceptional because 'among the multitude of interests by which he was surrounded, those which affected his personal well-being were not the most absorbing and important in his eyes'. He keeps silent for years about his love for Bathsheba and brushes off references to the subject – 'I must get used to such as that; other men have, and so shall I'. Boldwood 'who seemed so much deeper and higher and stronger in feeling than Gabriel' is really his moral inferior because he allows his love to turn into a monomania which blinds him to all responsibilities. In *The Mayor of Casterbridge* Hardy made a rather similar study, in greater detail, of a man who lets his individual passions, which he refuses to control, drive him outside the community. Boldwood is admirable because of his strength of feeling, but destructive and therefore evil because he has let himself become a fanatic. His infatuation causes him to neglect his farm (a symbolic abandonment of social responsibility) and finally drives him to the most extreme anti-social act, murder. That he is not, like Tess, hanged for it is an indication that Hardy still felt at this time that anti-social forces could be controlled and need not work through to full tragedy. The two destructive forces, Troy and Boldwood, end by annihilating each other and the community's shattered peace is restored.

The differing attitudes of the three men are illustrated strikingly in the symbolic storm scene – in many respects the central scene of the book. Troy has forced the labourers to get dead drunk (or 'look elsewhere for a winter's work') although he has been warned that the ricks are in danger. Boldwood allows his own ricks to remain exposed because he is absorbed in his despair over Bathsheba's marriage. It is afterwards said that 'a condition of mental disease seemed to afford the only explanation' for this 'unprecedented neglect'. Gabriel, on the other hand, risks his life, although he has been equally hurt by Bathsheba's rejection, to protect her ricks from the storm. His reasons for doing so are mixed:

> Seven hundred and fifty pounds in the divinest form that money can wear – that of necessary food for man and beast: should the risk be run of deteriorating this bulk of corn to less than half its value, because of the instability of a woman? 'Never, if I can prevent it', said Gabriel.

But there is also a deeper reason:

> It is possible that there was this golden legend under the utilitarian one: 'I will help to my last effort the woman I have loved so dearly.'

Bathsheba and the corn, the human beings who sustain the land and the food which sustains them, become at least equal in their value in Gabriel's eyes. The product of human labour and the value of unselfish human love are defended at the same time.

Bathsheba is significantly the only person who comes to help Gabriel. Throughout the action, although she treats him badly, she is dependent on his strength and endurance to help her through her personal disasters, just as she swallows her pride to appeal to him when the sheep have to be cured. Their relationship is grounded in the experience of years of shared labour – what Hardy calls 'similarity of pursuits' – in the care of the crops and animals, the well-being of the farm and those who work on it – which is what, in the end, matters most to them both. For Bathsheba is a much stronger character than Fancy; there are much deeper things in her than the passion for being admired. Her feeling for Gabriel, 'growing up in the interstices of a mass of hard prosaic reality' turns out to be 'the only love which is strong as death – that love which many waters cannot quench, nor the floods drown, beside which the passion usually called by the name is evanescent as steam'.

Gabriel can too easily be seen as the romanticised archetypal countryman. His name and occupation are relevant here. He is the traditional Good Shepherd, saving the flock from disease and new-born lambs from the cold. Yet his character, though strong and simple, is not so from any absence of skill or intelligence. He is only able to cure the sheep because he possesses a certain kind of knowledge which nobody else in the neighbourhood has. The labourers unanimously look up to him as 'a clever man in talents':

> We hear that ye can tell the time as well by the stars as we can by the sun and moon . . . and that ye can make sun-dials, and print folks' names upon their waggons almost like copper-plate, with beautiful flourishes.

Besides his familiarity with the traditional skills of outdoor life, Gabriel knows how to play the flute and read his small collection of books to some purpose – 'he had acquired more sound information by diligent perusal than many a man of opportunities has done from a furlong of laden shelves'. Like Bathsheba, he is gifted with a much higher degree of talent and energy than the rest of the community, and so is able to rise to a leading position within it. The simple, reductive pattern of an organic village society threatened by an alien intruder is inevitably complicated when we remember that Gabriel and Bathsheba are intruders themselves. Weatherbury is a sluggish place ('notoriously prone', says the Preface, to 'fuddling') and the people are 'as hardy, merry, thriving, wicked a set as any in the whole county'. In fact they are remarkedly like the shiftless Durbeyfield family, quite incapable of coping with the emergencies which come up naturally from time to time in any rural community. It is always Gabriel who has to get them out of their difficulties, like the fire, the storm, and the sheep-disease (as well as recalling them to a sense of decency when Joseph leaves Fanny's coffin outside the inn and gets drunk). Gabriel is himself a victim of one of these calamities when his sheep are destroyed. 'Sunk from his modest elevation as pastoral king' and left 'with the clothes he stood up in, and nothing more' he becomes a victim of the rural labour-market when he has to offer himself for work at the hiring fair. Like Bathsheba he has to pass through 'an ordeal of wretchedness' before he can find security. Suffering is as real in old-fashioned Wessex villages as it is in the cities and Christminster; Gabriel's great strength is in his ability to adapt and endure. It is through sheer initiative, mixed with luck, that he reaches his final successful and happy position, because as he says himself he was 'made for better things' than a life of mechanical toil.

Thus the rural community is not so much threatened from outside by the growth of urbanism as confronted with a series of internal crises which grow out of man's perpetual struggle with nature. In this struggle, those who are most likely to make a success of their lives are the resourceful and persevering, whose qualities are based on a real love and understanding of nature.

In the end the easy-going Weatherbury community, having expelled the destructive forces which menaced it, is revitalised by the two outsiders, Bathsheba and Gabriel. It is as if their eventual and long-postponed union – unromantic and unexciting, as Hardy stresses – has restored the desirable norm to the village; the norm of maintaining communal labour, looking after the sheep, getting food from the land. It is because both of them fundamentally want to live according to this norm that they possess a real basis for marriage, for they have both developed into mature human beings, who are prepared to grapple seriously with their responsibilities both in work and in love.

5 *The Return of the Native*

The Return of the Native has been vulgarised, in the popular mind, in very much the same way as *Wuthering Heights*. It is dreadfully easy to see the vast 'elemental' heath as a pseudo-romantic backcloth for human passions of an equally 'elemental' kind, and thus to cheapen and distort the real part the landscape plays in the writer's conception. Of course this is to some extent Hardy's own fault; the quality of his opening description of the heath and the rather theatrical figure of Eustacia, 'Queen of Night', brooding over the landscape incline us to visualise Egdon as a metaphysical entity, a dark and wild tract of land unrelated to any forms of human or animal life. But this abstraction is completely different from the heath as Hardy presents it in the whole book.

It is true that Egdon's sterility is contrasted with the productive agricultural life in the neighbouring valleys. It produces nothing but 'fern, furze, heath, lichens and moss' and reduces human labour to a few mechanical, barely productive tasks such as cutting the furze. Reclaiming it is an almost hopeless task, as we see from the description of Wildeve's Patch:

> a plot of land redeemed from the heath, and after long and laborious years brought into cultivation. The man who had discovered that it could be tilled died of the labour: the man who succeeded him in possession ruined himself by fertilising it. Wildeve . . . received the honours due to those who had gone before.

This indicates Wildeve's relation to the land, which is that of an exploiter, but it is also there to show that the heath can destroy people. It does destroy Mrs Yeobright, and later Eustacia and Wildeve himself; only those who have succeeded in forming the right relationship with it survive. Yet it is also 'a place perfectly accordant with man's nature . . . like man, slighted and enduring'. The heath can be humanised by people who respond to it fully; the eventual survivors are those who have been slighted and yet have the strength to endure.

Egdon in the novel as a whole is no mere tract of heather, the romantic stage-setting for violent emotions. It is a living soil which nourishes innumerable snakes and rabbits and butterflies and which has nourished several earlier human communities. Like Casterbridge, it is redolent of history, though only the faintest traces survive here – the Roman road, the barrows, the 'stone arrow-heads used by the old tribes on Egdon' and the 'ancient inhabitants; forgotten Celtic tribes ... dyed barbarians' who people Clym's mind as he walks on the heath. It also supports a few scattered 'outlandish hamlets' of uneducated cottage dwellers who keep up a number of traditional customs – erecting a maypole in pleasant weather on the cultivated fringes of the heath, village picnics and dancing, the mummers at Christmas, and most importantly the general lighting of bonfires on the fifth of November. This has a major symbolic importance because it exemplifies human energy and the refusal to be dominated by a forbidding environment:

To light a fire is the instinctive and resistant act of man when, at the winter ingress, the curfew is sounded throughout Nature. It indicates a spontaneous, Promethean rebelliousness against the fiat that this recurrent season shall bring foul times, cold darkness, misery and death. Black chaos comes, and the fettered gods of the earth say, Let there be light.

The heath-dwellers manage to adapt to life on Egdon because they refuse to let themselves be overwhelmed by it. The same is true of Thomasin when she finds herself alone, on a stormy night, on the heath:

To her there were not, as to Eustacia, demons in the air, and malice in every bush and bough ... Egdon in the mass was no monster whatever, but impersonal open ground. Her fears of the place were rational, her dislikes of its worst moods reasonable.

Thomasin, the 'fair, sweet and honest' country girl is radically different from Hardy's earlier heroines. She makes no extravagant demands on life, like Eustacia, but is content to fulfil herself naturally as a wife and mother (significantly hers is almost the only marriage in the novels that produces a child). Her first, mistaken marriage to Wildeve comes to an end without total disaster, leaving her free to marry Diggory Venn. The sub-plot of this novel is in many respects a parallel to the main action in *Far from the Madding Crowd*. Diggory is like Gabriel in his qualities of resourcefulness, understanding of the natural environment and loyalty to a woman who does not love him until experience has taught her to value him better. His basic qualities – also like Gabriel's – are 'good-nature, and an acuteness as extreme as it could be without verging on craft'. This acuteness is used several times in order to circumvent Wildeve, but always with a positive aim. It forces him to give up the purloined guineas, and to behave decently to Thomasin (a 'disinterestedness' in love so extreme that Eustacia 'almost thought it absurd'). And he is the only person who shows any commonsense in the final catastrophe, when Eustacia and Clym and Wildeve all fling themselves recklessly into the pool; Clym's life is only saved because of his presence of mind.

By making him a reddleman, a practitioner of a dying trade, Hardy might seem to be emphasising the positive values of a disappearing way of life:

> He was one of a class rapidly becoming extinct in Wessex, filling at present in the rural world the place which, during the last century, the dodo occupied in the world of animals. He is a curious, interesting, and nearly perished link between obsolete forms of life and those which generally prevail.

But in fact Hardy indicates that Diggory is capable of doing much better things. 'Why should such a promising being as this have hidden his prepossessing exterior by adopting that singular occupation?' As Diggory says, 'I am not red by birth, you know' – he is separable, as an individual, from the social role he adopts during most of the action. He was originally a small dairy-farmer, but became a reddleman 'for a freak' after Thomasin refused to marry him – a refusal in which questions of social status played some part:

> My aunt ... will want me to look a little higher than a small dairy-farmer, and marry a professional man.

After he does marry Thomasin he goes back to dairy-farming, loses his red exterior and resumes his normal place in the community's life. This solution was somewhat against Hardy's wishes:

The original conception of the story did not design a marriage between Thomasin and Venn. He was to have retained his isolated and weird character to the last, and to have disappeared mysteriously from the heath, nobody knowing whither – Thomasin remaining a widow.

But the ending we have is both more realistic and more meaningful than this would have been. It was not the 'isolated and weird' aspect of Diggory, his picturesque but static occupation as a reddleman, that Hardy truly valued, but his adaptability, his power to resist circumstances, his will to do good to the person he loves. In selling reddle he is practising a once useful and necessary, but now almost outmoded trade (the railways will shortly dispense with the need for it) whereas by returning to dairy-farming he is showing the power to break out of his fixed role and adapt himself to progress. He and Thomasin escape from the general catastrophe while the major characters are destroyed or broken, a sitution which is paralleled in Hardy's two next great works.

Wildeve is a counterpart to Troy in the earlier novel and Fitzpiers in the later one. Having gone through 'a lady-killing career' he is totally incapable of Venn's single-heartedness; in fact, as he languidly says to Eustacia:

I find there are two flowers where I thought there was only one. Perhaps there are three, or four, or any number as good as the first . . .

The only thing which can rouse him to an emotional fever for any one woman is to find that she is desired by somebody else:

To be yearning for the difficult, to be weary of that offered; to care for the remote, to dislike the near; it was Wildeve's nature always. This is the true mark of the man of sentiment.

It is fairly clear that Hardy is writing the last sentence with his tongue in his cheek. Wildeve, again like Troy, has had a good education but wantonly thrown it away:

He was brought up to better things than keeping the Quiet Woman. An engineer – that's what the man was, as we know; but he threw away his chance, and so 'a took a public-house to live. His learning was no use to him at all.

Being an innkeeper is in itself a somewhat suspect vocation, for Hardy's novels contain ample illustration of the dangers of drink. We have already seen how Troy uses it to stupefy himself and the labourers when the ricks are in peril; subsequent novels show its degrading effects upon Henchard, the Durbeyfields and Jude. Wildeve's profession, in fact, is almost as destructive as his emotions. The only fulfilment which he can find is a futile, romantic death.

Eustacia, of course, is Wildeve's emotional counterpart, although it is in both their natures that they should frequently grow tired of each other, neither of them being capable of a deep and real love. She is ready to work up a passion for Clym without even having seen him because he has just come from Paris – 'the centre and vortex of the fashionable world' – and therefore seems the answer to all her dreams. For Paris, and to a lesser extent Budmouth, exert the same emotional pull over her as Christminster does over Jude. 'The word Budmouth meant fascination on Egdon'. Of course the moral quality of Eustacia's yearning is much lower than Jude's; she sees town life as simple enjoyment:

> If I could live in a gay town as a lady should, and go my own ways, and do my own doings, I'd give the wrinkled half of my life.

What she does not realise is that Clym has given up his job as manager to a diamond merchant in Paris because he has turned completely against this conception of life.

> I cannot help it . . . I hate the flashy business . . . I get up every morning and see the whole creation groaning and travailing in pain . . . and yet there am I, trafficking in glittering splendours with wealthy women and titled libertines, and pandering to the meanest vanities.

Unfortunately Eustacia would be only too glad of the chance to be one of the 'wealthy women' for whom these 'glittering splendours' are manufactured. In her mind, Paris represents nothing except glamour and luxury. Hardy may have been remembering this many years later when he wrote of Jude's dreams of the 'gorgeous city' of Christminster: 'there was perhaps more of the painter's imagination and less of the diamond merchant's in his dreams thereof'. Eustacia's most bitter reproach to Clym after they are married is that he can offer her nothing but poverty:

All persons of refinement have been scared away from me since I sank into the mire of marriage. Is this your cherishing – to put me into a hut like this, and keep me like the wife of a hind?

The trouble is that her conception of 'refinement' is quite superficial. In her last speech she complains: 'How I have tried and tried to be a splendid woman, and how destiny has been against me!' Bathsheba also wanted to be a splendid woman, but gave up the idea when she realised that there were more important things in the world. This is something which Eustacia never finds out. Because she has no serious purpose in life, as she realises herself – 'Want of an object to live for – that's all is the matter with me' – she fritters her life away in a series of empty passions and idle adventures, such as her attempt at acting (which, like Troy's, is partly seen as the expression of an inauthentic personality, without the strength to stand on its own). Mrs Yeobright sums her up:

Miss Vye is to my mind too idle to be charming. I have never heard that she is of any use to herself or to other people.

Idleness is never, in Hardy, a neutral quality; it is always seen as destructive to others and to oneself.

Clym is deceived about Eustacia as much as she is about him. He imagines her as a 'romantic martyr to superstition' – the superstition he has come back to the heath to fight – and asks, 'Do you think she would like to teach children?' Even after he knows her better he imagines, absurdly, that she would be 'a good matron in a boarding-school'. Each of them is blinded by his own preoccupations, and projects imaginary qualities on to the other – a basis for marriage which is no less than disastrous. In the end, after he has lost everything, Clym understands that his mother was right:

Events had borne out the accuracy of her judgement, and proved the devotedness of her care. He should have heeded her for Eustacia's sake even more than for his own.

Hardy is not saying, of course, that one should always defer to one's parents in one's marriage choice. Mrs Yeobright's judgement has only a limited value; she can sense the falsity of Eustacia and Wildeve but is blind to Diggory's strength and cannot understand Clym's ideals. What he does want to emphasise is that a storm of emotion cannot be allowed to override all other human and social responsibilities. Eustacia and Clym, held together by nothing deeper than sexual attraction, live alone on the heath in an isolated cottage 'consuming their mutual affections at a fearfully prodigal rate'. Thomasin is not similarly absorbed by Wildeve but remains devoted to her baby and her relations. Clym, however, completely neglects his mother for several months and only tries to make up for this when it is too late. Mrs Yeobright is killed by a combination of forces but the central one is her feeling that Clym has rejected her. He realises this himself in the end, when her memory and his work have become the things that count most for him. Like Jude, he has allowed an unsuitable marriage to divert him from his principal purpose in life.

It should not really be difficult to understand Clym's function in a book whose language and theme contain so many foreshadowings of *Jude the Obscure*. The people comment on his plan to become a teacher that 'he had better mind his business' and such critics as D. H. Lawrence and Douglas Brown have accepted this as the author's own judgement. Yet the people need Clym more than they realise; as he comments to his mother when they hear that Eustacia has been attacked by Susan Nunsuch; 'Do you think I have turned teacher too soon?' Susan is the same woman who makes a wax image of Eustacia and roasts it on the night Eustacia dies. This is partly a healthy reaction, motivated by concern for her child and by an instinctive sense of Eustacia's falsity; Clym recognises that it is pointless to blame her when he says, 'there is no use in hating people – if you hate anything, you should hate what produced them'. What produced them is the primitive barbarism of the heath, as it is seen on that fatal night:

The gloom of the night was funereal; all nature seemed clothed in crape . . . She followed the path towards Rainbarrow, occasionally stumbling over twisted furze-roots, tufts of rushes, or oozing lumps of fleshy fungi, which at this season lay scattered about the heath like the rotten liver and lungs of some colossal animal.

This is the first indication in Hardy's novels that nature, when it is not controlled by human effort, can be a terrible and destructive force. And many human beings, like Susan, have not succeeded in rising very far above their environment, for her behaviour is not isolated. The wax image, that 'ghastly invention of superstition' is 'a practice well known on Egdon at that date'.

There are plenty of other superstitions to be got rid of. The people of Egdon nourish an ignorant dread not only of witches but also of reddlemen, who are seen by some as incarnations of the devil. The community on the heath belongs to 'the very rereward of thinkers'. At their best they are typified by the boy Charley, at their worst by Susan Nunsuch and Christian Cantle (who takes over the role of village idiot from Poorgrass and Leaf). In every case, they are wide open to exploitation from the more sophisticated; Charley is dazzled by Eustacia; the little boy Johnny Nunsuch is used by her as a cover for assignations; Christian is swindled over the guineas by Wildeve. The only person fully conscious of what is going on round him is Diggory, who is not a member of the most exploited group. When Clym decides to become 'a schoolmaster to the poor and ignorant, to teach them what nobody else will', his mother accuses him of going 'backward in the world by your own free choice' – which is what Diggory and Wildeve have both, mistakenly, done. But with Clym it is different; he knows that his success as a diamond merchant was valueless and replies with the question: 'Mother, what is doing well?' It is not possible for him to separate himself from the people among whom he grew up:

He wished to raise the class at the expense of individuals rather than individuals at the expense of the class. What was more, he was ready at once to be the first unit sacrificed.

Accordingly, he gives up his promising career because he sees that his real vocation is not in Paris but on Egdon Heath.

Of course, his relationship with the physical heath is so intimate that he cannot truly be himself when away from it.

If anyone knew the heath well it was Clym. He was permeated with its scenes, with its substance, and with its odours. He might be said to be its product.

His readjustment includes a period of working on the heath as a furze-cutter, which Douglas Brown sees as 'the end of Clym's pilgrimage'.[1] But this is not the end; it is only a stage. Eustacia is wrong, of course, to suppose it degrades him, but Clym himself is well aware that it is only a temporary substitute for his real work. His 'conscience would hardly have allowed him to remain in such obscurity while his powers were unimpeded'. The restricted, monotonous world he inhabits while he is working like this soothes him because it makes no intellectual demands on him, but if he had remained in it permanently he would have been regressing to a lower level of existence, like Diggory, letting his best capabilities waste. The work is good in itself, but well within his powers, and he takes it up only because he can do nothing more useful while he is partially blind.

Clym's blindness, which is never completely cured, is an emblem of his spiritual condition and of the images of light and darkness which keep recurring throughout the book. 'You are blinded, Clym', his mother tells him when he falls in love with Eustacia, the representative of darkness who nearly frustrates his best aims. Although he is the most enlightened character in the novel, he is intellectually blind in some respects right to the end. Yet ultimately Clym is seen as the noblest character in the book and as a genuine popular teacher, speaking 'in simple language' about 'the opinions and actions common to all good men'. Brown calls this teaching 'the traditional morality of Egdon' but it is a morality which the people of Egdon are only just beginning to grasp; some of them, like Susan, never will. They need to be taught something better than they have previously understood, and it is Clym's function to do this, rather like Diggory explaining to the little boy that there is nothing sinister about being a reddleman. In spite of his early mistakes and faults, he is still capable of this.

The answer to Clym's question: 'Wherefore is light given to him that is in misery?' – the title of one chapter and the text which Jude quotes on his deathbed – is contained in the heading to the next chapter, 'A lurid light breaks in upon a darkened understanding'. Clym goes on living; although he is miserable, to bring light to darkened minds. By the end of the book he is not only sick and half-blind, but isolated and celibate. Marriage is impossible for him because he would be 'the mere corpse of a lover' – 'God has set a mark upon me which wouldn't look well in a love-making scene'. When Thomasin and Diggory celebrate their wedding he does not join in but watches them at the window, with nobody missing him, because he feels he would be 'too much like the skull at the banquet'. He cannot find the simple happiness of Diggory and Thomasin, or Gabriel and Bathsheba, because he has moved beyond their world into an infinitely more complex one where 'thought is a disease of flesh'. It is necessary for him to stay close to his roots, as he does by working as a labourer on the heath, in order to keep his contacts with ordinary people, as many of Hardy's other intellectuals do not. But, in order to rise above a condition of simple labour, he has to forfeit his happiness. In the end he is a lonely and misunderstood preacher – perhaps rather like Hardy himself.

6 *The Mayor of Casterbridge*

The title of *The Mayor of Casterbridge* is particularly significant because in no other of Hardy's novels are the social and the personal so interlocked. The hero is both the individual man Michael Henchard whose violence and bouts of irresponsibility lead to the failure of all his relationships, and the leading citizen of the actual community Casterbridge whose energy brings about a meteoric rise and a spectacular fall. These two roles are inseparable; Henchard's public ruin goes along with his alienation from all those who were close to him, and this is not a coincidence but a fusion. The novel is about individuals struggling to express themselves through their social roles, about 'bettering oneself', rising in the world. The opposite way can be terrible; extremes of destitution and degradation are shown here more clearly than in any of the earlier books. The less ambitious characters try to avoid both extremes and are glad to be allowed to live respectably and in peace.

Henchard, it is said, begins life as 'a poor parish 'prentice . . . wi' no more belonging to 'en than a carrion crow'. But he rises through sheer intelligence to become a skilled labourer, and also to a fairly high degree of literacy – we first see him reading a ballad-sheet, the popular literature of his class. His wife Susan has not reached anything like the same educational level – 'she could write her own name, and no more'.* Her simplicity is 'the original ground of Henchard's contempt for her'; for like all Hardy's characters he is sensitive to the connections between education and 'getting on in the world'. When they reach Weydon-Priors he has got to the stage of resenting her bitterly 'because of my cursed pride and mortification at being poor'.

---

* Hardy seems to have forgotten the letter he makes her write to Henchard just before her death. But I think she is definitely meant to be much less intelligent than her husband.

His talents are wasted, he complains, through his having to support a family:

> I did for myself that way thoroughly ... I married at eighteen, like the fool that I was; and this is the consequence... I haven't more than fifteen shillings in the world, and yet ... if I were a free man again I'd be worth a thousand pound.

His public humiliation of Susan gradually develops to the point where he offers to sell her, and eventually he resigns her and the child to the sailor for five guineas.

The wife-selling scene was condemned as totally unrealistic in some quarters – the *Saturday Review* called it 'fiction stranger than truth'.[1] But in fact Hardy was keeping very close to the truth in his narrative; such sales were, if not exactly common, known about and accepted by ordinary people in the rural districts at this time:

> It was generally believed in bygone days that in this country a husband might lawfully sell his wife to another man, provided he conducted the transaction in some public place... The sales were duly reported in the newspapers of the period, without any special comment, as items of everyday news.[2]

So wrote the antiquarian William Andrews, who collected examples of such sales down to as late as 1887. Sabine Baring-Gould in 1900 knew people who had been involved in them:

> That this is so is due to rooted conviction in the rustic mind that such a transaction is legal and morally permissible.[3]

This is Susan's own view – 'she was by no means the first or last peasant woman who had religiously adhered to her purchaser, as too many rural records show'. Henchard, of course, knows that it is not legal, as do the people of Casterbridge, which is more advanced than the purely rural areas. But nobody, except the sophisticated Lucetta, is specially shocked by it; as the furmity-woman says, 'we don't gi'e it head-room, we don't, such as that'. Henchard is only acting through a recognised social form, here as elsewhere. If he had acknowledged it in Casterbridge, Hardy says, it would have been 'lightly regarded as the rather tall wild oat' – nothing more. But the disclosure helps to ruin him when its effect is added to other things, and in a sense this is no more than he deserves. Having begun by selling his wife and child he finds in the end, when he needs them, that he has no wife and no child. Having disposed of them for money, in order to free himself for a career, he finds that his money and career have both gone and, moreover, that they possess no real value for him when his human ties have been lost.

Susan's decision to go back to him is partly motivated by an ambition for her child not unlike Henchard's ambition for himself. Elizabeth's longing to be educated is cramped by their poverty; she can only develop it if she is in a secure position:

> They both were still in that strait-waistcoat of poverty from which she had tried so many times to be delivered for the girl's sake. The woman had long perceived how zealously and constantly the young mind of her companion was struggling for enlargement . . . The desire – sober and repressed – of Elizabeth-Jane's heart was indeed to see, to hear, and to understand. How could she become a woman of wider knowledge, higher repute – 'better', as she termed it – this was the constant inquiry of her mother.

The same desire for more knowledge, and to rise in the world (the two things are treated as inseparable) is shown by Farfrae, Elizabeth's masculine counterpart. He has left Scotland in order to 'see the warrld' and because he has no scope there for developing his new scientific skills; but his motives are also avowedly mercenary – to 'try my fortune', to get some of the prizes of life. Arriving in Casterbridge on the same day, it strikes them both, from their relatively sophisticated viewpoint, as 'an old-fashioned place'.

Casterbridge has often been somewhat idealised, which is all the easier to do as it is in many ways only a glorified village – 'the pole, focus, or nerve-knot of the surrounding country life'. According to Brown:

> Casterbridge is an image of Dorchester, the nearby town of Hardy's youth, and his presentation of it derives from local recollection, a turning from the precarious present back to a stable past.[4]

But the Casterbridge Hardy portrays is not stable, nor does he see the past simply as one timeless moment. The town is a continuous growth out of the old Roman settlement – 'it looked Roman, bespoke the art of Rome, concealed dead men of Rome' – and the skeletons and ancient remnants are as much part of the people's consciousness as the barrows are to the people of Egdon Heath. History filters down into the awareness of ordinary people and comes out in a distorted form through their everyday speech:

> Casterbridge is a old, hoary place o' wickedness, by all account. 'Tis recorded in history that we rebelled against the King one or two hundred years ago, in the time of the Romans, and that lots of us was hanged on Gallows Hill.

This remark, from the conversation in the Three Mariners on Farfrae's first evening, indicates that Casterbridge, for all its surface impression of 'great snugness and comfort' has plenty of brutality and hardship in its everyday life. The point is taken up by the next speaker:

> We be bruckle folk here – the best o' us hardly honest sometimes, what with hard winters, and so many mouths to fill, and God-a'mighty sending his little taties so terrible small to fill 'em with.

We get a strong impression from this introduction that ordinary people in Casterbridge are living only just above the poverty line. We see them 'put-to for want of a wholesome crust', their stomachs swollen like bladders from Henchard's bad bread. As the book continues we are made increasingly aware of the sinister aspects of Casterbridge – the amphitheatre with its long history of violence ('old tragedies, pugilistic encounters almost to the death'), the gallows, the two bridges where derelicts and suicides gather, the black river which flows through 'the seed-field of all the aches, rheumatisms, and torturing cramps of the year'. Also, because the community is so close to being purely rural, it is totally vulnerable to the fluctuations of weather and crops, for the time is 'in the years immediately before foreign competition had revolutionised the trade in grain. Famine years can have a disastrous effect on both merchants and farmers:

The people, too, who were not farmers, the rural multitude,
saw in the god of the weather a more important personage
than they do now. Indeed, the feeling of the peasantry in this
matter was so intense as to be almost unrealisable in these
equable days. Their impulse was well-nigh to prostrate themselves in lamentation before untimely rains and tempests,
which came as the Alastor of those households whose crime it
was to be poor.

Hardy never lets us forget the gulf of destitution which the
labourers can be plunged into. Henchard's business is ruined by
the uncertain weather, and because he has consulted a conjurer
about the harvest and relied on his forecast too implicitly. This is
a common practice among the superstitious country people, and
Henchard is a 'man of moods, glooms, and superstitions'.
Farfrae, on the other hand, consults no weather-prophets, but
calculates intelligently on the probabilities and is successful.
There cannot be much doubt that his methods are greatly
superior to the old-fashioned ones.

Brown thinks that in this novel the figure of the ideal countryman Oak 'has darkened into Henchard',[5] but the reverse is true;
he has been attenuated into Farfrae. In spite of obvious differences, Farfrae belongs to the same tradition as Hardy's earlier,
astute and resilient heroes who refuse to let themselves be extinguished by circumstances, and who bring new skills and intelligence to the community. His process for restoring bad grain, his
modern methods of management and the horse-drill which he
pioneers to 'revolutionise sowing' are all positive contributions to
the town's agricultural life. These skills are offset by a certain
poverty of feeling; he is unlike Oak and Diggory in not being
wholehearted in love. His rather lukewarm affections can be
switched from Elizabeth to Lucetta and back again, with no
apparent effort. But his emotional limitations are a guarantee
that he can remain safely inside the community; that he will
never, like Henchard, be driven to wretchedness or madness.
An early conversation pinpoints the difference between them.
Henchard says:

'I sank into one of those gloomy fits I sometimes suffer from . . .
when the world seems to have the blackness of hell, and, like

Job, I could curse the day that gave me birth'.
'Ah, now, I never feel like it', said Farfrae.

Henchard cannot, like Farfrae, adapt himself to any circumstances he finds himself in. He is like Boldwood is allowing his emotions to drive him over the borders of reason towards self-destruction, and also like Clym in his final self-hatred and loneliness. In the end, when he leaves the town 'to whose development he had been one of the chief stimulants', he feels like Cain, 'an outcast and a vagabond', although he insists stoically 'my punishment is *not* greater than I can bear'. Yet it is the worst of all punishments for him, because human contacts are more necessary for him than for most people:

He was the kind of man to whom some human object for pouring out his heat upon – were it emotive or were it choleric – was almost a necessity.

However, his violent individualism, and rapid emotional fluctuations, make it impossible for him to form any stable relationship. He never cares much for either Lucetta or Susan, and his attempts to create a substitute family – his affection for Farfrae, who reminds him of his dead brother, and for his supposed daughter Elizabeth – are too fitful to evoke a strong positive response. His feelings are at their purest when he realises that he loves Elizabeth, although she is not his real daughter, and is ready to put up with Farfrae for her sake. But by this time it is too late and he has thrown away her affection. He is also the kind of man who desperately needs recognition in society (this is his original reason for selling his wife). But although he does some good things when he is Mayor of Casterbridge he has all the contempt of the self-made man for his social inferiors, particularly when they are his intellectual inferiors too. This is why he despises Susan and bullies the mentally subnormal Abel Whittle. The same vein of brutal snobbery comes out when he abuses Elizabeth for being too considerate to servants:

Why do you lower yourself so confoundedly?... Making yourself a drudge for a common workman... Why, ye'll disgrace me to the dust!'

Being 'unduly sensitive on such points by reason of his own past' he bitterly resents anything in Elizabeth's speech or behaviour which reminds him of the ordinary labouring people from whom he has sprung:

One would think you worked upon a farm! One day I learn that you lend a hand in public-houses. Then I hear you talk like a clodhopper.

The same false notions of gentility make him bully her for using the Wessex dialect, though he speaks it himself – 'Good God, are you only fit to carry wash to a pig-trough, that ye use such words as these?' Conversely, he has a high respect for intelligence and education (this is one reason why he likes Farfrae) and his attitude to Elizabeth softens when he discovers that she has been educating herself:

Evidence of her care, of her endeavours for improvement, were visible all around, in the form of books, sketches, maps, and little arrangements for tasteful effects. Henchard had known nothing of these efforts.

In the end, he appeals to her to help him with his own inadequacies:

He said to her, 'Are miracles still worked, do you think, Elizabeth? I am not a read man. I don't know so much as I could wish. I have tried to peruse and learn all my life; but the more I try to know the more ignorant I seem.'

The final pathos and inner contradictions of his social striving are shown on the occasion of the royal visit when he parades himself, an ordinary workman and half-drunk, as if he were still Mayor of Casterbridge. It comes out most clearly in his splendid retort to Farfrae when the latter accuses him of having 'insulted Royalty':

'Royalty be damned!' said Henchard. 'I am as loyal as you, come to that!'

Of course he has not the slightest reverence for the monarchy, when it is set up as something opposed to him, but neither will he yield to anybody in professing the right, socially acceptable sentiments. The first half of his statement is the more sincere but the second is no less instinctive. Henchard can only express himself through the recognised forms of society; to be cut off from society means death.

Lucetta, the outsider within the community, imposes on it for a time through her richness and flashiness. Henchard's struggle for her with Farfrae is partly a social one, as he recognises when he threatens his rival. 'Your money and your fine wife no longer lift 'ee above me ... and my poverty does not press me down'. Conversation among ordinary Casterbridge people makes it clear that they too regard Farfrae's possession of her as a social asset. ''Tis wonderful how he could get a lady of her quality to go snacks wi' en in such quick time.' But the same people have no trouble in seeing that the qualities which she is admired for are purely external. 'Yet how folk do worship fine clothes!'

Lucetta resembles the earlier heroines in her frivolity and disregard of convention. But in her role as sophisticated woman of the world with a concealed sexual secret, she is less like them than like Mrs Charmond in *The Woodlanders*. Her relationship with Elizabeth, in which the 'woman of comparatively practised manner' temporarily dazzles the younger girl by her sophistication is also very like Mrs Charmond's with Grace.

Elizabeth provides a strong moral contrast to her. Disregarded and penniless, eclipsed in everyone's eyes by the flashier woman, she spends most of her time in obscurity, trying to broaden her mind. 'She read and took notes incessantly, mastering facts with painful laboriousness, but never flinching from her self-imposed task.' Lucetta, by contrast, seems to lead a life of elegant idleness, interested in nothing except flirtations and dress. Elizabeth, like the patient, rejected heroes of earlier novels, has to learn to control her own feelings; unlike Lucetta she cannot afford to make constant hysterical scenes. Indeed her suppression of her love for Farfrae is so stoical that she seems to have scarcely any real feelings at all. But if she is narrow and conventional in some respects – 'her craving for correctness of prudence was ... almost vicious' – this helps her to work out a strong though limited moral code, and also to remain safely within the community, like Farfrae, unlike her stepfather and Lucetta.

Brown identifies Lucetta as 'the Invader ... from outside the rural world' who brings 'a feeling of menace'[6] into the community with her. But Lucetta is not a strong enough figure to represent any real menace to Casterbridge, and her false way of life does no permanent damage to anyone but herself. As Henchard finally realises when she pleads with him not to expose her, she is 'very small deer to hunt'. Instead, her destruction is hatched in the slum inn at Mixen Lane, which represents a whole aspect of Casterbridge we have not seen directly before:

> Much that was sad, much that was low, some things that were baneful, could be seen in Mixen Lane. Vice ran freely in and out certain of the doors of the neighbourhood; recklessness dwelt under the roof with the crooked chimney; shame in some bow-windows; theft (in times of privation) in the thatched and mud-walled houses by the sallows. Even slaughter had not been altogether unknown here. In a block of cottages up an alley there might have been erected an altar to disease in years gone by. Such was Mixen Lane in the times when Henchard and Farfrae were Mayors.

The last sentence clinches what has gone before. Henchard and Farfrae, in their capacity as leading citizens, have largely ignored this wretchedness; the people retaliate by the crude and brutal skimmity-ride which will put both Henchard and Farfrae to shame. This aspect of muted class bitterness has been glimpsed before, in the crowds which gather to protest about the bad bread outside the hotel where the Mayor and Corporation are banqueting, or outside the court when the furmity-women reveals Henchard's past. Farfrae, too, has lost his original charm 'in the eyes of the poorer inhabitants' since growing rich. But the slum-dwellers, some of whom are prostitutes, are especially bitter when they find that the 'proud piece of silk and wax-work' Lucetta has a disreputable past, and the demonstration is primarily directed against her.

Casterbridge resembles the small towns of Mrs Gaskell and George Eliot (although it is much more concretely presented than Hollingford or St Ogg's) in its limitless capacity for backbiting and gossip, its eagerness to destroy a reputation – particularly a woman's reputation – on the merest hint of scandal. Up to this point it has still been possible to see the town Casterbridge in the same way as George Eliot's country communities, as a place with an essentially healthy though somewhat narrow and limited code. This incident forces us to take a considerably darker view. Lucetta is really guilty (unlike Molly or Maggie) but her punishment is much heavier than she deserves. The skimmity-ride is the community's brutal, direct and spectacular way of expressing what more genteel country towns would only have whispered. Lucetta dies because she is crushed out of existence by the weight of society's disapproval for her whole mode of life.

Also, of course, because it is necessary for her to be out of the way. Farfrae is now free to marry Elizabeth (the courtship is expressed symbolically through his giving her books) consoling himself for Lucetta's loss by reflecting that 'it was hard to believe that life with her would have been productive of further happiness'. The return of Newson at about this time gives an added emphasis to this point about Farfrae; he is another person who is good at making the best of things and so can fit into the community happily. Both of them are entirely different from Henchard, who thinks seriously of committing suicide when he is threatened with losing Elizabeth, and who when this loss becomes a certainty goes out alone to die on Egdon Heath.

In *The Return of the Native*, some years earlier, Hardy had written:

A well-proportioned mind is one which shows no particular bias; one of which we may safely say that it will never cause its owner to be confined as a madman, tortured as a heretic, or crucified as a blasphemer. Also, on the other hand, that it will never cause him to be applauded as a prophet, revered as a priest, or exalted as a king. Its usual blessings are happiness and mediocrity ... enabling its possessors to find their way to wealth, to wind up well, to step with dignity off the stage, to die comfortably in their beds.

He was writing about that other exile, Clym Yeobright, who, like Henchard, sometimes felt like cursing the day he was born. 'Happiness and mediocrity' are the portion of the lesser characters, who are looked at with a colder eye than in the earlier novel; Farfrae and Elizabeth are less vital human beings than Thomasin and Diggory Venn. Similarly, the community from which Henchard exiles himself has less positive value than the one which expels Boldwood in *Far from the Madding Crowd*. Henchard dies on Egdon Heath, the place in all Wessex where nature is least yielding to human endeavour, and his will is the ultimate expression of alienation, the desire that his name should be forgotten, the rejection of all the rituals through which society comes to terms with death.

Yet this is not quite the last word. Henchard is followed on his last journey out of Casterbridge by Abel Whittle, the half-idiot boy whom he has publicly humiliated. He is used to being deferential, but he takes no notice when Henchard tells him to leave him alone:

Then 'a said, 'Whittle, what do ye follow me for when I've told ye to go back all these times?' And I said, 'Because sir, I see things be bad with 'ee, and ye wer kind-like to mother if ye were rough to me, and I would fain be kind-like to you'. Then he walked on, and I followed; and he never complained at me no more.

Henchard does realise in the end that he has not been rejected by everyone. 'What, Whittle,' he said, 'and can ye really be such a poor fond fool as to care for such a wretch as I!' Even his will, which invokes on himself the curse he once called down on Farfrae – 'that no man remember me' – begins with the wish to spare Elizabeth pain. Farfrae and Elizabeth too, in their own way, try to help him, although they leave their efforts too late. Society, in this novel, still contains the possibilities of compassion. They were to become less and less in Hardy's more mature work.

7 The Woodlanders

It is easy to use a novel like *The Woodlanders* to support stereo-typed ideas of the relationship between country and town. The woods can be seen as a place of innocence, safety and natural fertility; the 'good' characters as simple country people, and Fitzpiers and Mrs Charmond as urban interlopers (in Brown's view their sinister qualities are heightened by Fitzpiers' being an intellectual). Grace is then the pivotal figure, who has to choose between town civilisation and country life in choosing between Fitzpiers and Giles.

Yet this interpretation of the novel is much too simple. The woods are productive and fruitful in certain seasons and under certain aspects, but this is only part of the truth:

> Here, as everywhere, the Unfulfilled Intention, which makes life what it is, was as obvious as it could be among the de-praved crowds of a city slum. The leaf was deformed, the curve was crippled, the taper was interrupted; the lichen ate the vigour of the stalk, and the ivy slowly strangled to death the promising sapling.

The flowering or fruit-bearing orchards are contrasted with dead and dying trees; during the storm which kills Giles the woods assume a quality of terror:

> Dead boughs were scattered about like ichthyosauri in a museum ... Next were more trees close together, wrestling for existence, their branches disfigured with wounds resulting from their mutual rubbings and blows ... Beneath them were the rotting stumps of those of the group that had been vanquished long ago, rising from their mossy setting like black teeth from green gums.

Nature is seen here from a post-Darwinian viewpoint; the trees have to struggle with their 'neighbours' in order to stay alive.

And in some aspects nature is not life-sustaining or even neutral but actively hostile to human beings, like the tree that kills John South:

> He says that it is exactly his own age, that it has got human sense, and sprouted up when he was born on purpose to rule him, and keep him as its slave.

To South this tree has become 'an evil spirit', and when it falls 'my poor life, that's worth houses upon houses, will be squashed out o' me'. Yet the relationship is more complex than that of destroyer and victim; South has perversely *identified* with the tree, which he claims was born at the same time as him, and when it is chopped down he dies. And his consciousness that his life is worth 'houses upon houses' reminds us that the tree is the landowner's property, which cannot legally be cut down without her permission, and that human lives and destinies (Giles's loss of the houses and Grace with them) are tied up inextricably with money and land. The woods belong to Mrs Charmond who can fell both trees and houses according to her caprice. When Giles is turned out of his cottage after South's death it is pulled down, and the apples in his garden rot. The wastage spreads in a reciprocal process from human to natural life; human beings, trees and houses are all connected with each other through the 'closely-knit interdependence of the lives' in the tiny village. The woods, like Egdon, are not a background but a complex and changing entity through which individual characters define themselves. Marty says that the young trees 'are very sorry to begin life in earnest – just as we be'. Grace is described to Fitzpiers as 'the tree your rainbow falls on' by Giles. The trees, whether viewed as subjects or as objects, are the medium through which the community lives and expresses itself.

The culture of this community is not merely simple, but primitive. Grace, at the rituals on Midsummer Eve, feels 'as if she had receded a couple of centuries in the world's history'. In fact a belief in the supernatural is deeply rooted among the less educated; hence the popular legends of 'white witches and black witches', 'equestrian witches and demons', John South's obsession about the tree, and the people's rationalisation of their instinctive distrust of Fitzpiers by claiming that he has 'sold his soul to the wicked one'.

Fitzpiers is also the centre of another kind of superstition, owing to his aristocratic descent. People value this quality, irrationally:

That touching faith in members of long-established families as such, irrespective of their personal condition or character, which is still found among old-fashioned people in the rural districts, reached its full perfection in Melbury.

Melbury's admiration for the upper classes and what he considers their superior refinement and culture leads him to sacrifice his daughter. Grace, too, is partly fascinated by the romantic aura from the past which surrounds Fitzpiers. Fitzpiers, despite his claims to be an emancipated intellectual, accepts this homage complacently: 'I feel as if I belonged to a different species from the people who are working in that yard.' His instinctive recoil from the normal patterns of life in the village makes him feel 'a profound distaste for the situation' and react boorishly when the neighbours come to congratulate him and Grace on their return from honeymoon. 'There must be no mixing in', he insists, 'with your people below'. His feeling of superiority to ordinary people is based much more on snobbishness than on intellectual pride.

The aristocratic background reminds us of Troy, whose behaviour to women is very like that of Fitzpiers. But in general he is even more like Wildeve, more subtly and fully portrayed. Like him, he is a 'man of sentiment', who is only stung into being interested in his wife when he thinks she has been unfaithful – 'he cultivated as under glasses strange and mournful pleasures that he would not willingly let die'. Hardy is echoing Wildeve's description of himself when he explains how Fitzpiers can feel attracted to Grace and other women simultaneously:

Yet here Grace made a mistake, for the love of men like Fitzpiers is unquestionably of such quality as to bear division and transference. He had indeed once declared, though not to her, that on one occasion he had noticed himself to be possessed by five distinct infatuations at the same time.

His attitude to women is that of the typical aristocrat; the episode with the 'hoydenish maiden of the hamlet' Suke Damson is strongly similar to Alec d'Urberville's behaviour with the Trantridge girls. Suke is a new type in Hardy's work, though one that was to become prominent in his next two novels – the amoral, noisy, casually promiscuous girl, totally realistically drawn with all 'the scratches and blemishes incidental to her outdoor occupation' who is as much a recognisable type of village girl as Marty. The harmful social effects of this liaison are emphasised; Suke's husband is forced to emigrate to conceal the disgrace and Fitzpiers, by way of retribution, narrowly escapes being caught in the hideous man-trap which was set to mutilate poachers only a generation before the novel begins. Indeed it is noteworthy that this, one of the most 'idyllic' of all Hardy's pictures of country life, contains the figure of Suke, the man-trap, and the operations of a primitive code of revenge.

Fitzpiers' affair with Mrs Charmond is quite different – not a casual sexual encounter but a decadent and sentimental romance. It subsists on 'infinite fancies, idle dreams, luxurious melancholies, and pretty, alluring assertions which could neither be proved nor disproved'. It is broadly similar to the relationship of Eustacia and Wildeve, and Mrs Charmond is recognisably a development from Lucetta – the rich, sophisticated, irresponsible woman who is destroyed through her sexual sins. She is 'a body who has smiled where she has not loved, and loved where she has not married', who has been an actress (this is associated here, as in Troy and Eustacia, with an inauthentic personality) but having married money can find nothing to interest her. Her sole idea of occupying herself when she is not flirting is to travel about the continent and write a diary of her impressions – 'but she cannot find energy enough to do it herself'. Her interests are as futile as her emotions, and these are both artificial and short-lived. 'Now for a winter of regrets and agonies and useless wishes, till I forget him in the spring.'

The essential falsity of the relationship is stressed from the beginning when she summons Fitzpiers to treat her for a non-existent ailment, as an excuse to flirt. We feel that in doing this she is making a mockery of his skill as a doctor, the one really valuable thing he possesses. Brown regards Fitzpiers as a typical useless intellectual, who eventually, to be reconciled with Grace, has to make the 'gesture (and how revealing a gesture!) of renouncing his studies'.[1] But the trouble with Fitzpiers is that he

is only playing at being an intellectual, allowing his desultory
reading to divert him from his real work:

> Dr Fitzpiers was a man of too many hobbies ... In the course
> of a year his mind was accustomed to pass in a grand solar
> sweep through the zodiac of the intellectual heaven ... One
> month he would be immersed in alchemy, another in poesy;
> one month in the Twins of astrology and astronomy; then in
> the Crab of German literature and metaphysics. In justice to
> him it must be stated that he took such studies as were immedi-
> ately related to his own profession in turn with the rest.

His metaphysical speculations as reported by Grammer Oliver,
sound rather empty:

> Let me tell you that Everything is Nothing. There's only Me
> and Not Me in the whole world.

However, his real intellectual achievements command admiration:

> One speciality of Fitzpiers was respected by Grace as much
> as ever: his professional skill. In this she was right. Had his
> persistence equalled his insight instead of being the spasmodic
> and fitful thing it was, fame and fortune need never have re-
> mained a wish with him.

After he has saved Grace's life she reflects: 'why could he not
have had more principle, so as to turn his great talents to good
account!' In fact there are indications towards the end that he
means to lead 'a new, useful, effectual life' as a doctor. Fitzpiers
can, with a little effort, find a positive role in the community;
Mrs Charmond cannot. 'It seemed to accord well with the fitful
fever of that impassioned woman's life that she should not have
found an English grave.'

Mrs Charmond has another role in the novel, that of the non-
productive landowner whose relationship with the land and her
tenants is entirely predatory. This is not an exaggeration; her
treatment of Giles over the houses is typical of the worst landlords. She owns the woods but dislikes and does not know her
way round them. It is taken for granted that people in the
Hintocks should work for her but – 'she takes no interest in the

village folk at all'. When she is forced into a direct relationship with any of them it is because she wants to deprive them of something – Marty's hair, Giles's home, Grace's husband. In each case she is acting not out of need but in order to gratify some trivial emotion – vanity, resentment, or sentimentality. Nothing is so important for her as to satisfy her caprice.

Contrasted are Giles and Marty, each of whom submits stoically to circumstances. Both of them endure a hopeless love without complaining and both can lose sight of their own suffering, physical and mental, in concentrating on the work which always has to be done. This work is not mechanical but as much of a skill as is Fitzpiers'; it is 'intelligent intercourse with Nature'. They understand the life of the trees, which to other people are only scenery, as no one else can:

> The casual glimpses which the ordinary population bestowed upon that wondrous world of sap and leaves called the Hintock woods had been with these two, Giles and Marty, a clear gaze. They had been possessed of its finer mysteries as of commonplace knowledge; had been able to read its hieroglyphs as ordinary writing; to them the sights and sounds of night, winter, wind, storm, amid those dense boughs, which had to Grace a touch of the uncanny, and even of the supernatural, were simple occurrences whose origin, continuance and laws they foreknew.

The second sentence indicates that their work, despised by the sophisticated, is actually very difficult and complex. The description of how they are not afraid of the woods under any aspect reminds us of Thomasin's fearlessness on Egdon Heath. Nature is frequently destructive but it has to be come to terms with because it is the basis of life (the false reaction is Mrs Charmond's drawing the curtains because she is depressed by a rainy day). Giles's wonderful skill, and his instinctive understanding of nature, are shown through his ordinary work in the woods with Marty:

> He had a marvellous power of making trees grow ... There was a sort of sympathy between himself and the fir, oak or beech that he was operating on; so that the roots took hold of the soil in a few days ... He put most of these roots towards

the south-west; for, he said, in forty years' time, when some great gale is blowing from that quarter, the trees will require the strongest holdfast on that side to stand against it and not fall.

Giles's work is thus set in its perspective in history (for history is no less real in the woods than in Casterbridge). He feels that he is working for something beyond himself and that the trees have a relation to other human beings, some of them not yet born, besides him. His work extends through the generations; this is what gives it its value. Although he is a much more tragic figure, Giles is very similar to the other skilled countrymen in Hardy's earlier novels, Oak and Diggory Venn. He has the same patience, the same skill, the same incapacity to love more than one person. This single-heartedness, while it makes him ready to die for Grace, is fatal to Marty's hopes, since she is no more capable than he is of transferring her love.

Marty is as skilled at copse work as Giles – she can make excellent spars with no practice – but this does not mean she is incapable of the kinds of work which society values more highly:

Nothing but a cast of the die of destiny had decided that the girl should handle the tool; and the fingers which clasped the heavy ash shaft might have skilfully guided the pencil or swept the string, had they only been set to do it in good time.

It is continually stressed that she is a person of vivid intelligence and great human potential. But her possibilities are never fulfilled, because of her subordinate social position and her unreturned love, and she remains 'always a lonely maid' up to the end. Other people usually forget or ignore her claims as a person – 'everybody thought of Giles; nobody thought of Marty'. Unlike Grace, and unlike Mrs Charmond – who, at the other extreme of the social scale, needs to think about nothing but her femininity – she is shut out from love and marriage. She desexualises herself (like Tess when she is abandoned by Angel) by sacrificing her hair to deck another woman. By the end of the novel this process has been completed:

The contours of womanhood so undeveloped as to be scarcely perceptible . . . she touched sublimity at points, and looked almost like a being who had rejected with indifference the attribute of sex for the loftier quality of abstract humanism.

Marty exists only through her work and is allowed no self-realisation apart from it. She carries 'the marks of poverty and toil', her arm is covered with 'old scratches from briars . . . purple in the cold wind'. Although Giles never loves her, she is 'his true complement in the other sex' through the language and values they share. Her final speech over his grave brings out the reality of their relationship, one built out of the homely details of common work and experience:

Whenever I plant the young larches I'll think that none can plant as you planted; and whenever I split a gad, and whenever I turn the cider wring, I'll say none could do it like you.

It is symbolic, too, that she should finally take over his tools and his work. Giles's character is ultimately made clear through his actions – 'you was a good man, and did good things'.

Grace, an almost neutral figure 'who combined modern nerves with primitive feelings' is balanced between these two groups. Her 'primitive feelings' are her love for the woods and for Giles; her 'modern nerves' are the false codes of conduct which have been instilled into her at school and also partly at home. Her father, believing that the idle 'refined' world of Fitzpiers and Mrs Charmond is intrinsically superior to that of the woodlanders, gives her an expensive education and, when this process is completed, cannot bear her to be reabsorbed into his own way of life. For Grace, who knows nothing about manual work, marriage is the only conceivable destiny, and marriage is more closely bound up with social status in this than in any other of Hardy's works. Melbury thinks that Grace is too fine for Giles, while Fitzpiers is not sure if she is fine enough for himself (the idea of 'a vulgar intimacy with a timber-merchant's pretty daughter' is the first one that crosses his mind). But Grace has been trained up to a point where she is indistinguishable on the surface from a member of Fitzpiers' own class: 'Won't money do anything', Giles says, 'if you've promising material to work upon?' Grace is in the position of a second-generation *nouveau riche* who is expected to ratify her position by marriage;

as such she cannot help feeling that she is being treated as a commodity:

'I, too, cost a good deal, like the horses and waggons and corn!' she said, looking up sorrily.

Her father replies with no ironic intention: 'Never mind. You'll yield a better return.' He sees a marriage with the aristocratic though impecunious Fitzpiers as the crown of his hopes for his daughter, and indeed the transaction is mutually beneficial:

Fitzpiers . . . while despising Melbury and his station, did not at all disdain to spend Melbury's money.

What Melbury has no idea of ('in the simple life he had led it had scarcely occurred to him that after marriage a man might be faithless') is that the ethos of the class which he so admires includes an exceedingly lax sexual code.

Grace, of course, is not just a tool of her father's, but the comparative weakness of her emotions makes her submit almost passively while her destiny is arranged for her. She has not the deep feelings of Giles or Marty; while she is still free to marry Giles she hesitates and lets the opportunity go. On the other hand she does have several positive feelings of affinity with the upper class; she is strongly attracted not only by Fitzpiers but also in the beginning by Mrs Charmond. It should incidentally be stressed that her education, on which so much emphasis is laid, seems to have been a paltry affair. She has read the right books and can juggle with the names of foreign authors (hence her enthusiasm for Mrs Charmond's silly scheme to publish a diary) but she has no genuine love or desire for knowledge as such. Her education is essentially a badge of social superiority; she has been to school with girls 'whose parents Giles would have addressed with a deferential Sir or Madam', and as Giles himself says, 'She's been accustomed to servants and everything superfine'. This accounts for her recoil from the jolly uninhibited manners at Giles's Christmas party (so similar to Fitzpiers' distaste for the neighbours' celebration) and from the tavern where Giles takes her, even after she thinks she has broken with her husband for good. Her sympathy with the world of Mrs Charmond and Fitzpiers does not of course mean that she can tolerate its sexual mores. On the contrary she has imbibed a prim boarding-school morality which makes her consider everything in the light of whether or not it is 'proper'. This helps to bring the tragic climax about.

Hardy had dealt with unhappy marriages several times in his earlier fiction – Bathsheba, Thomasin, Clym and Farfrae all make them – but in each case the unsuitable partner dies and the other is set free, usually to marry again. In *The Woodlanders* for the first time Hardy rejects this easy novelistic solution; Fitzpiers stays alive and Grace has to make the best of a bad job. Instead it is Giles who dies, and Grace is forced to realise that she has probably killed him. Naturally frigid, she has rejected him before her marriage, kept him at a distance afterwards ('I wish to keep the proprieties as well as I can') and finally driven him into the storm. There is a blinding moment of illumination when she understands what she has done:

> How selfishly correct I am always – too, too correct. Can it be that cruel propriety is killing the dearest heart that ever woman clasped to her own? . . . O, my Giles', she cried, 'what have I done to you!'

Her 'selfish correctness' is, in its own way, as negative and cruel as Fitzpiers' promiscuity. They are, in fact related; as both of them spring from a fear of deep commitments. Having been used with undeserved contempt by Fitzpiers, Grace is treated by Giles with an equally undeserved reverence. In sacrificing himself for the sake of her modesty he is treating her less like a human being than a plaster saint.

Grace's moment of insight cannot last, her feelings are too shallow. Almost immediately after Giles dies her false consciousness reasserts itself; she consoles herself by reciting prayers from the book 'which poor Giles had kept at hand mainly for the convenience of whetting his penkife'. The same book, later on, convinces her that she ought to go back to her lawful wedded husband. Her religiosity reaches its final point of fatuousness when she declares, after the man-trap incident: 'O, Edred, there has been an Eye watching over us tonight, and we should be thankful indeed!'

When she goes back to Fitzpiers Grace is, as Brown says, 'a diminished person'. After the first agonising remorse she ceases to worry about the extent of her responsibility for Giles's death. Indeed, once she is again on semi-flirtatious terms with her husband Giles has become a mere object to bait him with. 'I don't see why you should mind my having had one lover besides yourself in my life, when you have had so many.' The same is true of her pretence that she had been having an affair with Giles; this is prompted solely by spitefulness and in fact she realises that in making it she had 'wronged Winterborne's memory'. Her final reconciliation with Fitzpiers is not convincing; we have no reason apart from his own protestations to think he has changed:

> 'Well – he's her husband', Melbury said to himself, 'and let her take him back to her bed if she will!... But let her bear in mind that the woman walks and laughs somewhere at this very moment whose neck he'll be coling next year as he does hers tonight; and as he did Felice Charmond's last year, and Suke Damson's the year afore!... It's a forlorn hope for her, and God knows how it will end!'

Grace will be unhappy, we can scarcely doubt, and yet not much more unhappy than she deserves. The workmen's tart comments make it clear enough that what we are seeing is no triumphant vindication of the marriage-vow but a compromise; something shoddy and mean. And Marty's comment at Giles's grave finally puts Grace into the right perspective. 'She has forgot 'ee at last, although for her you died.'

So the novel appears to end on a note of defeat. Indeed one of the saddest things about *The Woodlanders* is that the community, unlike those in the earlier novels, seems to have almost no capacity for resistance. Its attitude towards those who exploit it is one of passive criticism or, worse still, of passive acceptance; the people cannot even imagine an active defiant revolt like the Casterbridge skimmity-ride. The only exception is Tim's mantrap, which is almost a joke. Natural laws fail to assert themselves. Fitzpiers gets off scot-free while the pure in heart suffer or die. And yet, at the very end, we feel that there is still an unspoken resilience which goes beyond individual lives, or the destruction of individual hopes. It is personified in Marty's lonely figure with her fresh flowers and her determination to continue Giles's work; it is felt on the morning of death through the trees which will live after Giles:

The whole wood seemed to be a house of death, pervaded by loss to its uttermost length and breadth. Winterborne was gone, and the copses seemed to show the want of him: those young trees, so many of which he had planted, and of which he had spoken so truly when he said that he should fall before they fell, were at that very moment sending out their roots in the direction that he had given them with his subtle hand.

The defeat seems total, but it is not total. Individuals are destroyed and yet the work which creates life continues; in the midst of death, there is life.

8 *Tess of the d'Urbervilles*

The understanding of *Tess* and *Jude* demands a radically different approach from that which is appropriate to Hardy's earlier
novels. Critics like Brown have seen *Tess* as the culmination of
Hardy's more characteristic art, with *Jude* as a kind of after-
thought which has little relation to his other works (and the
relative popularity of the two novels appears to bear out these
judgements). But in fact *The Woodlanders* marks the end of one
style of writing in Hardy – though of course there is no complete
break at any point in the series – and the two last great novels are
in a group by themselves. They share the themes of wandering
and isolation, of the impact of modern, progressive ideas on
encrusted conventions, and of 'the deadly war between flesh and
spirit', as Hardy expressed it in the 1895 Preface to *Jude*. This
war is enacted not only on the sexual plane but also in the
necessity for the flesh to submit to a life of brutalising labour
which the spirit can only weakly attempt to resist.

The extreme popularity of *Tess* owes something to the fact
that present-day readers have no trouble in grasping the central
point, about 'purity'. (It is much less easy to respond to the
central thesis of *Jude*, but that will be discussed in the next
chapter.) The revolutionary implications which were carried by
this argument in Hardy's time have become almost stale for us;
so much so that we are tempted by the last two novels to make
Hardy an apologist for a sexual code which would have shocked
him. (Tess is 'not quite indifferent to Alec's commonplace
charms . . . more than a stiff bundle of virtue',[1] proclaims Irving
Howe.) Hence the obsessive Angel-baiting, and the lengthy de-
fences of a thesis which no longer needs defending, in practically
all the modern criticism of *Tess*. In an earlier chapter I tried to
isolate the sexual theme in the novel (as far as this was possible).
The present chapter will try to combat some other critical misreadings and to arrive at a more balanced view of the whole.

The most common of these misreadings derives from the title –
that the novel centres on the significane of Tess's d'Urberville
blood. It is assumed that her tragedy consists in her family's loss
of its ancestral inheritance; that her being a real d'Urberville and
Alec a fake one symbolises the ruin and betrayal of the old
aristocracy by a new urban class bent on exploiting the land.
Many critics, for example Howe, see a deep significance in Alec's
unauthorised use of the d'Urberville name:

> That these cousins are not authentic offshoots of the aristocratic
> line, but *arriviste* bourgeois who have bought their way into
> the gentry and appropriated the name as a decoration, is a
> fine stroke.[2]

Brown writes:

> The appearance of the spurious country squire adds to the
> sense of jeopardy ... Alongside this image, there unfolds that
> of the old father's discovery of his ancient but unavailing
> ancestry: a disclosure of the community's past which helps to
> define what Tess represents in the ensuing tale, at the same
> time as it sharpens the intrusive and invading quality in Alec
> d'Urberville.[3]

All this implies that there is something intrinsically valuable
and authentic in the traditional aristocracy (Brown seems to
think it an integral part of the old-style agricultural community)
and that the falsity of Alec's name is the outward and visible sign
of his inward corruption (if not actually the worst of his crimes).
Disraeli had written about the manufacture of titles and the re-
duction of old aristocratic families to poverty, and the way is
wide open for a tory-democratic interpretation of *Tess* in which
the main enemy is seen as the merchant class and the interests of
aristocrats and ordinary people are one and the same. But
Hardy's treatment of the subject in his earlier writings makes this
highly improbable. Fitzpiers and Troy both have genuine aristocratic blood which helps them to dazzle the unsophisticated, but
their treatment of women is no different from that of the
'spurious' Alec. *Barbara of the House of Grebe* shows sadism,
weakness and madness among the nobility; real goodness only in
the plebeian hero. The villain of *A Laodicean*, Willy Dare, is an
illegitimate aristocrat like Troy; and a major theme of this novel
is the futility of living in dreams of a romantic past (symbolised

by the de Stancy castle) rather than coping with the demands of the modern world. This is made perfectly clear in the end when the castle burns down.

Hardy's attitudes had not changed when he came to write *Tess*. The d'Urbervilles were not a romantic fiction thrown in to lend colour to the narrative but were as much based on reality as the 'partly real, partly dream-country' of Wessex. There had been a real family with a similar name, the Turbervilles of Bere Regis 'whose swords founded their fortune in the Middle Ages'[4] and who had then been extinguished as a power in local affairs. By the mid-eighteenth century 'the last of the Turbervilles lay in a Putney churchyard',[5] but it is not improbable that various poor relations continued living obscurely in Dorset. 'You find such as I everywhere; 'tis a feature of our county', Tess says, and Hardy corroborated this in an interview with Raymond Blathwayt: 'there are many such cases about here. You will trace noble lineage in many a face'.[6] It is never suggested that Tess is superior to the other working people because of her ancestry. This would be unlikely, even in conventional terms, because many of them also spring from decayed landowning families, like the common-place Retty Priddle – 'Another dairy-girl was as good as she ... in that respect'.

Hardy's attitude to the historical d'Urbervilles is not romantic, quite the reverse. The portraits of Tess's ancestors are hideous and terrifying; their conduct was probably vicious as he stresses when Tess is seduced:

> One may, indeed, admit the possibility of a retribution lurking in the present catastrophe. Doubtless some of Tess d'Urberville's mailed ancestors rollicking home from a fray had dealt the same measure even more ruthlessly towards peasant girls of their time.

Alec has thus taken over the role of his namesakes, the brutal aristocrats who exploited and raped girls in the same social position as Tess. What matters is not the name but the function; the real class relationship of exploiter and victim. Alec is the modern aristocrat, enriched by trade rather than land but behaving in the same way as his historical predecessors and inheriting their title with everything else. A similar point is made when Tess's family are turned out:

Thus the Durbeyfields, once d'Urbervilles, saw descending upon them the destiny which, no doubt, when they were among the Olympians of the county, they had caused to descend many a time, and severely enough, upon the heads of such landless ones as they themselves were now.

It is evident that Hardy has no illusions either about the old aristocracy or about peasant life in the Middle Ages. Particular family fortunes have changed since the time of the d'Urbervilles; the inhumanity of the relationship between classes has not. Tess is no princess in rags, like Disraeli's Sybil, uncontaminated by the vulgar life around her and only waiting for the day when she can reclaim her inheritance. She is a typical village girl of her generation (typical in her character, circumstances and destiny) and her ancestry is also typical in a region where 'many of the present tillers of the soil were once owners of it'.

What, then, is the reason for Tess's d'Urberville ancestry if it is neither to emphasise her inherent nobility nor to romanticise the medieval social order? Almost certainly to illustrate the destructive role played by this kind of false consciousness in the lives of ordinary people, in this case the Durbeyfields after they know their descent. For, like *Jude*, this is in many respects a novel *about* false consciousness; Angel has it, and so in her excessive idealisation of Angel has Tess. In the Durbeyfields it takes the form of monumental delusions of grandeur which, like alcohol, help to prevent them from facing up to their actual and urgent problems. Joan's description of their new-found honours helps to show us her confused apprehension of history, her incurable tendency to shed 'a sort of halo, an occidental glow' over present and past:

We've been found to be the greatest gentlefolk in the whole county – reaching all back long before Oliver Grumble's time – to the days of the Pagan Turks – with monuments, and vaults, and crests, and 'scutcheons, and the Lord knows what all.

For John Durbeyfield this provides a welcome excuse not to support his family – 'he says, 'tis wrong for a man of such a high family as his to slave and drave at common labouring work'. For Joan, who blindly expects their rich 'cousin' Alec to welcome them, it provides an excuse for sending Tess into jeopardy. 'He'll marry her, most likely, and make a lady of her; and then she'll be what her forefathers was', she announces (marriage is most definitely linked with a rise or fall in the social scale here as elsewhere). Angel, despite his boasted radicalism, reacts very similarly. 'He always professed to despise ancient lineage', Hardy remarked to Blathwayt, 'and yet as a matter of fact he was delighted that Tess was a d'Urberville'. Tess herself is the person who shows least enthusiasm about her ancestry, particularly after it has led to her being seduced. She is thoroughly suspicious of 'd'Urberville air-castles' (a phrase carrying suggestions of Jude's ideal Christminster). Anyway she is only half a d'Urberville and her sex appeal, which is 'her mother's gift, and therefore unknightly, unhistorical' is obviously one of the main forces leading to her downfall:

'I have as much of mother as father in me!' she said. 'All my prettiness comes from her, and she was only a dairy-maid.'

If *Tess* is not about the degradation of the English aristocracy neither is it about 'the destruction of the English peasantry'[7] – the second ordinary critical fallacy. According to this reading Tess, the representative of the peasant class, is sent away from the happy valley of her childhood (the village May Day rituals are strongly emphasised in this interpretation) to be destroyed by the urban invader Alec and the intellectual Angel (who also, according to Brown, is 'the impassive instrument of some will, some purpose, stemming from the disastrous life of the cities'). Her ultimate degradation is symbolised at Flintcomb-Ash when she becomes a slave to the threshing-machine. But this interpretation is much too simple and gives an unjustified prominence to the machine and the towns, which in fact we scarcely see. The English peasantry as an independent class had long since ceased to exist; the so-called 'peasants' of the nineteenth century were mostly either small capitalist farmers or rural proletarians whom they employed. Durbeyfield belongs to an intermediate group but has made his position worse than it need have been by his shiftlessness. The copyholding class is unpopular with the farmers, anyway, and this leads to his family's being turned out on his death:

As the long holdings fell in they were seldom again let to similar tenants, and were mostly pulled down, if not absolutely required by the farmer for his hands. Cottagers who were not directly employed on the land were looked upon with disfavour, and the banishment of some starved the trade of others, who were thus obliged to follow.

The Durbeyfields are also objectionable to the local magnates for moral reasons:

> The father, and even the mother, had got drunk at times, the younger children seldom had gone to church, and the eldest daughter had made queer unions... The village had to be kept pure.

It is evident that the causes of their destitution are deeply rooted in the village community itself; their banishment is quite irrelevant to the lure of town life. They are in the same position as Giles, who loses his home when John Smith dies – victims not of the industrial process but of the traditional enemy, the land-owner. Nor is 'the beautiful Vale of Blackmore' quite the paradise which it appears. Historically, as Barbara Kerr notes, it was a centre of the labourers' rising in 1830 against near-starvation conditions.

> The very fertility of the Vale made human poverty seem more desperate; men languished but oxen, grasses and wild flowers, especially garlic and violets, flourished as nowhere else in the county.[8]

Fifty years later the Durbeyfields' situation shows that poverty in the region is no less a fact of life; the horse's death means that Tess has to be sacrificed to save her family from economic disaster. Tess is by no means the uneducated country girl that one might have expected; she has 'passed the Sixth Standard in the National School under a London-trained mistress' and inhabits a different mental world from her mother. 'When they were together the Jacobean and the Victorian ages were juxtaposed.' She 'had hoped to be a teacher at the school' (like Fancy Day) but circumstances force her to work with her hands. The conversation in the low inn which her parents frequent indicates how harsh these circumstances are:

'Tess is a fine figure o' fun ... but Joan Durbeyfield must mind that she don't get green malt in floor.'

'Figure of fun' is a phrase which is also used in *Under the Greenwood Tree* to describe Fancy, but in a context of infinite difference. If Tess had been a teacher she would no doubt have been treated with as much decorum as Fancy was, but as things are she is vulnerable to all the pressures society brings to bear upon wage-earners. The boozer's remark suggests that the community's consciousness is far from idyllic; everyone except Tess herself realises the danger in which she stands. Yet her departure from the valley is in a real sense a farewell to childhood, for until then she has had no life outside it. 'The Vale of Blackmore was to her the world, and its inhabitants the races thereof.' As a result of this first departure she becomes an exile and wanderer; banished from the old-style enclosed village she is turned into a rootless traveller more than any other of Hardy's figures but Jude.

Labour is seen in its most romanticised aspect at Talbothays, where Tess becomes the conventional 'dazzlingly fair dairymaid' in Angel Clare's eyes. It is not a false romanticism; Tess like all Hardy's positive characters really fulfils herself and is happy and skilled at her work. The independent value of this work is stressed constantly as when the milk is taken to the railway in order to nourish the people in towns. It makes no unnatural demands on the workers; the community is in 'perhaps the happiest of all positions in the social scale' and each labourer can freely express his or her own personality – as Angel discovers when he loses his preconceptions about 'the pitiable dummy known as Hodge':

The typical and unvarying Hodge ceased to exist. He had been disintegrated into a number of varied fellow-creatures – beings of many minds, beings infinite in difference.

But here the employment is only seasonal and the logical next step for Tess is 'to go to some arable farm where no divine being like Angel Clare was'. Marriage is again seen as partly an escape from intolerable social pressures. When the marriage breaks down she does find herself reduced to arable work, at Flintcomb-Ash. In this 'starve-acre place' the girls become the most exploited form of wage-labourers:

Female field-labour was seldom offered now and its cheapness made it profitable for tasks which women could perform as readily as men.

What follows is nothing less than a calvary of labour, something never shown before in Hardy, in which human beings are sustained by nothing but the sheer will to endure:

The whole field was in colour a desolate drab; it was a complexion without features, as if a face, from chin to brow, should be only an expanse of skin. The sky wore, in another colour, the same likeness; a white vacuity of countenance with the lineaments gone. So these two upper and nether visages confronted each other all day long, the white face looking down on the brown face, and the brown face looking up at the white face, without anything standing between them but the two girls crawling over the surface of the former like flies.

It is a terrifying image of annihilation; the idea of a face without features symbolises work drained of all human meaning, and the workers have been reduced to the status of flies. Only non-human forces, the cash nexus and raw nature, seem to have any independent power in this situation:

In the afternoon the rain came on again, and Marian said that they need not work any more. But if they did not work they would not be paid; so they worked on. It was so high a situation, this field, that the rain had no occasion to fall, but raced along horizontally upon the yelling wind, sticking into them like glass splinters till they were wet through.

Human beings are forced to accept their situation passively while the rain and wind, 'racing' and 'yelling', seem endowed with an active malevolent power of their own. But this is not the whole of their ordeal; the weather changes to snow and they are set reed-drawing – which is 'fearful hard work – worse than swede-hacking' – and which makes some of them physically break down. Their only way of sustaining themselves emotionally is to remember 'that happy green tract of land ... sunny, romantic Talbothays' where their working lives were qualitatively different from here.

Tess's ordeal on the threshing-machine has been regarded by some critics as the ultimate stage of her degradation; the machine being according to Brown an 'impersonal agent of destruction'[9] which has come from outside to shatter the traditional rhythms of agricultural life. Yet it is difficult to see how this work is any crueller than reed-drawing, or grubbing up swedes in the pitiless rain. Industrialism can certainly be brutal but then so can nature (remember the dying birds). Roy Morrell suggests that on this subject Hardy 'suspended judgement, feeling that the machine held at least possibilities for good'.[10] In *The Mayor of Caster-bridge* the machine was a positive force making for agricultural progress. The man-trap in *The Woodlanders* is obviously anti-human, but it is not modern; it is a machine rooted in centuries of rural history. The machine in *Tess*, which reduces her to a state of near-helplessness ('her knees trembling so wretchedly with the shaking . . . that she could scarcely walk') is destructive because it is only obliquely related to human needs and to human control. It has been introduced by a farmer in order to get the most out of his labourers; instead of cutting down their working hours it has made them slaves. Yet this is only one stage in Tess's calvary, and that not the final one, and many critics have tended grossly to overestimate its significance. (Hardy shows no consistent hatred of machinery, but rain, for example, is shown as a potent destructive force in *Far from the Madding Crowd*, *The Woodlanders*, this novel and *Jude*.) While she is working on the machine, Tess can still resist Alec; it is only when her family suffer the traditional fate of being turned out of their cottage that she is compelled to succumb.

Irving Howe writes:

> In contrast to Tess neither Alec nor Angel does meaningful work: Alec is a wastrel, Angel a dilettante. Neither lives under the lash of necessity, neither defines himself through craft or occupation.[11]

The emphasis is right, but the analysis somewhat misleading. Tess, as we have seen, only does humanly *meaningful* work at Talbothays, whereas at Flintcomb-Ash she is degraded to a mere wage-slave. Alec is diagnosed correctly as a wastrel. He is a cruder version of Fitzpiers, without his redeeming qualities; he has the same aristocratic name and aura, the same predatory attitude to women, and the scenes where he lays siege to Tess with honeyed words are strongly reminiscent of Fitzpiers' successful efforts to reinstate himself with Grace. Even his religion is spurious (contrasted with Mr Clare's) and his relationship with the land he farms is as hedonistic as are all his other relationships – one of 'enjoyment pure and simple'.

Angel is a very much more complex person and one whom it is easy to misunderstand. Critics of the most diverse kinds have united in abusing him; Irving Howe pronounces him an 'insufferable prig . . . Hardy feels . . . dislike towards everything Angel stands for'.[12] Actually Hardy treated him with much more sympathy than the critics, but he took great pains to emphasise his difference, his sense of distance from the ordinary workers at the dairy (symbolised by his eating apart from the rest). In so far as he allows himself to be ruled by snobbish emotions – as when he calls Tess 'an unapprehending peasant woman' – he really is contemptible, but when he is shown struggling to overcome the limitations of his background, to break down his own preconceptions, he is an authentic and sympathetic person. He has been denied a university education (like Jude) because of his rejection of dogma, but in trying to combine plain living and high thinking he is acting with the same positive purpose as Clym. The contrast between him and his brothers – 'hall-marked young men, correct to their remotest fibre', one of whom is 'all Church' and the other 'all College' – shows how far he is from being just a middle-class prig. His family worries about him, not just because of his unorthodox opinions but also because of his growing identification with farming people. 'A prig would have said that he had lost culture, and a prude that he had become coarse.' At this point he is not a dilettante but genuinely wants to absorb the values of ordinary people, marry among them, become one of themselves.

His response to Tess is a real and deep one although it is based on a misapprehension. In the end it turns out to be stronger than his prejudices – 'tenderness was absolutely dominant in Clare at last'. The trouble is that his feelings are, in the language of *Jude*, too 'spiritual' – 'with more animalism he would have been the nobler man'. This contempt for the 'flesh' – for the concrete stuff of humanity – means that, in Kettle's words, he 'gives abstract ideas or principles a priority over the actual needs of specific situations'[18] – exactly as Sue does in abandoning Jude. For, like Sue, he boasts of being an intellectual radical without having the true courage of his convictions:

> With all his attempted independence of judgement this advanced and well-meaning young man ... was yet the slave to custom and conventionality when surprised back into his early teachings.

'Custom and conventionality' – the dead weight of Victorian intellectual hypocrisy – is what brings about the disaster. Angel's tragedy is that he does not really know where he stands in relation to this hypocrisy until it is too late, and Tess has been sacrificed. His failure to live up to his ideals would have been less tragic if the ideals in themselves had been less good. For Angel is an intellectual pioneer, like Clym, and – like Clym – is held back from fulfilling himself by an anachronistic weakness and prejudice. In spite of everything Angel is one of Hardy's nobler characters. He is limited by the past, but he can point forward into the future. This is clearly illustrated in one of his early conversations with his father:

> 'What is the good of your mother and me economising and stinting ourselves to give you a University education, if it is not to be used for the honour and glory of God?', his father repeated.
> 'Why, that it may be used for the honour and glory of man, father.'

Angel is speaking here with Hardy's own voice, anticipating the world of *Jude the Obscure*.

9 *Jude the Obscure*

Hardy's last and most abused novel is, even today, one of the most undervalued. The contemporary critics hated it. 'It is simply one of the most objectionable books that we have ever read in any language whatsoever',[1] said the *New York Bookman*, in one of the milder comments, and the Bishop of Wakefield 'was so disgusted with its insolence and indecency'[2] that he threw it into the fire. The attacks were mainly concentrated on Hardy's attitudes to religion and marriage and on a few passages which were supposed to be obscene. The Christminster theme was largely overlooked in these reviews, although Edmund Gosse sneered 'does the novelist really think it was the duty of the heads of houses to whom Jude wrote his crudely pathetic letters to offer him immediately a fellowship?'[3] As Hardy himself said, when he came to look back on this painful period in the 1912 Postscript:

> The sad feature of the attack was that the greater part of the story – that which presented the shattered ideals of the two chief characters . . . was practically ignored.

Even nowadays, those who prefer to concentrate on Hardy's more 'idyllic' fiction find it a shock to their sensibilities. Douglas Brown speaks of its 'failure of total imaginative organisation'[4] and sums up:

> *Jude the Obscure* has deflected attention away from Hardy's most distinguished and personal contribution to the English novel, and towards a small part of his achievement . . . That part, however serious, is less distinguished, and it cannot stand comparison with the achievements of his greatest contemporaries.[5]

It seems a failure to Brown because it is not, like the earlier novels, based on rural society but begins with the flight from it:

The opening book of *Jude* is Hardy's finest narrative of a countryman's struggle towards the civic milieu: something needed to complete the pattern of his work ... It is a grim but necessary complement to the simpler, more affirmative novels.

My own view is that *Jude* is not only Hardy's greatest novel but also one of the very greatest in the language, a creative achievement on the same level as *Middlemarch, Great Expectations, The Rainbow* and *Wuthering Heights.* It is not an easy novel to understand even today, when we flatter ourselves on having got beyond the prejudices which blocked its acceptance with Hardy's first readers, but, when we do understand it, it speaks to our own condition more clearly than any other work of its time.

One reason for its unpopularity was its rejection of the earlier sunnier concept of nature which we find in *Under the Greenwood Tree.* Nature here is red in tooth and claw, based solely upon the survival of the fittest. 'Cruelty is the law pervading all nature and society', says Phillotson, 'and we can't get out of it if we would'. So Jude, 'a boy who could not himself bear to hurt anything' is forced to kill the pig for money, and the trapped rabbit to save it from pain. And the poor rabbit's situation 'caught in a gin ... bearing its torture' exactly parallels that of Jude and Sue in which 'the normal sex-impulses are turned into devilish domestic gins and springes to noose and hold back those who want to progress'. These traps are social as well as domestic – 'the social moulds civilisation fits us into have no more relation to our actual shapes than the conventional shapes of the constellations have to the real star-patterns'. Jude can no more escape from the consequences of his disastrous marriage than he can break out of his class and become a student at Christminster. It seems in the darkest moments as if the whole scheme of things is actively thwarting all human desires:

There is something external to us which says, 'You shan't!' First it said, 'You shan't learn!' Then it said, 'You shan't labour!' Now it says, 'You shan't love!'

If nature in general is so forbidding, it is not surprising that in its particular manifestation in the village home of Jude's childhood it should seem bleak and repellent. The action takes place in several different parts of Wessex, linked by the railways which have now become a familiar feature of life, but there are only two real emotional poles, Christminster and Marygreen, the great university city and the obscure village in the countryside twenty miles away. In the opening chapters Jude is a typical agricultural child, following a traditional children's vocation, one of the 'boys who in lone wheat-fields scare the rooks'[6] whom Matthew Arnold saw as part of the landscape round Oxford. The farmer he works for, 'the great Troutham' is a petty tyrant very like Groby in *Tess*, who beats him for not being harsh enough to the birds. The whole field has 'only the quality of a work-ground' for Jude; agricultural work of this kind is not life-enhancing but negative, as he would much rather be at school. His deepest reaction is 'how ugly it is here!' for the landscape is utterly different from Talbothays or from the Hintock woods:

> The fresh harrow-lines seemed to stretch like the channellings in a piece of new corduroy, lending a meanly utilitarian air to the expanse, taking away its gradations, and depriving it of all history.

The field does possess a history, in fact, but it is not an inspiring one:

> Under the hedge which divided the field from a distant plant-ation girls had given themselves to lovers who would not turn their heads to look at them by the next harvest; and in that ancient corn-field many a man had made love-promises to a woman at whose voice he had trembled by the next seed-time after fulfilling them in the church adjoining.

This glimpse into the village's sexual mores seems to fore-shadow Jude's destiny; his seduction and 'coarse conjugal life' with Arabella – the pigbreeder's daughter who is a natural development from Suke Damson and the Amazons in *Tess*, and who seems to be the *reductio ad absurdum* of the stereotyped 'pure' country girl.

Jude and Sue, the children of broken marriages, have each lived in Marygreen for years but neither really belongs there, Jude having been 'deposited by the carrier from a railway station southward, one dark evening' – rather like his own son later on in the book. Their ancestors are buried there but they know virtually nothing about them, except that one of them was hanged on a gibbet nearby. Any feeling of continuity with the past has been shattered:

Many of the thatched and dormered dwelling-houses had been pulled down of late years, and many trees felled on the green.

Even the church has been demolished by 'a certain obliterator of historic records' and an ugly new substitute raised in its place.

Situated as he is, with no close family or local ties, it is absolutely necessary for the boy to attach himself to a tradition. Christminster comes to fill this place in his mind years before he has seen it; it is represented in his imagination only by hearsay and vague blurs of light. He heroically teaches himself Latin and Greek and theology in the hope of being recognised and valued there at some unspecified date. At the same time he is training to be a stone-mason, a trade which Hardy regards at least as highly as his studies:

He was a handy man at his trade, an all-round man, as artisans in country towns are apt to be. In London the man who carves the boss or knob of leafage declines to cut the fragment of moulding which merges in that leafage, as if it were a degradation to do the second half of one whole.

Jude's work has a kind of wholeness and creativity which is really valuable; in his own way he is a genuine artist in stone. The same idea is emphasised when he goes to the yard, the 'little centre of regeneration' which shows how much the university is dependent on the labour of ordinary Christminster people; it is 'a centre of effort as worthy as that dignified by the name of scholarly study within the noblest of the colleges'. But this work also exposes him to the rain and cold weather which lead to his fatal illness:

Moving the blocks always used to strain me, and standing in trying draughts in buildings before the windows are in, always gave me colds, and I think that began the mischief inside.

Christminster exploits his labour without compunction while denying him any chance to develop his other talents. (But it would have been no better in Marygreen; people are exploited there, too, by Farmer Troutham and the quack Vilbert. The exploitation of urban building workers only takes on another form.)

Christminster in this book exists on three levels. It is partly the 'city of light' which Jude dreams about, and which in Arnold's quoted words 'keeps ever calling us to the true goal of all of us, to the ideal, to perfection'. Then there is the towns-people's Christminster, much older than the university, repre-sented by the shabby suburb of Beersheba and having a cynical attitude to the local establishment:

> Yes, 'tis a serious-minded place. Not but there's wenches in the streets o' nights . . .'

And finally there is the conventional Christminster as the outside world sees it; the Christminster of smart students, archaic processions, honorary degrees conferred on 'illustrious gents' who have done nothing to merit them, ceremony and pomp. The ritualistic element is especially important, for this is Oxford after the Tractarian movement, and the Anglo-Catholic sensi-bility is a crucial factor in determining the codes of morals pre-sented in this book. To Jude, coming up with his head filled with dead languages and no less dead theology, it is significant as 'a city in whose history such men as Newman, Pusey, Ward, Keble, loom so large'. This official and formal Christminster is an extension of ruling class consciousness; the place where its children are sent to absorb its own values of class exclusiveness, bookish scholasticism and a neurotic awareness of sin.* To Hardy its rituals are empty, and its codes so narrow as to become often actively cruel. 'A nest of commonplace schoolmasters', Sue calls it, 'whose characteristic is timid obsequiousness to tradition'. Jude cannot possibly break into this closed circle even though, in the beginning, his mind is imbued with what he takes to be its values. He only really becomes aware of the unbridgeable gap between the two Christminsters when he actually comes to work at the place of his dreams:

* The Oxford Movement was extraordinarily unaware of the needs of working-class people. Somerville records a visit to Oxford in which he saw a certain clergyman who 'was called Potato Dick . . . in consequence of his having spoken at some public meeting approvingly of five millions of the poor *rejoicing* on potatoes'.

Only a wall divided him from those happy young contempories of his with whom he shared a common mental life ...
Only a wall – but what a wall! ... He was as far from them
as if he had been at the antipodes. Of course he was. He was a
young workman in a white blouse, and with stone-dust in the
creases of his clothes; and in passing him they did not even see
him, or hear him, rather saw through him as through a pane of
glass at their familiars beyond.

Hardy uses the same imagery to describe the situation of people
living in back streets behind the colleges:

The little houses were darkened to gloom by the high collegiate
buildings, within which life was so far removed from that of
the people in the lane as if it had been on opposite sides of
the globe; yet only a thickness of wall divided them.

The university lives on the labour of ordinary people, while
coldly denying their human reality. Jude understands this only
after the wreck of his hopes:

He saw that his destiny lay not with these, but among the
manual toilers in the shabby purlieu which he himself occupied, unrecognised as part of the city at all by its visitors and
panegyrists, yet without whose denizens the hard readers could
not read nor the high thinkers live.

These are the people who work on the crumbling college
fabrics and relax in the seedy taverns of Beersheba, who gather
to watch the processions and are kept in order by the police.
They are no less real for being unacknowledged in the formal
history of Christminster:

He only heard in part the policeman's further remarks, having
fallen into thought on what struggling people like himself had
stood at that Crossway, whom nobody ever thought of now.
It had more history than the oldest college in the city. It was
literally teeming, stratified, with the shades of human groups,
who had met there for tragedy, comedy, farce; real enactments
of the intensest kind ... These struggling men and women
before him were the reality of Christminster, though they knew
little of Christ or Minster. That was one of the humours of
things. The floating population of students and teachers, who

did know both in a way, were not Christminster in a local sense at all.

Jude's first impression of Sue is as part of the tradition – he pictures her becoming his 'companion in Anglican worship'. On first seeing her in the ecclesiastical shop he reflects: 'a sweet, saintly, Christian business, hers!' Of course this impression is totally false; Sue is a sceptic who designs church texts for a living while keeping her employers in the dark about her real sympathies. Like all of Hardy's characters who do useless work for which they are unsuited she is to this extent a sham, inauthentic (Jude in his later years reacts strongly against ecclesiastical work.) From this inauthenticity follows a similar inauthenticity of feelings; she plays with both Jude and Phillotson and has no convictions strong enough to stand up to a shock. Hardy calls her 'an epicure in emotions'. Like other neurotic women in his novels, and like Angel, she derives pleasure from self-torture, as Jude finally realises when he accuses her of 'indulging in the luxury of the emotion raised by an affected belief'.

Hardy said in the original Preface that the novel was about 'a deadly war waged between flesh and spirit', a definition which is slightly too compressed because Jude is shown continually trying to reconcile the two claims. Like Tess, he is a strong and authentic person who is helplessly trapped between two sexual partners, one over-sensual and one over-spiritual. Arabella stands for the flesh. Unlike Sue she is completely genuine in her crude way (her job as a barmaid, doling out the strong drink which incapacitates Jude, is a splendid expression of her personality). She only loses this genuineness when she reappears, like Alec, thinly disguised as a convert, and she quickly abandons this when she sees that religion is difficult to combine with sex. Sue, on the other hand, is pushed by religion into a state where her natural frigidity is intensified into a hysterical rejection of sexual fulfilment. 'We should mortify the flesh – the terrible flesh.' But sacrificing the flesh, Hardy saw, also means sacrificing the intellect. Angel ruins his marriage because he is in the grip of conventional views about chastity and the double standard. Sue rejects Jude and forces herself into Phillotson's bed because her intellect has broken and she no longer has the courage to be happy in a socially unorthodox way.

Hardy's view of marriage was so widely misrepresented at the time that it is worth quoting his own definition from the 1912 Preface:

My opinion . . . is . . . that a marriage should be dissolvable as soon as it becomes a cruelty to either of the parties, being then essentially and morally no marriage.

And Sue says to Phillotson, 'For a man and woman to live on intimate terms when one feels as I do is adultery, in any circumstances, however legal'. This, and the whole tenor of his earlier work, should make it clear that Hardy was attacking, not permanent and loving relationships, but the profound misconceptions which made marriage an institution or sacrament unrelated to human needs.

Although his preoccupation with mistaken marriages dates from very early in his career, he had solved it, up to *The Woodlanders*, in the conventional manner, as we have seen, by making the unwanted partners die. His last three novels show a much greater realism and freedom from literary stereotypes, a recognition of the new divorce laws and an awareness that these are nevertheless futile while people retain a false conception of human relationships. The protagonists in these novels are committed to utterly incongruous marriages whose consequences remain with them till the end of their lives. Tess (though legally married to Angel) is made to feel that Alec is her 'husband in nature'; she can only break this tie by killing him and thereby bringing about her own death. Sue is also reduced to the point of wanting Phillotson to die, but both he and Arabella live on whereas Jude dies, and Sue will never find peace again 'till she's as he is now'.

In a sense it is the official Christminster, the microcosm of a false society, which kills them; just as it kills the children. Little Time, though his father dreams of making him a student, is not impressed by the university. 'Are the great old houses gaols?' His attitude is partly a total rejection of life which can only be paralleled in the darkest of Hardy's fiction; it is as if he had had a prophetic glimpse into the next twenty-five years when he spoke of 'the coming universal wish not to live'. But in fact the suicide is much less closely related to Hardy's metaphysical preoccupations than to the actual unavailing struggle to find a way of subsisting in Christminster. The shabby family trails round trying to find lodgings and is told 'we don't let where there are children', and yet another child is coming 'to bring us all into *more* trouble', as it inevitably seems to the little boy. For this was the common situation of Victorian working-class families; the great questions facing them were how to provide for the vast numbers of unwanted children and what the future of these children would be. Trying to answer these questions, Tess prostitutes herself and little Time decides that he and his generation had better not live. It is striking a familiar note: 'Let the day perish wherein I was born.'

Official Christminster is not concerned with what happens to Jude and his family. Outside the house where the children die two clergymen are talking, not about them, but about 'the eastward position' (for altars). 'Good God – the eastward position', Jude says, 'and all creation groaning!' This is the most extreme example of the separation between the official language of Christminster and the language of ordinary human need. It sparks off Jude's final complete disillusionment with the attitudes he once revered:

> The theologians, the apologists, and their kin the meta-physicians, the high-handed statesmen, and others, no longer interest me. All that has been spoilt for me by the grind of stern reality.

Sue, however, reacts by using this false, ritualistic-religious language to channel her feelings of grief and remorse. The sense of sin, the dogma of indissoluble marriage, the belief in a punishing God which are nourished by Christminster all combine to drive her hysterically into sacrificing Jude and herself. Phillotson realises this and uses it for his own advantage:

> She's affected by Christminster sentiment and teaching. I can see her views on the indissolubility of marriage well enough, and I know where she got them.

The only apparent alternative to Christminster is Marygreen, where Jude goes back for his last meeting with Sue. But any sense he ever had of belonging there has been almost destroyed:

He himself went further into the church. Everything was new, except a few pieces of carving preserved from the wrecked old fabric, now fixed against the new walls. He stood by these: they seemed akin to the perished people of that place who were his ancestors and Sue's.

The church, the symbol of their separation, offers only a false shelter. He goes out, exposing himself to the rain, like Giles, this time with the deliberate intention of killing himself:

There are cold spots up and down Wessex in autumn and winter weather; but the coldest of all when a north or east wind is blowing is the crest of the down by the Brown House... Here in the teeth of the north-east wind and rain Jude now pursued his way.

Nature and man-made civilisation are equally destructive. After this there is nothing left for him but to die in the midst of the traditional Christminster celebrations, the Remembrance games.

By this time his original ideal of Christminster seems undermined beyond redemption. In so far as this ideal was conventional, it has indeed been destroyed by the juxtaposition of empty Christminster traditions with the reality of Christminster working-class life. But there is a third level on which Christminster resolves the contradiction – the dream-university which means, essentially, whatever ordinary people want it to mean. This university can only exist in the future, as Jude realises when he is dying:

When we were at our own best, long ago – when our minds were clear, and our love of truth fearless – the time was not ripe for us! Our ideas were fifty years too soon to be any good to us.

Yet it is also built into the actual university, as Sue tells him:

You are one of the very men Christminster was intended for when the colleges were founded; a man with a passion for learning, but no money, or opportunities, or friends. But you were elbowed off the pavement by the millionaires' sons.

This is why Jude retorts to the man who tells him that 'such places be not for such as you – only for them with plenty o' money': 'There you are wrong. They are for such ones!' And Jude, unlike Sue, never surrenders in his mind to the system. He tells her, 'I *would* have died game!' – and he does. His speech to the crowd of artisans expresses his final conviction:

> It was my poverty and not my will that consented to be beaten. It takes two or three generations to do what I tried to do in one.

Humanity, then, is not faced solely by a 'coming universal wish not to live'. It is rather confronted with a choice of possibilities, and Jude's ideal may well be stronger than the little boy's sense of damnation. It is an ideal of a society of integrated human beings, in which spirit and flesh, intellectual and physical labour, can be fused into a harmonious whole. Asking Clym's question, 'Wherefore is light given to him that is in misery?' on his deathbed, he knows that it is because his task was to reach out to the future. Jude dies, but the ideal is not destructible. Years later, in the 1912 Preface, Hardy wrote:

> I was informed that some readers thought ... that when Ruskin College was subsequently founded it should have been called the College of Jude the Obscure.

It was a token of the kind of society to which Hardy looked, not back, but forward, into our own struggling world.

Conclusion

We have seen that the crisis in rural society was not a new one, although it grew sharper in the years between Hardy's birth and the end of the century. During this time a number of forces coalesced to make society primarily industrial and to drive many thousands of labourers into leaving the land. This meant that the countryside, and the character of its people, changed very much in order to adapt to the new conditions. The basic facts are recorded in the censuses of the time and in Royal Commission reports. These are given substance by the studies, memoirs and novels which have been looked at here.

There were two traditions of English rural writing. The more conventional was centred on the stereotype of a changeless Arcadia, inhabited by a race of 'peasants' who were happy precisely because they were limited, and who could therefore be patronised even while they were being praised – 'the pitiable dummy known as Hodge'.

After the depressions and during the rise of industrialism a whole school of thought saw this Arcadia threatened by new and frightening social pressures which were destroying the old rural civilisation. But although the sense of a crisis was sharper, it was not a new thing. Thomas More had expressed the same fear three centuries earlier when he wrote in *Utopia*:

> Your sheep that were wont to be so meek and tame, and so small eaters, now, as I hear say, be become so great devourers and so wild, that they eat up, and swallow down the very men themselves. They consume, destroy and devour whole fields, houses and cities . . . they throw down houses; they pluck down towns, and leave nothing standing but only the church to be made a sheephouse.

Goldsmith's *Deserted Village* (1769), written well before industrialism had become a force to be reckoned with, spoke about an exodus in very similar terms:

> A time there was, ere England's griefs began,
> When every rood of ground maintained its man . . .
> But times are altered, trade's unfeeling train
> Usurp the land, and dispossess the swain . . .
> These, far departing, seek a kinder shore,
> And rural mirth and manners are no more.

The real causes of rural depopulation and suffering are to be found in a longer and more general history, and are rooted in the nature of rural society itself. They were not suddenly imported by Free Trade or the growth of towns (which, as we have seen, the labourers tended to regard as liberating influences) but had existed, in varying forms, from the earliest times. The alternative, less easily appealing tradition, of country writing, reveals the true nature of the England into which Hardy and his predecessors were born; a society which included illiteracy and illegitimacy; starvation wages, unemployment, exploitation and fear.

This realistic tradition had been steadily building up, since at least the eighteenth century. It is there in the early verse of the labourer-poet Stephen Duck (1705–56):

> Let those who feast at ease on dainty Fare
> Pity the Reapers, who their Feasts prepare:
> For Toils scarce ever ceasing press us now;
> Rest never does, but on the Sabbath show;
> And barely that our Masters will allow.
> Think what a painful life we daily lead;
> Each morning early rise, go late to Bed;
> Nor, when asleep, are we secure from Pain;
> We then perform our labours o'er again.
> Our mimic Fancy ever restless seems;
> And what we act awake, she acts in Dreams.

The pastoral tradition is explicitly challenged by Crabbe in *The Village*:

> I grant indeed that fields and flocks have charms
> For him that grazes and for him that farms;
> But when amid such pleasing scenes I trace
> The poor laborious natives of the place,
> And see the mid-day sun, with fervid ray,
> On their bare heads and dewy temples play;

> While some, with feebler heads and fainter hearts,
> Deplore their fortune, yet sustain their parts;
> Then shall I dare these real ills to hide
> In tinsel trappings of poetic pride?

In Wordsworth, elements of this realism are combined with a philosophical attachment to Nature as the source of innocence and truth. In John Clare (1793–1864) there is a comparable fusion of realistic observation and recognition of the transforming power of poetry:

> While threshing in the dusty barn
> Or squashing in the ditch to earn
> A pittance that would scarce allow
> One joy to smooth my sweating brow
> Where drop by drop would chase and fall
> Thy presence triumphed over all.

This presence is poetry, incongruous in the village which he knows too well to idealise:

> Bred in a village full of strife and noise,
> Old senseless gossips, and blackguarding boys,
> Ploughmen and threshers, whose discourses led
> To nothing more than labour's rude employs,
> 'Bout work being slack, and rise and fall of bread
> And who were like to die, and who were like to wed.

This kind of recognition was important, but afterwards came a critical period of transition from this kind of verse to the more extended observation of the novel. We have seen the extent to which much early rural fiction was determined by older stereotypes, or by the limitation of its attention to the problems of the landowning class. We noticed George Eliot's difficulties when she came to extend the social range of this fiction. My central argument is that Hardy is the first writer to achieve the necessary range and realism of the novel of English country life. But to understand this achievement, it was necessary to look, not only at the literary tradition, but at the important body of observations and factual accounts which indicate the deepening recognition of reality in his own generation and in that immediately preceding it.

This work, as we saw, was a matter of direct observation, of people recording, not stereotypes, but the facts which they saw and knew. This does not mean that they saw everything there was to see; for example, most of them seemed quite unaware of the 'interesting and better-informed class' which was so important to Hardy, and saw the country poor as an undifferentiated mass, 'the typical and unvarying Hodge'. It is also important to remember that they wrote in different parts of the country, and that conditions varied very widely from region to region; indeed much of the most important social history of rural England is essentially regional. But by going through this enormous body of material one can establish a more precise sense of the actualities of English country life, and of its representative literature, as a necessary preliminary to the detailed study of Hardy.

Some of these writers were working within the context of a wider argument; Somerville and Caird were advocating Free Trade and scientific farming, Marx and Engels a Socialist revolution. Another very common attitude was that a return to feudalism was the only solution; there are traces of this in Howitt as well as in several contemporary novelists. Jefferies, on the other hand, was a born countryman who went on throughout his life writing about the countryside for its own sake. In the course of accumulating a vast mass of knowledge about the social and physical structure of rural Wiltshire, he gradually formulated a philosophy of his own – at first commonplace, later startlingly revolutionary – based on these facts.

After 1870, commentators tended to concentrate on the exodus of the labourers. Arch, who was partly responsible for it, believed that the people would only come back to the land if they were given a share in its ownership, with an absolute security of homes and of jobs. Hardy and Jefferies strongly supported this, and even Haggard, who generally saw things from the farmers' viewpoint, thought that allotments or small-holdings were the one way of stemming the tide. But it was nearly impossible to achieve this aim, and most village people eventually gave it up in despair. By the end of the century the exodus had gone far enough for Haggard to feel (paving the way for several modern interpretations of Hardy) that English rural society was on the verge of collapse.

Haggard's survey resembles some of the earlier accounts in being written largely as propaganda. He was so convinced of the evils of town life and the necessity for a return to a society based upon agriculture that he even disliked popular education, which most other writers considered essential. Cobbett had also disliked it, for different reasons, as Howitt noted:

> The labourer, to his fancy, ought to be nothing but a stout, plodding animal, well fed on bread, beef and beer.[1]

Whereas Howitt and most of the writers who followed him thought that education would make the working classes more content with their situation, Haggard, who shared the farmers' point of view, knew that it was making the labourers discontented and accelerating their drift from the land.

There were many other differences between the critics. Everybody could agree about the evils of bad housing, or immorality, but not about such things as the influence of towns. Were they really centres of corruption or did they have a healthy effect on the villages round them, like the industrial cities in the north, or like Swindon? Was agricultural machinery a liberating force or – like the threshing-machine in *Tess* – a new means of enslavement? Were the farmers or labourers the greater sufferers from the depression? Was it right for children to work on the land, like the boy Jude, or to be educated and move away?

Writing 'The Dorsetshire Labourer' in 1883, before his major novels had appeared, Hardy answered some of these questions with a greater sensitivity than most other critics had shown. He was keenly aware of the facts of rural living through his own experience and that of his neighbours; as we have seen the social history of nineteenth-century Dorset was the material on which the Wessex Novels are based. This is why he concentrated so intently on the economics of Henchard's downfall, or the social and cultural forces which destroy Giles and Tess. When he tried to evaluate the changes which were taking place in his county, and to suggest what was best for its future, he found that no simple solutions were possible. He wanted to preserve the consciousness of local traditions and history, and (like George Bourne) the villages' old crafts and skills. But he also wanted the countryside to share in the national progress, and he had no illusions about the recent or remote past. Also (unlike Haggard) he blamed the farmers for dispossessing the class which had done most to keep an indigenous village culture alive.

As a novelist, he showed the same reluctance to give easy answers. The tradition of country fiction available to him reflected many of the same distortions as the non-fiction we have described. Mrs Tonna, Disraeli and Kingsley were all writing as propagandists, the first two from a definitely anti-industrial standpoint. Jefferies found it difficult to write novels which were fully distinguished from journalism or to escape from conventional 'romance'. In *The Dewy Morn*, the figure of the nature-goddess Felise jostles uneasily with the detailed descriptions of petty tyranny in a small village. *Amaryllis* is a more consistent work, but it is outside the mainstream of the English novel because of its formlessness.

In most of these novels, as we have seen, the majority of country people were treated as mere lay figures and their problems handled in a very superficial way. Holme Lee's wretchedly bad novel *A Poor Squire*, written as late as 1882, can find only this to say about the depression:

'It's God's judgements is at the bottom of all the troubles and losses that have befallen us these six or seven years back.' The tears had come into the old woman's eyes with the recollection of these troubles and losses – a serious catalogue – but they dried as quickly under the parching, unsympathetic cheerfulness of Lady Loftus, who assured her that a more favourable season was the general expectation of the country.[2]

The poor are here shown as pious, resigned and with absolutely no comprehension (any more than the author herself) of the real problems the countryside faced.

Margaret Woods, as we saw, was working within a tradition of far greater economic and sexual realism. But for all its good qualities, *A Village Tragedy* is written from an essentially alienated position. In this story of the girl from outside the village who is destroyed by its ethos, the whole tone is rather like an anthropological study and there can therefore be no full identification with the ordinary people who are ostensibly the subject of the book.

George Eliot was the first great novelist to write about the problems of country life seriously. There are several limitations in her treatment; her novels are usually set some way back in the past and this historical distancing mirrors her tendency to idealise old-fashioned village life in *Silas Marner* and *Adam Bede*. Yet these two novels convincingly describe the 'intermediate class' which so preoccupied Hardy, and make it the moral centre of the action. The critic in the *Saturday Review* summarised the greatness of her achievement by commenting that she had made ordinary people seem real for the first time. In *Middlemarch* her method is quite different; farmers and labourers are only glimpsed on the fringe of the action and the focus is upon members of the educated classes like Dorothea and Lydgate, who are struggling in their own sphere to do good to mankind.

The closest parallel in Hardy's work is Clym Yeobright, who is very much the same kind of frustrated idealist. But in Hardy's novels the teacher-figure is comparatively rare. Instead he tended to concentrate, to an increasing extent, on the people who needed to be taught, the despised and rejected, all those who had been considered unworthy of a place in literature up to that time. 'There is no part of the population for whom so little is done, and of which so little is thought',[3] William Howitt had written, and half a century later Haggard echoed his judgement. 'The farm labourer is looked down upon . . . and consequently looks down upon himself.'[4] Yet this class was not to be despised; it had produced men like Joseph Arch and Alexander Somerville, and Hardy knew from his own day-to-day experience that the uncouth and ineducable 'Hodge' was a caricature. Jefferies understood the same thing and said it over and over again; in 'Country Literature' he pleaded for the villages to be supplied with the best books available and in *The Dewy Morn* ridiculed the idea of giving the half-starved labourers bad pictures. The contradiction is only a superficial one. 'Is not art rather in the man than on the wall?'

> Up in the north they say there is a district where the labourers spend their idle hours in cutting out and sticking together fiddles. I do not care twopence for a fiddle as a fiddle; but still I think if a labouring man coming home from plough, and exposure to rough wind, and living on coarse fare, can still have spirit enough left to sit down and patiently carve out bits of maple wood and fit them together into a complete and tunable fiddle, then he must have within him some of the true idea of art, and that fiddle is in itself a work of art.[5]

This is very much the same as Hardy's feeling about the music of the Mellstock choir. He shared Jefferies' dislike of the idea of art for art's sake, 'on the wall'; this is why he was hostile to Christminster, and to intellectuals like Fitzpiers and Angel who are lacking in human response. The kind of creation which he valued was spontaneous, an expression of the whole personality; the woodland skills of Giles and Marty are 'art in the man'. His concern with human wholeness led him to feel (like Ruskin) that men cannot produce good work of any kind unless they are themselves good. Hardy's objection to Victorian rural society was that it denied and inhibited human potential and reduced people to wage-slaves whose work was deprived of human meaning and joy.

This extension of range is Hardy's most evident contribution to the novel. In his works, the people of the English villages become at last something more than a background to the action; in his later novels, in fact, they became its centre. It is common for critics to talk about Hardy's 'rustic chorus', whose function, apparently, is to supply gnomic comments on the real, important action. But the word chorus is totally misplaced, as the function of these people is much more vital. In *Under the Greenwood Tree* they are the musicians who make up the centrally significant choir. In *Far from the Madding Crowd* and *The Mayor of Casterbridge* they represent the community in terms of which the characters and destinies of individual persons are defined and worked out. In *The Return of the Native* they are the magnet which draws Clym back to Egdon; it is through educating them that he wants to improve the world. But we have seen that this is the only Hardy novel in which the hero occupies the position of teacher. In his three final novels, his identification with the ordinary, uneducated or half-educated people is much more complete. Giles, the representative woodlander, is presented as a complete human contrast to the alienated aristocrat Fitzpiers. Tess is a representative of exploited and betrayed country girls. Jude is an 'obscure' working man struggling for the educational heritage which has for centuries been denied to his class. Towards the end, we glimpse the possibility of many thousands like him who will continue the struggle. Hardy is less interested in the exceptional human being (as Kingsley, Disraeli and George Eliot had all been) than in finding qualities and potentialities for good among what were known as the common people. It is the 'exceptional' individuals (like Fitzpiers, Angel and Sue) who are ultimately seen as failures, because their intellectual awareness is not matched by an awareness of human and social responsibilities. The stress is rather on what the more ordinary, more warm-hearted people (like Giles, Marty, Tess and Jude) *could* have achieved, if they had not been frustrated.

There are flaws in even the greatest of the novels, of course. Just as his attempts to write 'well' often clashed with his attempts to write naturally, so the new things he was trying to say frequetly conflicted with the conventional demands of the Victorian plot. *Desperate Remedies* was written because Meredith had told him that the public expected intrigue in a novel, and as late as *The Woodlanders* some elements of the conventional novel persist. It was only when he had decided that he no longer cared what the public thought that he produced his two lonely and maligned masterpieces, *Tess* and *Jude*.

This study of rural England and its literature must close with an emphasis on the complexity of Hardy's achievement and attitude. Complex they were bound to be, because it was a complex situation and because Hardy was too intelligent and too close to the problem to come up with slogans for answers. He could not say, 'Back to the land!', like Haggard, because he was too well aware of the harm done by centuries of near-feudal tyranny, but at the same time it hurt him to see what was best in provincial and village culture decline. He did not want to see country people become part of 'the depraved crowds of a city slum',[6] but neither did he want them to go on digging up swedes in the rain for a pittance, without education or human respect. Christminster is hardly a typical industrial town but his attitude to it is significant; the city, like the university, can become a force for good even if it is not one at present. So can the countryside, if it is organised for the sake of the men and women who live and work there.

In the last resort Hardy had no slogans, only values. It was not possible for him to write propaganda, only to record the facts as he felt them and knew them. There is a tradition that the characters in his books 'were all real people', and we have seen how these novels were built out of the actual situation in rural Wessex; real villages, real towns, real history. Hardy's greatness lies in the fact that he transformed into literature a whole area of central human experience which had never yet been explored. In one sense, his work was the climax of the realistic tradition of country writing which we have traced from the beginnings. In another sense, it was its transformation. For the whole problem must be seen as part of a prolonged cultural crisis.

The achievement of a growing realism, centred in the lives of ordinary people, was much more than a matter of documentation. It required an imaginative re-creation, from the inside, of what for generations had been the thwarted humanity, the inarticulate fullness of emotion, of such men and women as Jude and Tess. Nor, as we have seen, was this any simple creation of lay figures. His first attempts can be seen in that way, and of course, if the rural characters could be isolated some of the most difficult human questions need not arise. It was not only an existing but a growing and struggling humanity that Hardy wished to describe. From *The Return of the Native* on, the recognition of simple humanity is extended and complicated by questions of education, mobility, and aspiration, beyond the customary rural ways. This is what I have seen as the highest kind of realism, and Hardy's permanent achievement as a novelist. To see what was really there, beyond the conventional stereotypes, was difficult enough. But to see what was moving and growing, not only within individuals, but within a whole society on the edge of further difficult change and growth, required an imaginative insight of the highest order: a penetration to what was potential yet thwarted, active but though slighted, enduring, in late nineteenth-century England. In this final recognition Hardy became, not only our most important country novelist, but a major writer whose insights and concerns are still at the centre of our experience.

Appendix—
Population Movements in some
Dorsetshire Parishes 1840–1900

It is worth while to take a look at the population movements within a cross-section of Dorsetshire parishes to get some idea of what was meant by the common talk of a flight from the countryside. Take for example Cranborne, Bere Regis, and Fordington, which were named by the *Victoria County History* as three of the five Dorset parishes where housing was worst. Cranborne was described by Somerville in 1843 as the centre of an area 'where many people are unemployed, where all are ill fed and ill paid, and where many starve until sent off ten miles to the Union Workhouse'.[1] At that time, according to the 1841 census, the popuation was 2551. For most of the rest of the century, it dwindled steadily, and fifty years later, when Hardy portrayed it as the scene of Tess's seduction, he described it as 'Chaseborough, a decayed market-town'. The figure recorded in the 1891 census was 2511 – a drop of forty people in fifty years.

A roughly similar movement took place in Bere Regis – Hardy's Kingsbere and the seat of the illustrious Turberville family, which he called a 'half-dead townlet' and 'a little, one-eyed, blinking sort o' place' in *Tess*. Its population was 1169 in 1841; it fluctuated and sometimes reached slightly higher levels during the next sixty years but was down to just over a thousand in 1901.

The parish of Fordington St George, which was really a small village tagged on to the east end of Dorchester, was the nearest thing Dorset had to an industrial slum. In *The Mayor of Casterbridge*, set in the early forties, Hardy describes it under the name of Durnover and gives a detailed account of life in Mill Street (Mixen Lane) – the most wretched district in the place, which 'lay close to the open country . . . commanding a view across the moor of airy uplands and corn-fields, and mansions of the great'. The worst part was later pulled down, but at the time which Hardy was writing about, and which he remembered from childhood, it was a violent and vicious slum. It was also the most unhealthy place in the whole county – 'In a block of cottages up an alley there might have been erected an altar to disease in years gone by'.

These conditions were brought to light by a remarkable man who was the vicar of Fordington for over fifty years, the Reverend Henry Moule (1801–80). He was the original of Angel Clare's father and Hardy described him as 'a Dorset-shire parson whose name still lives enshrined in the hearts of thousands'.² During the terrible cholera epidemic of 1854 Moule fought the disease almost single-handed and at the same time wrote a series of eight public letters to Prince Albert de-manding government action to clear up the slums. These letters give a vivid and faithful picture of the normal conditions of life in the area surrounding Mill Street. The district was centred on a pond where the filth of the whole neighbourhood was dumped, though people drew most of their water from it 'for washing, and sometimes even for culinary purposes'.³ In Mill Street itself 'the floors of the houses lie considerably below the highest elevation of the pond, and some of them even below its bed'. The cottages were crowded out; Moule found one where 'nine per-sons were sleeping in the single bedroom' and sanitation was primitive or non-existent. 'The filth and vice involved in this one feature of the case', he wrote, 'can scarcely be conceived'. In these circumstances, once the cholera germ had been brought to the district, it was not surprising that it spread so rapidly or that there were so many deaths.

Yet this slum always had a much higher population than any other parish in Dorchester and the records show that it went on climbing throughout the century. After 1871 it grew by leaps and bounds, by almost a thousand per decade, until 1901 it stood at over six thousand. What was the reason for this astound-ing increase at a time when many Dorsetshire parishes were dwindling and other parishes, inside Dorchester itself, standing still? Hardy explained some of its attractiveness in *The Mayor of Casterbridge*:

Mixen Lane was the Adullam of all the surrounding villages. It was the hiding place of those who were in distress, and in debt, and trouble of every kind. Farm-labourers and other peasants, who combined a little poaching with their farming, and a little brawling and bibbing with their poaching, found themselves sooner or later in Mixen Lane. Rural mechanics too idle to mechanise, rural servants too rebellious to serve, drifted or were forced into Mixen Lane.

In fact, in a predominantly rural district, Fordington had the same kind of pull as an industrial town. Moule said that the bulk of the inhabitants were 'mechanics, labourers, and paupers from this and many other parishes'. Not all of them were petty criminals, of course. Hardy made it clear that many of those driven into Fordington were the dispossessed copyholders with whom he sympathised more than any other class:

Amid so much that was bad needy respectability also found a home. Under some of the roofs abode pure and virtuous souls whose presence there was due to the iron hand of necessity, and to that alone. Families from decayed villages – families of that once bulky, but now nearly extinct, section of village society called 'liviers', or lifeholders – copyholders and others whose roof-trees had fallen for some reason or other, compelling them to quit the rural spot that had been their home for generations–came here, unless they chose to lie under a hedge.

Other Dorset parishes which grew during these sixty years were Weymouth with its tourist trade, Swanage, the centre of the Purbeck marble industry (where quarrying was revived for the needs of church restorers), and Portland which had a very flourishing stone trade. The increase here was particularly large; from just under three thousand in 1841 it multiplied to over fifteen thousand in 1901. According to the *Victoria County History* its growth in the nineties could be 'attributed mainly to the construction of the breakwater and to other Government works'.[4]

These instances of growth were, however, exceptional in a county where any kind of industry was scattered and rare. Other towns which had been quite large by Dorset standards tended to show a dramatic fall in population – Beaminster, portrayed in *Tess* as Emminster, the home of the Clare family; Puddletown,

Hardy's Weatherbury; Cerne Abbas, whose population was more than halved. Marnhull, which appears as Tess's native village Marlott, suffered less badly because it had a quarry and a minor building stone industry. Its population fell from 1464 to 1286, a definite but comparatively small drop.

However, the typical unit in the Dorsetshire countryside was not a village of this size but one with less than five hundred inhabitants. Such villages have been estimated as comprising more than 70 per cent of all parishes in the county in 1901.[5] Statistics for a few of them will give some idea of the underlying pattern. Wool – the Wellbridge of *Tess* and another ancient Turberville seat – had a population of 505 in 1841. In 1901 it was 497 – just eight less. Other small villages declined rather more sharply – Minterne Magna, the Great Hintock of *The Woodlanders*; Okeford Fitzpaine, which appears in the same novel as Oakbury Fitzpiers, the former seat of the Fitzpiers family; Stinsford, where Hardy was born and which he rechristened Mellstock; Tolpuddle, where agricultural trade unionism had its baptism of fire.

The tendency in these villages was for the population to decline slowly but steadily after 1841, or else to reach a peak in 1851 or 1871 and to decline after that. The movements are very small but also very significant. They show that by the end of the century the population had fallen back to its 1841 level or, more commonly, to something distinctly lower. Very large losses were rare; it was more usual for Dorsetshire villages to dwindle slowly, or to remain nearly stagnant. But when we remember the great increase in national population during these sixty years it becomes apparent that the population of these villages stood still, when it would normally have been expected to grow. They were not depopulated, as is often loosely said, but the entire natural increase was creamed off by the people's compulsion or wish to migrate.

Table 5: Population of Dorset 1841–1901

1841	1851	1861	1871	1881	1891	1901
175,274	184,380	189,015	195,774	191,028	194,568	202,984

Table 6: Population of Dorchester by Parishes 1841–1901

	1841	1851	1861	1871	1881	1891	1901
All Saints	692	814	946	923	912	813	894
Holy Trinity	1354	1549	1601	1625	1565	1301	1178
St Peter's	1203	1150	1213	1307	1389	1372	1336
Fordington	2937	3147	3258	3277	4095	5076	6224

Table 7: Population of certain Dorset parishes, 1841–1901

	1841	1851	1861	1871	1881	1891	1901
Beaminster	3270	2832	2614	2585	2130	1915	1702
Bere Regis	1169	1242	1189	1253	1284	1144	1014
Cerne Abbas	1342	1343	1185	1164	925	834	643
Cranborne	2551	2737	2656	2562	2317	2511	2464
Marnhull	1464	1481	1444	1453	1396	1415	1286
Minterne Magna	354	396	380	352	322	339	306
Okeford Fitzpaine	675	643	685	701	602	557	600
Portland	2852	5195	8468	9907	10,061	9443	15,199
Puddletown	1168	1297	1241	1249	1175	1077	961
Stinsford	392	373	357	352	339	278	278
Swanage	1990	2139	2004	2151	2357	2674	3455
Tolpuddle	368	354	401	360	305	288	282
Weymouth	2669	2957	3515	3828	3630	3591	4497
Wool	505	545	590	602	509	521	497

All figures are taken from the census returns between 1841 and 1901 inclusive.

Notes

Introduction

1. F. E. Hardy, *The Later Years of Thomas Hardy* (London, 1930) p. 208.
2. For evidence, see L. Lerner and J. Holmstrom, *Thomas Hardy and his Readers* (London, 1968) p. 42.
3. *Saturday Review*, 29 May 1886, quoted in Lerner and Holmstrom, op. cit., p. 49.
4. *Cosmopolis*, January 1896, quoted in Lerner and Holmstrom, p. 121.
5. Douglas Brown, *Thomas Hardy* (London, 1954; rev. ed., 1961) p. 89.
6. Irving Howe, *Thomas Hardy* (London, 1968) p. 1.
7. A. J. Guerard, *Thomas Hardy* (London, 1949) pp. 17–18.
8. Brown, op. cit., p. 65.
9. Arnold Kettle, *Introduction to the English Novel* (London, 1953) II 54, 58.
10. John Holloway, *The Charted Mirror* (London, 1950) pp. 95–96.

Part One

Chapter 1

1. Sir James Caird, *English Agriculture in 1850–1* (London, 1852) p. 517.
2. Ibid., p. 511.
3. Ibid., p. 513.
4. Ibid., p. 518.
5. J. D. Chambers and G. E. Mingay, *The Agricultural Revolution 1750–1880* (London, 1966) p. 107.
6. F. M. L. Thompson, *English Landed Society in the Nineteenth Century* (London, 1963) p. 25.

7. C. S. Orwin and E. H. Whetham, *History of British Agriculture 1846–1914* (London, 1964) p. 48.
8. Thompson, op. cit., p. 27.
9. Orwin and Whetham, op. cit., p. 82.
10. Quoted by Lord Ernle, *English Farming Past and Present* (London, 1912) Appendix x.
11. Supplementary Report to the Royal Commission on the Housing of the Working Classes, 1884–5.
12. Joseph Arch, *Life* (London, 1898) p. 29.
13. See A. Peacock, *The Revolt of the Fields in East Anglia*, an 'Our History' pamphlet, 49/50, spring/summer 1968.
14. Orwin and Whetham, op. cit., p. 94.
15. Arch, op. cit., p. 67.
16. Quoted by Lady Warwick in her introduction to Arch's *Life*.
17. J. P. D. Dunbabin, 'The Revolt of the Field' in *Past and Present* (Nov. 1963) p. 70.
18. Chambers and Mingay, op. cit., p. 195.
19. Quoted by Arthur Clayden in *The Revolt of the Field* (London, 1874) p. 50.
20. Arch, op. cit., p. 96.
21. Ibid., p. 313.
22. Chambers and Mingay, op. cit., p. 197.
23. Quoted by Peacock, op. cit., p. 8.
24. Alfred Marshall (the Cambridge economist), quoted by Peacock, op. cit., p. 13.

Chapter 2

1. Mary Burrows, *Sketches of our Village* (Ipswich and London, 1852) p. 3. This includes several bad imitations of Goldsmith.
2. 'The Dorsetshire Labourer', in *Longman's Magazine* (July, 1883). Reprinted in Harold Orel, *Thomas Hardy's Personal Writings* (London, 1967).
3. Quotations are from Hardy's obituary of Barnes in the *Athenaeum* (16 Oct. 1886) and an essay on Barnes in *The English Poets* (London, 1918). Both are reprinted in Orel.

4. Francis Kilvert, *Diary 1870–79*, ed. William Plomer (London, 1938–40) II 441–2.
5. William Barnes, *Poems of Rural Life in the Dorset Dialect* (London, 1879).
6. William Howitt, *The Rural Life of England* (London, 1838).
7. William Howitt, *The Year-Book of the Country* (London, 1850).
8. Alexander Somerville, *The Whistler at the Plough* (Manchester, 1852).
9. Friedrich Engels, *Condition of the Working Class in England in 1844* (London, 1892), chap. 11, 'The Proletariat on the Land'.
10. Karl Marx, *Capital* (London, 1887) II 23, section E, 'The British Agricultural Proletariat'.
11. Henry Rider Haggard, *Rural England* (London, 1902).

Chapter 3

1. All three letters are reprinted in *The Toilers of the Field* (London, 1892).
2. *Victoria County History of Wiltshire* (London, 1959) IV 84.
3. Ibid., p. 77.
4. Quoted in Engels, op. cit.
5. Reprinted in *The Toilers of the Field*.
6. All these essays are reprinted in *The Hills and the Vale* ed. Edward Thomas (London, 1909).
7. *Hodge and his Masters* (London, 1880).
8. *The Scarlet Shawl* (London, 1874).
9. *Restless Human Hearts* (London, 1875).
10. *World's End* (London, 1877).
11. *Greene Ferne Farm* (London, 1880).
12. *The Dewy Morn* (London, 1884).
13. *After London* (London, 1885).
14. *Amaryllis at the Fair* (London, 1887).
15. 'Lives and Works of Richard Jefferies' *Scrutiny*, Mar. 1938, p. 435. This essay has been reprinted in *A Selection from Scrutiny*, ed. F. R. Leavis (Cambridge, 1968).
16. Brown, op. cit., pp. 142–3.
17. In *The Life of the Fields* (London, 1884).

18. In *The Open Air* (London, 1885).
19. 'Field Words and Ways', in *Field and Hedgerow* (London, 1889).
20. All these essays are in *Field and Farm* ed. S. J. Looker (London, 1957).

Chapter 4

1. *Saturday Review*, 13 Apr. 1861. Reprinted in Lerner and Holmstrom, *George Eliot and her Readers* (London, 1966).
2. Frances Trollope, *Town and Country* (London, 1848).
3. Mortimer Collins, *The Village Comedy* (London, 1878).
4. Margaret Oliphant, *A Country Gentleman and his Family* (London, 1886).
5. Cuthbert Bede, *Our New Rector* (London, 1861).
6. John Mills, *The Old English Gentleman* (London, 1854).
7. Holme Lee, *A Poor Squire* (London, 1881).
8. R. D. Blackmore, *Cripps the Carrier* (London, 1876).
9. Thomas Dolby, *Floreston* (London, 1839) p. 240.
10. 'Charlotte Elizabeth', *Helen Fleetwood* (London, 1841).
11. Benjamin Disraeli, *Coningsby* (London, 1844).
12. Charles Kingsley, *Yeast* (London, 1851).
13. Benjamin Disraeli, *Sybil* (London, 1845).
14. Marx and Engels, *The Communist Manifesto* (London, 1886).
15. Charles Kingsley, *Alton Locke* (London, 1852).
16. William Howitt, *The Hall and the Hamlet* (London, 1848).
17. William and Mary Howitt, *Stories of English and Foreign Life* (London, 1853).
18. William Howitt, *The Man of the People* (London, 1860).
19. William Howitt, *Woodburn Grange* (London, 1867).
20. Elizabeth Gaskell, *North and South* (London, 1855).
21. Elizabeth Gaskell, *Cranford* (London, 1853).
22. Elizabeth Gaskell, *Wives and Daughters* (London, 1866).
23. Anthony Trollope, *Doctor Thorne* (London, 1858).
24. F. E. Hardy, *Early Life of Thomas Hardy* (London, 1928) p. 129.
25. 'The Natural History of German Life', repr. in *Essays of George Eliot* (London, 1968).
26. George Eliot, *Felix Holt* (London, 1866).

27. George Eliot, *Scenes of Clerical Life* (Edinburgh, 1858).
28. George Eliot, *Adam Bede* (Edinburgh, 1859).
29. George Eliot, *The Mill on the Floss* (Edinburgh, 1860).
30. George Eliot, *Silas Marner* (Edinburgh, 1861).
31. George Eliot, *Middlemarch* (Edinburgh, 1871–3).
32. George Eliot, *Daniel Deronda* (Edinburgh, 1876).

Chapter 5

1. Edwin Waugh, *Poems and Lancashire Songs* (London, 1859) p. 101.
2. Royal Commission on the Employment of Children, Young Persons and Women in Agriculture (First Report, 1869) 1 x.
3. Ibid., p. 95.
4. 'Field-Faring Women', repr. in *The Toilers of the Field*.
5. Margaret Louisa Woods, *A Village Tragedy* (London, 1887).
6. W. L. Courtney, *The Feminine Note in Fiction* (London, 1904) p. 138.
7. Repr. in Lerner and Holmstrom, op. cit., p. 85.
8. Ibid., p. 81.
9. Interview with Raymond Blathwayt in *Black and White*, 27 Aug. 1892. Repr. in Lerner and Holmstrom, p. 90–7.
10. Arnold Kettle, *Introduction to the English Novel*, op. cit., 11 60.
11. Quoted in interview with Raymond Blathwayt, op. cit.
12. Arnold Kettle, *Hardy the Novelist* (Swansea, 1967). Should be read in full.

Part Two

Chapter 1

1. Hermann Lea, *Thomas Hardy's Wessex* (London, 1913) p. xvii.
2. General Preface to the Wessex Novels, repr. in Orel.
3. Haggard, op. cit., 1 257.
4. *Victoria County History of Dorset* (London, 1908) p. 275.
5. Caird, op. cit., p. 57.
6. H. C. Darby and R. W. Finn (*The Domesday Geography of South-West England* (Cambridge, 1967) p. 127.

7. *Victoria County History*, op. cit., p. 275.
8. Ibid., p. 281.
9. Haggard, 1 265.
10. *Victoria County History*, p. 284.
11. Somerville, op. cit., p. 91.
12. Ibid., p. 380.
13. Wilhelm Hasbach, *History of the English Agricultural Labourer* (London, 1908) p. 411.
14. Caird, p. 72.
15. Quoted in Haggard, 1 282.
16. Somerville, p. 27.
17. *Victoria County History*, p. 285.
18. Somerville, p. 32.
19. Ibid., p. 35.
20. This and all other quotations from Hardy in this chapter are taken from 'The Dorsetshire Labourer' unless otherwise stated. In February 1883 Longman's Magazine published the first of a series of articles 'in which the peasantry of different parts of the United Kingdom will be discussed by writers with special local knowledge'. Only five of these articles ever appeared, but the series was a distinguished one and included an essay by Jefferies on the Wiltshire labourers as well as Hardy's. The other articles, which are well worth reading, are about Ireland, Scotland and Wales.
21. Hasbach, op. cit., p. 412.
22. *Victoria County History*, p. 262.
23. John Saville, *Rural Depopulation in England and Wales 1851–1951* (London, 1957) p. 44.
24. Arch, op. cit., p. 100.
25. Dunbabin, op. cit., p. 68.
26. Haggard, op. cit., 1 268.
27. *Victoria County History*, p. 263.

Chapter 3

1. *Early Life*, op. cit., p. 81.
2. *Desperate Remedies* (London, 1871) VII.
3. Quotations from Brown in this chapter are from the section on *Under the Greenwood Tree* in *Thomas Hardy* (op. cit.).

Chapter 5

1. Quotations from Brown are from his section on the *Return of the Native* in *Thomas Hardy*.

Chapter 6

1. *Saturday Review*, 29 May 1886, repr. in Lerner and Holmstrom.
2. William Andrews, *Bygone England* (London, 1892) p. 199.
3. Sabine Baring-Gould, *In a Quiet Village* (London, 1900) p. 134.
4. Brown, op. cit., p. 64.
5. Ibid., p. 63.
6. Douglas Brown, *Hardy's Mayor of Casterbridge* (London, 1962) p. 31.

Chapter 7

1. Quotations from Brown in this chapter are from his section on *The Woodlanders* in Thomas Hardy.

Chapter 8

1. Howe, op. cit., p. 116.
2. Ibid., p. 114.
3. Brown, p. 91.
4. Barbara Kerr, *Bound to the Soil: A Social History of Dorset* (London, 1968) p. 124.
5. Ibid., p. 125.
6. Lerner and Holmstrom, p. 93.
7. Kettle, *Introduction to the English Novel*, op. cit., II 49.
8. Kerr, op. cit., p. 11.
9. Brown, op. cit., p. 94.
10. Roy Morrell, *Thomas Hardy: The Will and the Way* (Kuala Lumpur, 1965) p. 30.
11. Howe, op. cit., p. 122.
12. Ibid., p. 123.
13. Kettle, *Hardy the Novelist*, op. cit., p. 10.

Chapter 9

1. *New York Bookman*, Jan. 1896, repr. in Lerner and Holmstrom.
2. Letter to the *Yorkshire Post*, 8 June 1896, repr. in Lerner and Holmstrom.
3. *Cosmopolis*, Jan. 1896, repr. in Lerner and Holmstrom.
4. Brown, op. cit., p. 100.
5. Ibid., p. 90.
6. Matthew Arnold, *The Scholar Gypsy*.
7. Somerville, p. 138.

Conclusion

1. William Howitt, *The Man of the People* (London, 1860) II 263.
2. Holme Lee, *A Poor Squire* (London, 1882) I 160–1.
3. *Rural Life of England*, op. cit., I 155.
4. *Rural England*, op. cit., II 540.
5. *The Dewy Morn*, op. cit., II 239.
6. *The Woodlanders*.

Appendix

1. Somerville, p. 156.
2. Interview with Blathwayt, op. cit., in Lerner and Holmstrom, p. 94.
3. Henry Moule, *Paupers, Criminals and Cholera at Dorchester in 1854* (reprinted as a monograph, Guernsey, 1968).
4. *Victoria County History*, op. cit., p. 269 n.
5. Saville, op. cit., p. 72.

Select Bibliography

This consists of works read and consulted, including but not restricted to those cited in the text.

OUTLINE

A: Texts

   1. By Hardy
   2. By other writers

B: Secondary sources

   1. Studies of Hardy
   2. Studies of other nineteenth century writers on rural life
   3. Historical and related studies

A: *Texts*

1. Hardy, Thomas:
   Desperate Remedies (London, 1871).
   Under the Greenwood Tree (London, 1872).
   A Pair of Blue Eyes (London, 1873).
   Far from the Madding Crowd (London, 1874).
   The Hand of Ethelberta (London, 1876).
   The Return of the Native (London, 1878).
   The Trumpet-Major (London, 1880).
   A Laodicean (London, 1881).
   Two on a Tower (London, 1882).
   The Mayor of Casterbridge (London, 1886).
   The Woodlanders (London, 1887).
   A Group of Noble Dames (London, 1891).

Tess of the d'Urbervilles (London, 1891).
Jude the Obscure (London, 1896).
Collected Poems (London, 1962).
'The Dorsetshire Labourer', *Longman's Magazine*, July 1883.
Personal Writings, ed. Harold Orel (London, 1967).

2. Arch, Joseph, *Life* (London, 1898).
Ashby, Joseph, and King, Bolton, 'Statistics of some Midland Villages', *Economic Journal*, Mar. and June 1893.
Ashby, M. K., *Joseph Ashby of Tysoe* (Cambridge, 1961).
Austen, Jane, *Emma* (London, 1816).
Baring-Gould, Sabine, *Dartmoor Idylls* (London, 1896).
Bede, Cuthbert, *Our New Rector* (London, 1861).
Black, William, *Green Pastures and Piccadilly* (London, 1877).
Blackmoor, R. D., *Cripps the Carrier* (London, 1876).
Bourne, George, *The Bettesworth Book* (London, 1901).
— *Memoirs of a Surrey Labourer* (London, 1907).
Bronte, Emily, *Wuthering Heights* (London, 1847).
Burrows, Mary, *Sketches of our Village* (Ipswich and London, 1852).
Caird, James, *English Agriculture in 1850–1* (London, 1852).
Charlesworth, Mrs, *Book for the Cottage* (London, 1848).
— *Ministering Children* (London, 1854).
— *The Cottage and its Visitor* (London, 1856).
Cobbett, William, *Rural Rides* (London, 1830).
Cobbold, Richard, *Margaret Catchpole, a Suffolk Girl* (London, 1845).
Collins, Mortimer and Frances, *The Village Comedy* (London, 1878).
Disraeli, Benjamin, *Coningsby* (London, 1844).
— *Sybil* (London, 1845).
Dolby, Thomas, *Floreston* (London, 1839).
Eliot, George, *Scenes of Clerical Life* (Edinburgh, 1858).
— *Adam Bede* (Edinburgh, 1859).
— *The Mill on the Floss* (Edinburgh, 1860).
— *Silas Marner* (Edinburgh, 1861).
— *Felix Holt* (London, 1866).

Eliot, George, *Middlemarch* (Edinburgh, 1871–3).
— *Daniel Deronda* (Edinburgh, 1876).
— *Essays*, ed. T. Pinney (London, 1963).
Gaskell, Elizabeth, *Mary Barton* (London, 1848).
— *Cranford* (London, 1853).
— *North and South* (London, 1855).
— *Wives and Daughters* (London, 1866).
Haggard, Henry Rider, *Rural England* (London, 1902).
Hatton, Joseph, *Cruel London* (London, 1878).
Howitt, Mary, *Wood Leighton* (London, 1836).
— *Sowing and Reaping* (London, 1841).
Howitt, William, *The Rural Life of England* (London, 1838).
— *The Hall and the Hamlet* (London, 1848).
— *The Year-Book of the Country* (London, 1850).
— *The Man of the People* (London, 1860).
— *Woodburn Grange* (London, 1867).
Howitt, William and Mary, *Stories of English and Foreign Life* (London, 1853).
Jefferies, Richard, *The Scarlet Shawl* (London, 1874).
— *Restless Human Hearts* (London, 1875).
— *World's End* (London, 1877).
— *Wild Life in a Southern County* (London, 1879).
— *The Gamekeeper at Home* (London, 1880).
— *Greene Ferne Farm* (London, 1880).
— *Hodge and his Masters* (London, 1880).
— *Round about a Great Estate* (London, 1880).
— *Nature near London* (London, 1883).
— *The Story of my Heart* (London, 1883).
— *The Dewy Morn* (London, 1884).
— *The Life of the Fields* (London, 1884).
— *After London* (London, 1885).
— *The Open Air* (London, 1885).
— *Amaryllis at the Fair* (London, 1887).
— *Field and Hedgerow* (London, 1889).
— *The Toilers of the Field* (London, 1892).
— *Hills and the Vale*, ed. Edward Thomas (London, 1909).
— *Spring of the Year*, ed. Samuel J. Looker (London, 1964).

— *The Old House at Coate*, ed. Looker (London, 1948).

— *Field and Farm*, ed. Looker (London, 1957).

Kilvert, Francis, *Diary 1870–79*, ed. William Plomer (London, 1938–40).

Kingsley, Charles, *Yeast* (London, 1851).

— *Alton Locke* (London, 1852).

Lee, Holme, *Country Stories* (London, 1872).

— *A Poor Squire* (London, 1882).

Marx, Karl, *Capital* (London, 1887).

Oliphant, Margaret, *A Country Gentleman and his Family* (London, 1886).

Sewell, William, *Hawkstone* (London, 1845).

Somerville, Alexander, *Autobiography of a Working Man* (London, 1848).

— *The Whistler at the Plough* (Manchester, 1852).

Surtees, R. S., *Jaunts and Jollities* (London, 1838).

Tonna, Charlotte Elizabeth, *Helen Fleetwood* (London, 1841).

Trollope, Anthony, *The Warden* (London, 1855).

— *Barchester Towers* (London, 1857).

— *Doctor Thorne* (London, 1858).

— *Framley Parsonage* (London, 1861).

— *Orley Farm* (London, 1862).

— *The Small House at Allington* (London, 1864).

— *The Last Chronicle of Barset* (London, 1867).

Trollope, Frances, *The Vicar of Wrexhill* (London, 1837).

— *Town and Country* (London, 1848).

Woods, Margaret, *A Village Tragedy* (London, 1887).

— *The Vagabonds* (London, 1894).

— *Weeping Ferry* (London, 1898).

B. Secondary sources

1. Studies of Hardy

Abercrombie, L., *Thomas Hardy, A Critical Study* (London, 1912).

Blunden, Edmund, *Thomas Hardy* (London, 1941).

Brown, Douglas, *Thomas Hardy* (London, 1954).

— *Thomas Hardy: 'The Mayor of Casterbridge'* (London, 1962).

Cecil, Lord David, *Hardy the Novelist* (London, 1943).

Chase, M. E., *Thomas Hardy from Serial to Novel* (Minneapolis, 1927).

Child, Harold, *Thomas Hardy* (London, 1916).

Deacon, Lois, and Coleman, Terry, *Providence and Mr Hardy* (London, 1966).

Duffin, H. C., *Thomas Hardy* (Manchester, 1916).

Gardner, W. H., *Some Thoughts on 'The Mayor of Caster-bridge'* (Oxford, 1930).

Grimsditch, H. B., *Character and Environment in the Novels of Thomas Hardy* (London, 1925).

Guerard, A. J., *Thomas Hardy* (London, 1949).

Hardy, Evelyn, *Thomas Hardy* (London, 1954).

Hardy, F. E., *The Early Life of Thomas Hardy* (London, 1928).

— *The Later Years of Thomas Hardy* (London, 1930).

Hawkins, Desmond, *Thomas Hardy* (London, 1950).

Holland, Clive, *Thomas Hardy* (London, 1933).

Holloway, John, *The Victorian Sage* (London, 1953).

— *The Charted Mirror* (London, 1960).

Howe, Irving, *Thomas Hardy* (London, 1968).

Johnson, Lionel, *The Art of Thomas Hardy* (London, 1894).

Johnson, Trevor, *Thomas Hardy* (London, 1968).

Kettle, Arnold, *Introduction to the English Novel* (London, 1951–53).

— *Hardy the Novelist* (Swansea, 1967).

Lea, Hermann, *Thomas Hardy's Wessex* (London, 1913).

Lerner, L., and Holmstrom, J., *Thomas Hardy and his Readers* (London, 1968).

Maxwell, Donald, *The Landscape of Thomas Hardy* (London, 1928).

McDowall, A. S., *Thomas Hardy: A Critical Study* (London, 1931).

Morrell, Roy, *Thomas Hardy: The Will and the Way* (Kuala Lumpur, 1965).

Paterson, John, *The Making of 'The Return of the Native'* (Berkeley, 1963).

Pinion, F. B., *A Hardy Companion* (London, 1968).

Purdy, R. L., *Thomas Hardy: A Bibliographical Study* (London, 1954).

Rutland, William, *Thomas Hardy* (Oxford, 1938).

Skilling, M. R., *Hardy's Mellstock on the Map* (Dorchester, 1968).

Stewart, J. I. M., *Eight Modern Writers* (Oxford, 1963).

Tanner, Tony, 'Hardy's "Tess of the d'Urbervilles"', *Critical Quarterly*, autumn 1968.

Weber, Carl, *Hardy of Wessex* (New York, 1940).

Webster, Harvey Curtis, *On a Darkling Plain* (Chicago, 1947).

Williams, Randall, *The Wessex Novels of Thomas Hardy* (London, 1924).

Williams, Raymond, 'Thomas Hardy', *Critical Quarterly*, winter 1964.

Wing, George, *Hardy* (Edinburgh, 1963).

2. *Studies of other writers*

Arkell, Reginald, *Richard Jefferies* (London, 1933).

Beer, Gillian, 'Charles Kingsley and the Literary Image of the Countryside', *Victorian Studies,* Mar. 1965.

Besant, Walter, *Eulogy of Richard Jefferies* (London, 1888).

Courtney, W. L., *Feminine Note in Fiction* (London, 1904).

Haight, G. S., *George Eliot, a biography* (Oxford, 1968).

Hardy, Barbara, *Novels of George Eliot* (London, 1959).

Keith, W. J., *Richard Jefferies, a critical study* (London, 1965).

Leavis, Q. D., 'Lives and Works of Richard Jefferies', *Scrutiny*, Mar. 1938.

Lee, Amice, *Laurels and Rosemary: the life of William and Mary Howitt* (London, 1955).

Lerner, L., and Holmstrom, J., *George Eliot and her Readers* (London, 1966).

Looker, S. J., and Porteous, C., *Richard Jefferies, Man of the Fields* (London, 1965).

Pollard, Arthur, *Mrs Gaskell: Novelist and Biographer* (Manchester, 1965).

Sadleir, Michael, *Trollope: a Commentary* (London, 1927).

Salt, H. S., *Richard Jefferies* (London, 1894).

Stephen, Leslie, *George Eliot* (London, 1902).

Thale, Jerome, *Novels of George Eliot* (New York, 1959).

Thomas, Edward, *Richard Jefferies* (London, 1909).

Williams, Raymond, 'The Knowable Community in George Eliot's Novels', *Novel*, spring 1969.

3. Historical and Related Studies

Andrews, William, *Bygone England* (London, 1892).

Arch, Joseph, *A word of counsel to the new electors of Warwickshire* (London, 1885).

Ashby, A. W., *A hundred years of Poor Law administration in a Warwickshire village* (Oxford, 1912).

— *Allotments and Smallholdings in Oxfordshire* (Oxford, 1917).

Ashby, A. W., and Byles, P. G., *Rural Education* (Oxford, 1923).

Ashby, M. K., *The Country School* (London, 1929).

Baring-Gould, Sabine, *Old Country Life* (London, 1890).

— *In a Quiet Village* (London, 1900).

Barnes, William, *Poems of Rural Life, in the Dorset Dialect* (London, 1844).

Bell, Adrian, *The Open Air: an anthology of English Country Life* (London, 1936).

Bourne, George, *Change in the Village* (London, 1912).

— *The Wheelwright's Shop* (Cambridge, 1923).

— *A Small Boy in the Sixties* (Cambridge, 1927).

Boyd, Andrew, *Recreations of a Country Parson* (London, 1866).

Caird, James, *High Farming* (Edinburgh, 1849).

— *The Landed Interest and the Supply of Food* (London, 1878).

— *The British Land Question* (London, 1881).

Clayden, Arthur, *The Revolt of the Field* (London, 1874).

Chambers, J. D., and Mingay, G. E., *The Agricultural Revolution 1750–1880* (London, 1966).

Darby, H. C., and Finn, R. W., *The Domesday Geography of South-West England* (Cambridge, 1967).

Deane, P. M., and Cole, W. A., *British Economic Growth 1688–1959* (Cambridge, 1962).

Dunbabin, J. P. D., 'The Revolt of the Field', *Past and Present*, Nov. 1963.

Engels, Friedrich, *Condition of the Working Class in England in 1844* (London, 1892).

Ernle, Lord, *English Farming, Past and Present* (London, 1912).

Garnier, R. M., *History of English Landed Interest* (London, 1892–3).

— *Annals of the British Peasantry* (London, 1895).

Haggard, Henry Rider, *A Farmer's Year* (London, 1899).

Hasbach, Wilhelm, *History of the English Agricultural Labourer* (London, 1908).

Hoskyns, C. C. W., *Talpa: or the Chronicles of a Clay Farm* (London, 1852).

Hudson, W. H., *Nature in Downland* (London, 1900).

— *Hampshire Days* (London, 1903).

Kerr, Barbara, *Bound to the Soil: A Social History of Dorset, 1750–1918* (London, 1968).

Orwin, C. S., and Whetham, E. H., *History of British Agriculture 1846–1914* (London, 1964).

Peacock, A., *The Revolt of the Fields in East Anglia*, an 'Our History' pamphlet, 49/50, spring/summer 1968.

Royal Commission Reports
Employment of Children, Young Persons and Women in Agriculture, 1867.
Agricultural Depression, 1879 and 1893.
Housing of the Working Classes, 1884.

Saville, John, *Rural Depopulation in England and Wales, 1851–1951* (London, 1957).

Thompson, F. M. L., *English Landed Society in the Nineteenth Century* (London, 1963).

Victoria County History of Dorset (London, 1908).

Victoria County History of Wiltshire (London, 1959).

Waugh, Edwin, *Poems and Lancashire Songs* (London, 1859).

Williams, Raymond, 'Literature and Rural Society', *The Listener*, 16 Nov. 1967.

Index